Joint Workshop on Automatic Knowledge Base Construction and Web-scale 2012

(AKBC-WEKEX 2012)

Held at the 2012 Conference of the North American Chapter of the Association for Computational Linguistics: Human Language Technologies (NAACL-HLT 2012)

Montreal, Quebec, Canada
3 – 8 June 2012

ISBN: 978-1-62276-591-1

Printed from e-media with permission by:

Curran Associates, Inc.
57 Morehouse Lane
Red Hook, NY 12571

Some format issues inherent in the e-media version may also appear in this print version.

Printed by Curran Associates, Inc. (2012)

For permission requests, please contact the Association for Computational Linguistics
at the address below.

Association for Computational Linguistics
209 N. Eighth Street
Stroudsburg, Pennsylvania 18360

Phone: 1-570-476-8006
Fax: 1-570-476-0860

acl@aclweb.org

Additional copies of this publication are available from:

Curran Associates, Inc.
57 Morehouse Lane
Red Hook, NY 12571 USA
Phone: 845-758-0400
Fax: 845-758-2634
Email: curran@proceedings.com
Web: www.proceedings.com

Introduction

Recently, there has been a significant amount of interest in automatically creating large-scale knowledge bases (KBs) from unstructured text. The Web-scale knowledge extraction task presents a unique set of opportunities and challenges. The resulting knowledge bases can have the advantage of scale and coverage. They have been enriched by linking to the Semantic Web, in particular the growing linked open dataset (LOD). These semantic knowledge bases have been used for a wide variety of Natural Language Processing, Knowledge Representation, and Reasoning applications such as semantic search, question answering, entity resolution, ontology mapping etc. The automatic construction of these KBs has been enabled by research in areas including natural language processing, information extraction, information integration, databases, search and machine learning. There are substantial scientific and engineering challenges in advancing and integrating such relevant methodologies.

With this year's workshop, we would like to resume the positive experiences from two previous workshops: AKBC-2010 and WEKEX-2011. The joint AKBC-WEKEX workshop will serve as a forum for researchers working in the area of automated knowledge harvesting from text. By having invited talks by leading researchers from industry, academia, and the government, and by focusing particularly on vision papers, we aim to provide a vivid forum of discussion about the field of automated knowledge base construction. For more details on the workshop, please visit: http://akbcwekex2012.wordpress.com/

James Fan, Raphael Hoffman, Aditya Kalyanpur, Sebastian Riedel, Fabian Suchanek, Partha Talukdar

Organizers:

James Fan (IBM Research)
Raphael Hoffman (University of Washington)
Aditya Kalyanpur (IBM Research)
Sebastian Riedel (University of Massachusetts, Amherst)
Fabian Suchanek (Max-Planck Institute for Informatics)
Partha Pratim Talukdar (Carnegie Mellon University)

Steering Committee:

Oren Etzioni (University of Washington)
Andrew McCallum (University of Massachusetts, Amherst)
Fernando Pereira (Google Research)
Gerhard Weikum (Max-Planck Institute for Informatics)

Invited Speaker:

Nilesh Dalvi (Yahoo Research)
Bonnie Dorr (DARPA)
Oren Etzioni (University of Washington)
James Fan / Aditya Kalyanpur (IBM Research)
Ed Hovy (University of Southern California/ISI)
Andrew McCallum (University of Massachusetts, Amherst)
Fernando Pereira (Google Research)
Tom Mitchell (Carnegie Mellon University)
Patrick Pantel (Microsoft Research)
Chris Re (University of Wisconsin, Madison)
Steffen Staab (University of Koblenz)

Program Committee:

Soren Auer (University of Leipzig)
Ken Barker (IBM Research)
Peter Clark (Vulcan Inc.)
Amol Deshpande (University of Maryland)
Anhai Doan (University of Wisconsin, Madison)
Oren Etzioni (University of Washington)
Tony Fader (University of Washington)
Alfio Gliozzo (IBM Research)
Alon Halevy (Google Research)
Ed Hovy (University of Southern California/ISI)
Zack Ives (University of Pennsylvania)
Vladimir Kolovski (Novartis)
Xiao Ling (University of Washington)

Andrew McCallum (University of Massachusetts, Amherst)
Goran Nenadic (University of Manchester)
Patrick Pantel (Microsoft Research)
Marius Pasca (Google Research)
Chris Re (University of Wisconsin, Madison)
Alan Ritter (University of Washington)
Sunita Sarawagi (IIT Bombay)
Sameer Singh (University of Massachusetts, Amherst)
Martin Theobald (Max-Planck Institute for Informatics)
Gerhard Weikum (Max-Planck Institute for Informatics)
Limin Yao (University of Massachusetts, Amherst)

Table of Contents

Workshop Program

Thursday, June 7, 2012

8:30–9:00	Opening Remarks
9:00–9:45	Invited Talk: Oren Etzioni
9:45–10:30	Invited Talk: Patrick Pantel
10:30–11:00	Break
11:00–11:45	Invited Talk: Andrew McCallum
11:45–12:30	Invited Talk: James Fan / Aditya Kalyanpur
12:30–14:00	Lunch
14:00–14:45	Poster Quick Presentations
14:45–15:30	Top 3 Talks
15:30–16:00	Break
16:00–18:00	Poster Session

Friday, June 8, 2012

9:00–9:45	Invited Talk: Fernando Pereira
9:45–10:30	Invited Talk: Tom Mitchell
10:30–11:00	Break
11:00–11:45	Invited Talk: Chris Re
11:45–12:30	Invited Talk: Steffen Staab

Friday, June 8, 2012 (continued)

12:30–14:00	Lunch
14:00–14:45	Invited Talk: Ed Hovy
14:45–15:30	Invited Talk: Nilesh Davi
15:30–16:00	Break
16:00–16:30	Invited Talk: Bonnie Dorr
16:30–18:00	Unconference

Towards Distributed MCMC Inference in Probabilistic Knowledge Bases

Mathias Niepert, Christian Meilicke, Heiner Stuckenschmidt
Universität Mannheim
Mannheim, Germany
{firstname}@informatik.uni-mannheim.de

Abstract

Probabilistic knowledge bases are commonly used in areas such as large-scale information extraction, data integration, and knowledge capture, to name but a few. Inference in probabilistic knowledge bases is a computationally challenging problem. With this contribution, we present our vision of a distributed inference algorithm based on conflict graph construction and hypergraph sampling. Early empirical results show that the approach efficiently and accurately computes a-posteriori probabilities of a knowledge base derived from a well-known information extraction system.

1 Introduction

In recent years, numerous applications of probabilistic knowledge bases have emerged. For instance, large-scale information extraction systems (Weikum and Theobald, 2010) aim at building knowledge bases by applying extraction algorithms to very large text corpora. Examples of such projects include KNOWITNOW (Cafarella et al., 2005), TEXTRUNNER (Etzioni et al., 2008), YAGO (Suchanek et al., 2007; Hoffart et al., 2011; Hoffart et al., 2010), and NELL (Carlson et al., 2010a; Carlson et al., 2010b). These systems face challenges of scalability both in terms of the degree of uncertainty and the sheer size of the resulting knowledge bases. Most of these projects combine pattern learning and matching approaches with some form of logical reasoning, with the majority of the systems employing weighted or unweighted first-order Horn clauses (Suchanek et al., 2007; Carlson et al., 2010a). More recently, random walk algorithms were applied to NELL's knowledge base to infer novel facts (Lao et al., 2011) and both pattern matching and reasoning algorithms were distributed on the HADOOP platform to enrich YAGO (Nakashole et al., 2011).

Similar to the distributed processes building indices for web search engines, there are distributed algorithms continuously building indices for structured knowledge (Carlson et al., 2010a). A combination of learned and manually specified common-sense rules is an important factor for the quality of the indexed knowledge. For the inference component of a large-scale information extraction system we propose a sampling approach consisting of two continuously running processes. The first process aggregates minimal conflict sets where each such set contradicts one or more of the common-sense rules. These conflicts are generated with relational queries and pattern-based approaches. The second component of the system is a sampling algorithm that operates on hypergraphs built from the minimal conflict set. The hypergraph is first decomposed into smaller disconnected sub-hypergraphs to allow distributed processing. Theoretical results on sampling independent sets from hypergraphs are leveraged to construct an ergodic Markov chain for probabilistic knowledge bases. The Markov chains are continuously run on the various connected components of the conflict hypergraph to compute a-posteriori probabilities of individual logical statements which are in turn stored in a large relational index. While this is still work in progress, we have developed the theory, implemented the respective algorithms, and conducted first experiments.

2 Related Work

The presented representational framework is related to that of Markov logic (Richardson and Domingos, 2006) as the semantics is based on log-linear distributions. However, in this work we make the notion of consistency explicit by defining a log-linear distribution over consistent knowledge bases, that is, knowledge bases without logical contradictions. Moreover, the semantics of the knowledge bases is that of description logics which are commonly used for knowledge representation and exchange. There is existing work on distributing large-scale information extraction algorithms. For instance, pattern matching and reasoning algorithms were distributed on the HADOOP platform to enrich YAGO (Nakashole et al., 2011). However, these algorithms are not MCMC based and do not compute a-posteriori probabilities of individual statements. GraphLab (Low et al., 2010) is a recently developed parallel framework for distributing machine learning algorithms similar to MapReduce but better suited for classical learning algorithms. GraphLab was used to implement two parallel Gibbs samplers (Gonzalez et al., 2011). The approach is similar in that it identifies components of the graph (using graph coloring algorithms) from which one can sample in parallel without losing ergodicity. While not a distributed algorithm, query aware MCMC (Wick and McCallum, 2011) is a related approach in that it exploits the locality of the query to make MCMC more efficient.

3 Log-Linear Knowledge Bases

We believe that the common-sense rules should be stated in a representation language whose syntax and semantics is well-understood and standardized so as to support data and rule exchange between systems. Description logics are a commonly used representation for knowledge bases. There are numerous tools and standards for representing and reasoning with knowledge using description logics. The description logics framework allows one to represent both facts about individuals (concept and role assertions) as well as axioms expressing schema information. Log-linear description logics integrate description logics with probabilistic log-linear models (Niepert et al., 2011). The syntax of log-linear DLs is equivalent to that of the underlying DL except that it is possible to assign weights to general concept inclusion axioms (GCIs), role inclusion axioms (RIs), and assertions. We will use the term axiom to denote GCIs, RIs, and concept and role assertions. A log-linear knowledge base $\mathcal{K} = (\mathcal{K}^{\mathsf{D}}, \mathcal{K}^{\mathsf{U}})$ is a pair consisting of a deterministic knowledge base $\mathcal{K}^{\mathsf{D}}$ and an uncertain knowledge base $\mathcal{K}^{\mathsf{U}} = \{(c, w_c)\}$ with each c being an axiom and w_c a real-valued weight assigned to c. The deterministic KB contains axioms that are known to hold and the uncertain knowledge base contains the uncertain axioms. The greater the a-priori probability of an uncertain axiom the greater its weight. A set of axioms $\mathcal{A}$ is *inconsistent* if it has no model. A set of axioms $\mathcal{A}'$ is a *minimal inconsistency preserving subset* if it is inconsistent and every strict subset $\mathcal{A}'' \subset \mathcal{A}'$ is consistent.

The semantics of log-linear knowledge bases is based on probability distributions over consistent knowledge bases – the distribution assigns a non-zero probability only to consistent sets of axioms. For a log-linear knowledge base $\mathcal{K} = (\mathcal{K}^{\mathsf{D}}, \mathcal{K}^{\mathsf{U}})$ and a knowledge base $\mathcal{K}'$ with $\mathcal{K}^{\mathsf{D}} \subseteq \mathcal{K}' \subseteq \mathcal{K}^{\mathsf{D}} \cup \{c : (c, w_c) \in \mathcal{K}^{\mathsf{U}}\}$, we have that

$$\mathrm{Pr}_{\mathcal{K}}(\mathcal{K}') = \begin{cases} \frac{1}{Z} \exp\left(\sum_{\{c \in \mathcal{K}' \setminus \mathcal{K}^{\mathsf{D}}\}} w_c\right) & \text{if } \mathcal{K}' \textit{ consistent;} \\ 0 & \text{otherwise} \end{cases}$$

where Z is the normalization constant of the log-linear distribution $\mathrm{Pr}_{\mathcal{K}}$.

The weights of the axioms determine the log-linear probability (Koller and Friedman, 2009; Richardson and Domingos, 2006). The marginal probability of an axiom c given a log-linear knowledge base is the sum of the probabilities of the consistent knowledge bases containing c. Please note that an axiom with weight 0, that is, an a-priori probability of 0.5, which is not in conflict with other axioms has the a-posteriori probability of 0.5. Given these definitions, a Monte Carlo algorithm must sample consistent knowledge bases according to the distribution $\mathrm{Pr}_{\mathcal{K}}$. This seems daunting at first due to the reasoning complexity, the size of web-extracted knowledge bases, and the presence of

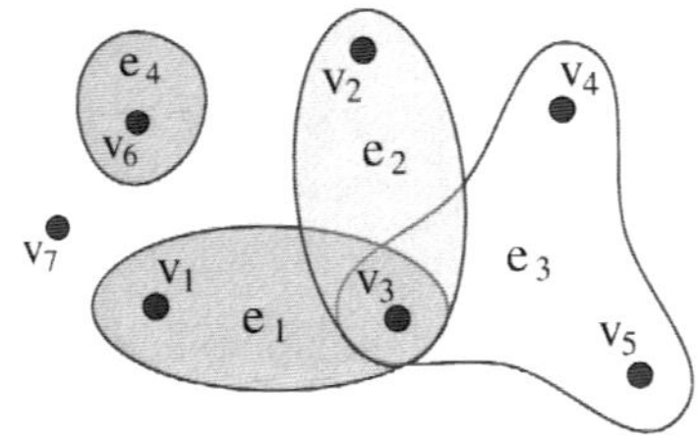

Figure 1: Hypergraph with 7 vertices (axioms) and 4 edges (conflict sets). Both the maximum degree of the hypergraph and the size of the largest edge are 3.

deterministic dependencies. However, we describe an approach with two separate distributable components. One that generates *minimal conflict sets* and one that leverages these conflict sets to build parallel Markov chains whose global unique stationary distribution is $\Pr_{\mathcal{K}}$.

4 Independent Sets in Hypergraphs

A hypergraph $G = (V, E)$ consists of a vertex set V and a set E of edges, where each edge is a subset of V. Let $m = \max\{|e| : e \in E\}$ be the size of the largest edge and let $\Delta = \max\{|\{e \in E : v \in e\}| : v \in V\}$ be the maximum degree of the graph. An independent set X in the hypergraph G is a subset of the vertex set V with $e \nsubseteq X$ for all $e \in E$. Let v be a vertex, let e be an edge with $v \in e$, and let $X \subseteq V$. If $v \notin X$ but, for all $u \in (e \setminus \{v\})$, we have that $u \in X$, then v is said to be *critical* for the edge e in X. Figure 1 depicts a hypergraph with 7 vertices and 4 edges.

Let $\mathcal{I}(G)$ be the set of all independent sets in the hypergraph G and let $\lambda \in \mathbb{R}_+$ be a positive parameter. The distribution π on $\mathcal{I}(G)$ is defined as

$$\pi(X) = \lambda^{|X|} / \sum_{X' \in \mathcal{I}(G)} \lambda^{|X'|}.$$

The problem of counting independent sets in graphs and hypergraphs (Dyer and Greenhill, 2000) was initially motivated by problems in statistical physics. While NP-hard in general, approximately counting independent sets in graphs is possible in polynomial time using the Markov Chain Monte Carlo method whenever a rapidly mixing Markov chain is available (Jerrum and Sinclair, 1996). Leveraging the theory of sampling independent sets from hypergraphs for efficient inference in probabilistic knowledge bases is straight-forward once the connection between consistent knowledge bases and independent sets in conflict hypergraphs is made.

5 Sampling Consistent Knowledge Bases

The set of inconsistency preserving subsets of a log-linear KB is denoted by $\mathcal{S}(\mathcal{K})$. This set is iteratively computed over the entire knowledge base consisting of *both* the known and the uncertain axioms. The conflict hypergraph is the projection of the minimal conflict sets onto the set of uncertain axioms.

Definition 1. *Let $\mathcal{K} = (\mathcal{K}^{\mathsf{D}}, \mathcal{K}^{\mathsf{U}})$ be a log-KB base and let $\mathcal{S}(\mathcal{K})$ be the set of all minimal conflict sets in $\mathcal{K}$. The* conflict hypergraph *$G = (V, E)$ of $\mathcal{K}$ is constructed as follows. For each axiom c in $\{c : (c, w_c) \in \mathcal{K}^{\mathsf{U}}\}$ we add one vertex v_c to V. For each minimal conflict set $S \in \mathcal{S}(\mathcal{K})$ we add the edge $\{v_c : c \in S \cap \{c : (c, w_c) \in \mathcal{K}^{\mathsf{U}}\}\}$ to E.*

Example 2. *Let* Student *and* Professor *be concepts,* hasAdvisor *an object property; and* Peter, Anna, *and* Bob *be distinct individuals. Now, let* $\mathcal{K}^{\mathsf{D}} = \{v_0 := \mathsf{Range(hasAdvisor)} \sqcap \mathsf{Student} \sqsubseteq \bot,\ v_0' := \{\mathsf{Anna}\} \sqcap \mathsf{Student} \sqsubseteq \bot\}$ *and*

$$\mathcal{K}^{\mathsf{U}} = \left\{ \begin{array}{l} v_1 := \langle \mathsf{hasAdvisor(Anna, Peter)}, 0.8 \rangle, \\ v_2 := \langle \mathsf{hasAdvisor(Bob, Peter)}, 0.5 \rangle, \\ v_3 := \langle \mathsf{Student(Peter)}, 0.1 \rangle, \\ v_4 := \langle \mathsf{Student} \sqcap \mathsf{Professor} \sqsubseteq \bot, 0.9 \rangle, \\ v_5 := \langle \mathsf{Professor(Peter)}, 1.0 \rangle, \\ v_6 := \langle \mathsf{Student(Anna)}, 0.1 \rangle, \\ v_7 := \langle \mathsf{Professor(Bob)}, 0.4 \rangle \end{array} \right\}$$

Axiom v_0 expresses that advisors cannot be students and axiom v_0' expresses that Anna is not a student. Here, we have that $\mathcal{S}(\mathcal{K}) = \{\{v_0, v_1, v_3\}, \{v_0', v_6\}, \{v_0, v_2, v_3\}, \{v_3, v_4, v_5\}\}$. Figure 1 depicts the corresponding conflict hypergraph.

There is a one-to-one correspondence between independent sets of the hypergraph and consistent knowledge bases. Hence, analogous to sampling independent sets from hypergraphs we can now sample conflict-free knowledge bases from the *conflict hypergraph*. The difference is that each vertex v_c is weighted with w_c. Let $G = (V, E)$ be the conflict hypergraph and let m be the size of the largest edge in G. The following Markov chain $\mathcal{M}^{\mathsf{w}}(\mathcal{I}(G))$ samples independent sets from the conflict hypergraph taking into account the weights of the axioms. If the chain is in state $X^{(t)}$ at time t, the next state $X^{(t+1)}$ is determined according to the following process:

- Choose a vertex $v_c \in V$ uniformly at random;
- If $v_c \in X^{(t)}$ then let $X^{(t+1)} = X^{(t)} \setminus \{v_c\}$ with probability $1/(\exp(w_c)+1)$;
- If $v_c \in X^{(t)}$ and v_c is not critical in $X^{(t)}$ for any edge then let $X^{(t+1)} = X^{(t)} \cup \{v_c\}$ with probability $\exp(w_c)/(1+\exp(w_c))$;
- If $v_c \in X^{(t)}$ and v_c is critical in $X^{(t)}$ for a unique edge e then with probability $(m-1)\exp(w_c)/(2m(\exp(w_c)+1))$ choose $w \in e \setminus \{v_c\}$ uniformly at random and let $X^{(t+1)} = (X^{(t)} \cup \{v_c\}) \setminus \{w\}$;
- Otherwise let $X^{(t+1)} = X^{(t)}$.

The following theorem is verifiable by showing that the Markov chain $\mathcal{M}^{\mathsf{w}}(\mathcal{I}(G))$ is aperiodic and irreducible and that $\Pr_{\mathcal{K}}$, projected onto the set of uncertain axioms, is a reversible distribution for the Markov chain.

Theorem 3. *Let $\mathcal{C} = (\mathcal{K}^{\mathsf{D}}, \mathcal{K}^{\mathsf{U}})$ be a log-linear knowledge base with conflict hypergraph G. Let $\Pr : \wp(\{c : (c, w_c) \in \mathcal{K}^{\mathsf{U}}\}) \rightarrow [0,1]$ be a probability distribution. Then, $\Pr(U) = \Pr_{\mathcal{K}}(\mathcal{K}^{\mathsf{D}} \cup U)$ for every $U \subseteq \{c : (c, w_c) \in \mathcal{K}^{\mathsf{U}}\}$ if and only if $\Pr$ is the unique stationary distribution of $\mathcal{M}^{\mathsf{w}}(\mathcal{I}(G))$.*

The first component of the proposed approach accumulates minimal inconsistency preserving subsets. These minimal conflict sets can be efficiently computed with relational queries and pattern-based approaches and, therefore, are distributable. For instance, consider the common-sense rule "Students cannot be PhD advisors." To compute the sets of statements contradicting said rule, we process the conjunctive query "$\mathsf{hasAdvisor}(x,y) \wedge \mathsf{Student}(y)$." Each returned tuple corresponds to a minimal inconsistency preserving subset, that is, a set of statements that together contradicts the known rule. For instance, let us assume we execute the query "$\mathsf{hasAdvisor}(x,y) \wedge \mathsf{Student}(y)$" for the knowledge base in Example 2. The returned tuples are $(\mathsf{Anna}, \mathsf{Peter})$ and $(\mathsf{Bob}, \mathsf{Peter})$ corresponding to the minimal conflict sets $\{v_0, v_1, v_3\}$ and $\{v_0, v_2, v_3\}$. Again, since we can iteratively accumulate these sets of conflicts using relational joins we can distribute the process, for instance using a MAPREDUCE platform.

In order to facilitate distributed processing, the global conflict hypergraph is decomposed into its connected components. For instance, the conflict hypergraph in Figure 1 can be decomposed into the sub-hypergraphs induced by the partition of the nodes $\{\{v_1, v_2, v_3, v_4, v_5\}, \{v_6\}, \{v_7\}\}$. Markov chain for independent sets of hypergraphs are continuously run on the various conflict sub-hypergraphs to (re-)compute the a-posteriori probabilities of the statements.

6 Experiments

To assess the practicality of the approach, we conducted preliminary experiments focusing on the data and common-sense rules of the PROSPERA system due to the availability of recent results[1] (Nakashole et al., 2011). Each logical rule of the PROSPERA system was translated to a relational database query returning the minimal conflict sets *violating* said rule. For instance, for the common-sense PROSPERA rule "A student can have only one alma mater that she/he graduated from (with a doctoral degree)," the following relational query is executed: $\mathsf{graduatedFrom}(x,y) \wedge \mathsf{graduatedFrom}(x,y') \wedge \neg(y = y')$. For the rule "The advisor of a student must be older than her/his student" the query is $\mathsf{hasAdvisor}(x,y) \wedge \mathsf{bornOn}(x,y') \wedge \mathsf{bornOn}(y,y'') \wedge (y' > y'')$. Analogously, these queries can be formulated for the type constraints used by the PROSPERA system. Figure 2 depicts a subset of the minimal conflict sets in the academic domain of PROSPERA involving the object Albert Einstein.

For the preliminary experiments we used the academic domain facts that were extracted by PROSPERA without reasoning, and employed the common-sense rules mentioned in the description of PROSPERA[1] (Nakashole et al., 2011). The knowledge base has 384,816 bornOn, 59,933 facultyAt, 154,874 graduatedFrom, and 5,606 hasAcademicAdvisor assertions. Each assertion was assigned an a-priori probability of 0.5 except for bornOn assertions contained in YAGO which were

[1] http://www.mpi-inf.mpg.de/yago-naga/prospera/

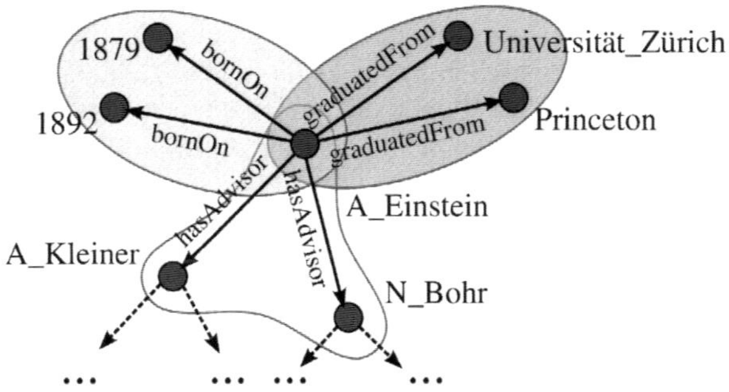

Figure 2: A knowledge base fragment with object A_Einstein and its properties. Some of the minimal conflicts between property assertions (edges in the graph) are indicated by hyperedges.

sampling	$\|E\|$	m	Δ	t_s	MMR	p@1
no	-	-	-	-	0.35	0.24
yes	102.3	2.5	13.4	1.3	0.88	0.82

sampling	$\|E\|$	m	Δ	t_s	MMR	p@1
no	-	-	-	-	0.60	0.37
yes	250.2	2.4	27.0	2.2	0.86	0.81

Table 1: Empirical results for the probabilistic query graduatedFrom(Individual, x) (top) and hasAcademicAdvisor(Individual, x) (bottom). The values are averaged over 100 repetitions of the 50 probabilistic queries. t_s: seconds to compute samples for one connected component; MRR: mean reciprocal rank measure values; p@1: precision @ 1.

assigned an a-priori probability of 0.75. To build a gold standard for the evaluation, we selected 50 academics randomly for which the actual PhD advisor or the alma mater was present in the data. To compute the minimal conflict sets, we processed the join queries using a relational database system. After the construction of the conflict hypergraphs we ran the Markov chains for 10^5 iterations on the individual connected components.

In order to evaluate the marginal a-posteriori probabilities we computed the mean reciprocal rank measure (MRR) of the ranking induced by the computed marginal probabilities and compared it to the expected value of the MRR when no sampling is performed. The MRR measure (for example, see (Lao et al., 2011)) is defined as the inverse rank of the highest ranked correct result in a set of results. More formally, for a set of queries Q we have

$$\text{MRR} = \frac{1}{|Q|} \sum_{q \in Q} \frac{1}{\text{rank of first correct answer}}.$$

Table 1 list the averaged results of 100 experiments each with 50 queries. The columns $|E|$, m, and Δ are the averaged properties of the conflict hypergraphs the Markov chain was run on. t_c is the time needed to execute the relational queries for one connected component. The increase in MRR and precision@1 of the ranking induced by the a-posteriori probabilities over the initial ranking without sampling is statistically significant (paired t-test, $p < 0.01$). These results are encouraging and we are optimistic that they can be improved when individual a-priori weights of assertions are available.

7 Discussion

Log-linear knowledge bases integrate description logics with probabilistic log-linear models. Since it is possible to express knowledge both on the schema and the instance level it allows the *explicit* representation of background knowledge that is already used implicitly by several information extraction systems such as PROSPERA. These systems employ the common-sense rules to ensure a high-quality knowledge base amid a high degree of uncertainty in the extraction process. The presented approach based on the generation of minimal conflict sets and hypergraph sampling is a first step towards a distributed sampling algorithm for structured knowledge extraction. We are also working on incorporating temporal information into the knowledge base (Dylla et al., 2011). We have developed the theory, namely the adaptation of Markov chains for independent sets in hypergraphs so as to incorporate individual node weights, implemented the respective algorithms, and conducted first experiments with the YAGO and PROSPERA datasets and rules. The robust implementation and distribution of the presented algorithms on a HADOOP cluster will be the main objective of future work. Moreover, in many real-world applications, the conflict hypergraph might not be decomposable without the removal of edges. Nevertheless, there are several hypergraph partitioning approaches that one could employ to find an finer-grained decomposition of the conflict hypergraph. We will also compare the presented approach to existing probabilistic inference algorithms such as belief propagation.

References

Michael J. Cafarella, Doug Downey, Stephen Soderland, and Oren Etzioni. 2005. Knowitnow: Fast, scalable information extraction from the web. In *Proceedings of the Conference on Human Language Technology Conference and Conference on Empirical Methods in Natural Language Processing (HLT-EMNLP)*.

A. Carlson, J. Betteridge, B. Kisiel, B. Settles, E.R. Hruschka Jr, and T.M. Mitchell. 2010a. Toward an architecture for never-ending language learning. In *Proceedings of the 24th Conference on Artificial Intelligence (AAAI)*, pages 1306–1313.

A. Carlson, J. Betteridge, R. C. Wang, E. R. Hruschka, and T. M. Mitchell. 2010b. Coupled semi-supervised learning for information extraction. In *Proceedings of the Third ACM International Conference on Web Search and Data Mining (WSDM 2010)*.

M. Dyer and C. Greenhill. 2000. On markov chains for independent sets. *Journal of Algorithms*, 35(1):17–49.

M. Dylla, M. Sozio, and M. Theobald. 2011. Resolving temporal conflicts in inconsistent rdf knowledge bases. In *14. GI-Fachtagung Datenbanksysteme für Business, Technologie und Web (BTW)*, pages 474–493.

O. Etzioni, M. Banko, S. Soderland, and D.S. Weld. 2008. Open information extraction from the web. *Communications of the ACM*, 51(12):68–74.

Joseph Gonzalez, Yucheng Low, Arthur Gretton, and Carlos Guestrin. 2011. Parallel gibbs sampling: From colored fields to thin junction trees. In *In Artificial Intelligence and Statistics (AISTATS)*.

J. Hoffart, F. M. Suchanek, K. Berberich, and G. Weikum. 2010. YAGO2: A Spatially and Temporally Enhanced Knowledge Base from Wikipedia. Research report, Max-Planck-Institut für Informatik.

J. Hoffart, F. M. Suchanek, K. Berberich, E. Lewis-Kelham, G. de Melo, and G. Weikum. 2011. Yago2: exploring and querying world knowledge in time, space, context, and many languages. In *Proceedings of the 20th international conference on World wide web (WWW)*, pages 229–232.

M. Jerrum and A. Sinclair. 1996. The markov chain monte carlo method: an approach to approximate counting and integration. In *Approximation algorithms for NP-hard problems*, pages 482–520. PWS Publishing.

D. Koller and N. Friedman. 2009. *Probabilistic Graphical Models: Principles and Techniques*. MIT Press.

N. Lao, T. Mitchell, and W. W. Cohen. 2011. Random walk inference and learning in a large scale knowledge base. In *Proceedings of the Conference on Empirical Methods in Natural Language Processing (EMNLP)*, pages 529–539.

Yucheng Low, Joseph Gonzalez, Aapo Kyrola, Danny Bickson, Carlos Guestrin, and Joseph M. Hellerstein. 2010. Graphlab: A new parallel framework for machine learning. In *Conference on Uncertainty in Artificial Intelligence (UAI)*.

N. Nakashole, M. Theobald, and G. Weikum. 2011. Scalable knowledge harvesting with high precision and high recall. In *Proceedings of the 4th International Conference on Web Search and Data Mining (WSDM)*, pages 227–236.

M. Niepert, J. Noessner, and H. Stuckenschmidt. 2011. Log-linear description logics. In *Proceedings of the 22nd International Joint Conference on Artificial Intelligence (IJCAI)*, pages 2153–2158.

M. Richardson and P. Domingos. 2006. Markov logic networks. *Machine Learning*, 62(1-2).

F. M. Suchanek, G. Kasneci, and G. Weikum. 2007. Yago: A Core of Semantic Knowledge. In *Proceedings of the 16th International World Wide Web Conference (WWW)*, pages 697–706.

G. Weikum and M. Theobald. 2010. From information to knowledge: harvesting entities and relationships from web sources. In *Proceedings of the 29th Symposium on the Principles of Database Systems (PODS)*, pages 65–76.

Michael L. Wick and Andrew McCallum. 2011. Query-aware mcmc. In *proceedings of the 25th Conference on Neural Information Processing Systems (NIPS)*, pages 2564–2572.

Collectively Representing Semi-Structured Data from the Web

Bhavana Dalvi
School of Computer Science
Carnegie Mellon University
Pittsburgh, PA 15213
bbd@cs.cmu.edu

William W. Cohen
School of Computer Science
Carnegie Mellon University
Pittsburgh, PA 15213
wcohen@cs.cmu.edu

Jamie Callan
School of Computer Science
Carnegie Mellon University
Pittsburgh, PA 15213
callan@cs.cmu.edu

Abstract

In this paper, we propose a single low-dimensional representation of a large collection of table and hyponym data, and show that with a small number of primitive operations, this representation can be used effectively for many purposes. Specifically we consider queries like set expansion, class prediction etc. We evaluate our methods on publicly available semi-structured datasets from the Web.

1 Introduction

Semi-structured data extracted from the web (in some cases extended with hyponym data derived from Hearst patterns like "X such as Y") have been used in several tasks, including set expansion (Wang and Cohen, 2009b; Dalvi et al., 2010) automatic set-instance acquisition (Wang and Cohen, 2009a), fact extraction (Dalvi et al., 2012; Talukdar et al., 2008)), and semi-supervised learning of concepts (Carlson et al., 2010). In past work, these tasks have been addressed using different methods and data structures. In this paper, we propose a single low-dimensional representation of a large collection of table and hyponym data, and show that with a small number of primitive operations, this representation can be used effectively for many purposes.

In particular, we propose a low-dimensional representation for entities based on the embedding used by the PIC algorithm (Lin and Cohen, 2010a). PIC assigns each node in a graph an initial random value, and then performs an iterative update which brings together the values assigned to near-by nodes, thus producing a one-dimensional embedding of a graph. In past work, PIC has been used for unsupervised clustering of graphs (Lin and Cohen, 2010a); it has also been extended to bipartite graphs (Lin and Cohen, 2010b), and it has been shown that performance can be improved by using multiple random starting points, thus producing a low-dimensional (but not one-dimensional) embedding of a graph (Balasubramanyan et al., 2010).

2 The PIC3 Representation

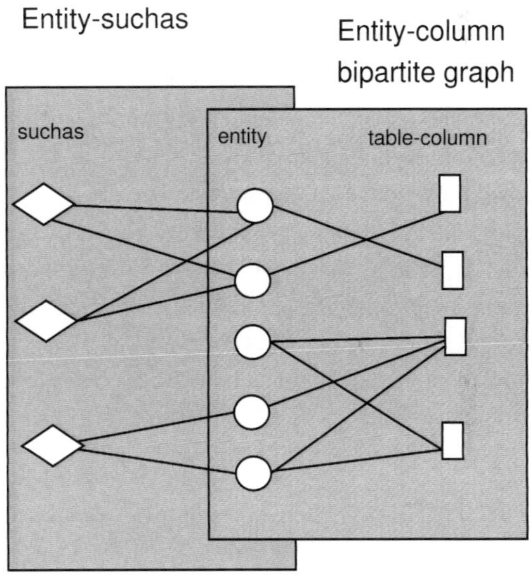

Figure 1: Entities on the Web

We use PIC to produce an embedding of a tripartite graph, in particular the data graph of Figure 1. We use the publicly available (Dalvi et al., 2012) entity-tableColumn co-occurrence dataset and Hyponym Concept dataset. Each edge derived from the entity-tableColumn dataset links an entity name with an identifier for a table column in which the entity name appeared. Each edge derived from the Hyponym Concept Dataset links an entity X and a concept Y with which it appeared in the context of a Hearst pattern (weighted by frequency in a large web corpus). We combine these edges to form a tripartite graph, as shown in Figure 1. Occurrences of entities with hyponym (or "such as") concepts form a bipartite graph on the left, and occurrences of entities in various table-columns form the bipartite graph on the right. Our hypothesis is that entities co-occurring in multiple table columns or with similar suchas concepts probably belong to the same class label.

Since we have two bipartite graphs, entity-tableColumn and entity-suchasConcept, we create bipartite PIC embeddings for each of these in turn (retaining only the part of the embedding relevant to the entities). Specifically, we start with m random vectors to generate m-dimensional PIC embedding. Since we have two bipartite graphs, entity-tableColumn and entity-suchasConcept, we create PIC embeddings for each of them separately. The embedding for entities is then the concatenation of these separate embeddings (refer to Algorithm 1). Below we will call this the PIC3 embedding.

Figure 2 shows the schematic diagrams for final and intermediate matrices while creating the PIC3 embedding. We have experimented with a version of this algorithm in which we create PIC embeddings of the data by concatenating the dimensions first instead of computing separate embeddings and later concatenating them. We observed that the version showed in Algorithm 1 performs as good as or better than its variant.

Algorithm 1 Create PIC3 embedding

function Create_PIC3_Embedding(E, X_T, X_S, m): X_{PIC3}
Input: E: Set of all entities,
X_T: Co-occurrence of E in table-columns,
X_S: Co-occurrence of E with suchasConcepts,
m: Number of PIC dimensions per bipartite graph
Output: X_{PIC3}: 2*m dim. PIC3 embedding of E.
$X_{PIC3} = \phi$
t = a small positive integer
for d = 1 : m **do**
    V_0 = randomly initialized vector of size $|E| * 1$
    V_t = *PIC_Embedding*(X_T, V_0, t)
    Add V_t as d^{th} column in X_{PIC3}
end for
for d = 1 : m **do**
    V_0 = randomly initialized vector of size $|E| * 1$
    V_t = *PIC_Embedding*(X_S, V_0, t)
    Add V_t as d^{th} column in X_{PIC3}
end for
end function

Our hypothesis is that these embeddings will cluster similar entities together. E.g. Figure 3 shows a one dimensional PIC embedding of entities belonging to the two classes "city" and "celebrity". The value of embedding is plotted against its entity-index, and color indicates the class of an entity. We can clearly see that most entities belonging to the same class are clustered together. In the next section, we will discuss how the PIC3 embedding can be used for various semi-supervised and unsupervised tasks.

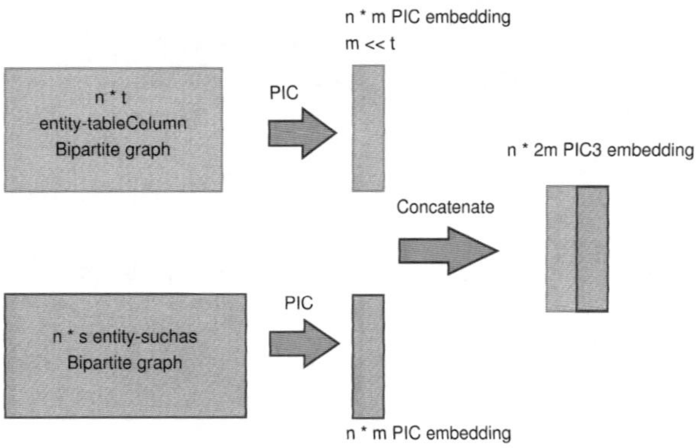

Figure 2: Schematic diagram of matrices in the process of creating PIC3 representation (n : number of entities, t : number of table-columns, s : number of suchas concepts and m : number of PIC dimensions per bipartite graph).

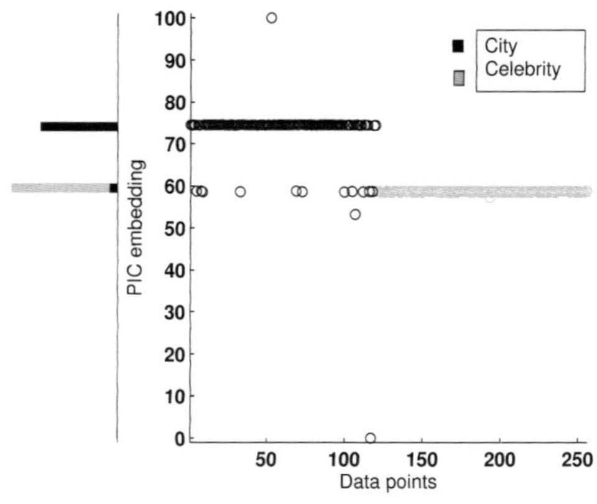

Figure 3: One dimensional PIC embedding for 'City' and 'Celebrity' classes

3 Using the PIC3 Representation

In this section we will see how this PIC3 representation for entities can be used for three different tasks.

3.1 Semi-supervised Learning

In semi-supervised transductive learning, a few entities of each class are labeled, and learning method extrapolates these labels to a larger number of unlabeled data points. To use the PIC3 representation for this task, we simply learn a linear classifier in the embedded space. In the experiments below, we experiment with using labeled entities Y_n from the NELL Knowledge Base (Carlson et al., 2010). We note that once the PIC3 representation has been built, this approach is much more efficient than applying graph-based iterative semi-supervised learning methods (Talukdar and Crammer, 2009; Carlson et al., 2010).

3.2 Set Expansion

Set expansion refers to the problem of expanding a set of seed entities into a larger set of entities of the same type. To perform set expansion with PIC3 representation, we find the K nearest neighbors of the centroid of the set of seed entities using a KD-tree (refer to Algorithm 2). Again, this approach is more efficient at query time than prior approaches such as SEAL (Wang and Cohen, 2009b), which ranks nodes within a graph it builds on-the-fly at set expansion time using queries to the web.

Algorithm 2 Set Expansion with K-NN on PIC3

```
1: Input: Q: seed entities for set expansion ,
   X_PIC: low dimensional PIC3 embedding of E
2: Output: Q' : Expanded entity set
3: k = a large positive number
4: Q_c = centroid of entities in Q
5: Q' = Find-K-NearestNbr(Q_c, X_PIC, k)
```

3.3 Automatic Set Instance Acquisition (ASIA)

This task takes as input the name of a semantic class (e.g.,"countries") and automatically outputs its instances (e.g., "USA" , "India" , "China" etc.). To perform this task, we look up instances of the given class in the hyponym dataset, and then perform set expansion on these - a process analogous to that used in prior work (Wang and Cohen, 2009a). Here, however, we again use Algorithm 2 for set expansion, so the entity-suchasConcept data are used only to find seeds for a particular class Y. Again this method requires minimal resources at query time.

Dataset	Toy_Apple	Delicious_Sports
$\|X\|$: # entities	14,996	438
$\|C\|$: # table-columns	156	925
$\|(x, c)\|$: # (x, c) edges	176,598	9192
$\|Y_s\|$: # suchasConcepts	2348	1649
$\|(x, Y_s)\|$: # (x, Y_s) edges	7683	4799
$\|Y_n\|$: # NELL Classes	11	3
$\|(x, Y_n)\|$: # (x, Y_n) pairs	419	39
$\|Y_c\|$: # manual column labels	31	30
(c, Y_c): # (c, Y_c) pairs	156	925

Table 1: Table datasets Statistics

4 Experiments

Although PIC algorithm is very scalable, in this paper we evaluate performance using smaller datasets which are extensively labeled. In particular, we use the Delicious_Sports, Toy_Apple and Hyponym Concept datasets made publicly available by (Dalvi et al., 2012) to evaluate our techniques. Table 1 shows some statistics about these datasets. Numbers for $|Y_s|$ and $|(x, Y_s)|$ are derived using the Hyponym Concept Dataset.

4.1 Semi-supervised Learning (SSL)

To evaluate the PIC embeddings in terms of predicting NELL concept-names, we compare the performance of an SVM classifier on PIC embeddings (named SVM+PIC3) vs. the original high-dimensional dataset (named SVM-baseline). In SVM-baseline method the hyponyms and table-columns associated with an entity are simply used as features. The number of iterations t for PIC and number of dimensions per view m were set to $t = m = 5$ in these experiments. (Experiments with $m > 5$ showed no significant improvements in accuracy on Toy_Apple dataset.)

Figure 4 shows the plot of accuracy vs. training size for both datasets. We can see that SVM+PIC3 method is better than SVM-Baseline with less training data, hence is better in SSL scenarios. Also note that PIC3 embedding reduces the number of dimensions from 2574 (Delicious_Sports) and 2504

(Toy_Apple) to merely 10 dimensions. We checked the rank of the matrix which we use as PIC3 representation to make sure that all the PIC embeddings are distinct. In our experiments we found that an m dimensional embedding always has $rank = m$. This is achieved by generating a new random vector V_0 using distinct randomization seeds each time we call the PIC embedding procedure (see Line 7 and 12 in Algorithm 1).

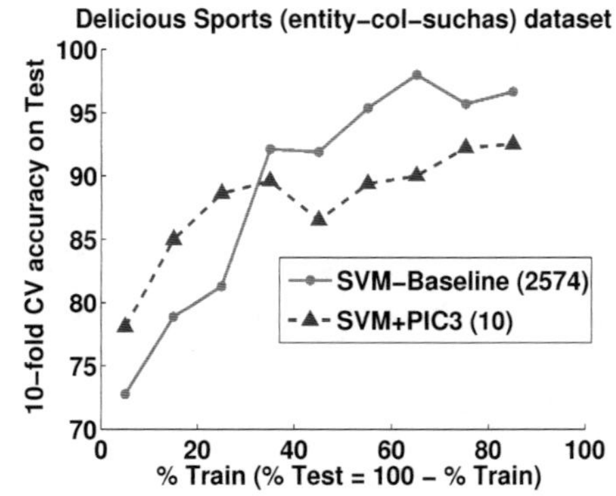

(a) Delicious_Sports dataset

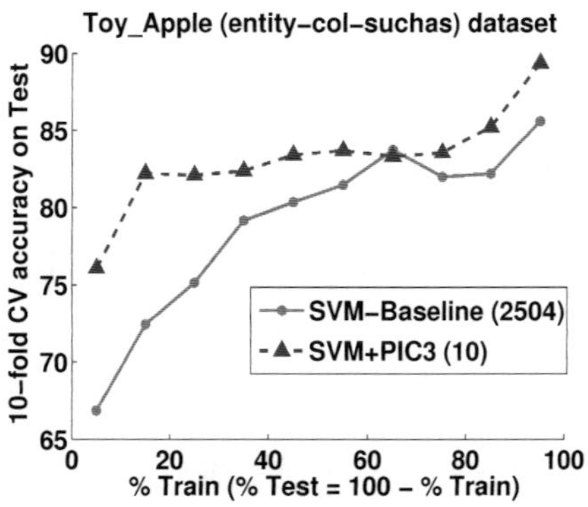

(b) Toy_Apple dataset

Figure 4: SSL Task : Comparison of SVM+PIC3 vs. SVM-Baseline

4.2 Set Expansion

We manually labeled every table column from Delicious_Sports and Toy_Apple datasets. These labels are referred to as Y_c in Table 1. This also gives us labels for the entities residing in these table-columns. We use the set of entities in each of these table columns as "a set expansion query" and evaluate "the expanded set of entities" based on manual labels. The baseline runs K-Nearest Neighbor on the original high-dimensional dataset (referred to as K-NN-Baseline).

As another baseline, we adapt the MAD algorithm (Talukdar and Crammer, 2009), a state-of-the art semi-supervised learning method. Similar to a prior work by (Talukdar et al., 2010), we adapt MAD for unsupervised learning by associating each table-column node with its own id as a label, and propagating these labels to other table-columns. MAD also includes a "dummy label", so after propagation every table-column T_q will be labeled with a weighted set of table-column ids $T_{s_1}, ...T_{s_n}$ (including its own id), and also have a weight for the "dummy label". We denote MAD's weight for associating table-column id T_s with table column T_q as $P(T_s|T_q)$, and consider the ids $T_{s_1}, ...T_{s_k}$ with a weight higher than the dummy label's weight. We consider e_1, e_2, ... e_n, the union of entities present in columns $T_{s_1}...T_{s_k}$, and rank them in descending order score, where $score(e_i, T_q) = \sum_{j:e_i \in T_{s_j}} P(T_{s_j}|T_q)$. Figure 5 shows Precision-

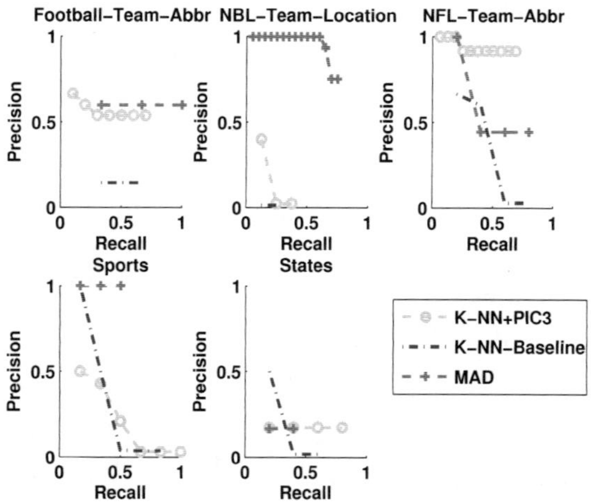

Figure 5: Set Expansion Task : Precision recall curves

Recall curves for all 3 methods, on sample set expansion queries. These plots are annotated with manual column-labels (Y_c). For most of the queries, K-NN+PIC3 performs as well as K-NN-Baseline and is comparable to MAD algorithm. Table 2 shows the running time for all three methods. K-NN+PIC3 method incurs a small amount of preprocessing time (0.02 seconds) to create embeddings and compared to other two methods it is very fast at the query time. The numbers show total query time for 881 Set Expansion queries and 25 ASIA queries (described below).

Method	Total Query Time (s)	
	Set Expansion	ASIA
K-NN+PIC3	12.7	0.5
K-NN-Baseline	80.1	1.4
MAD	38.2	150.0

Table 2: Comparison of Run Time on Delicious_Sports

4.3 Automatic Set Instance Acquisition

For the automatic set instance acquisition (ASIA) task, we use concept-names from Hyponym Concept Dataset (Y_s) as queries. Similar to the Set Expansion task, we compare K-NN+PIC3 to the K-NN-Baseline and MAD methods.

To use MAD for this task, the concept name Y_s is injected as label for the ten entities that co-occur most with Y_s, and the label propagation algorithm is run. Each entity e_i that scores higher than the dummy label is then ranked based on the probability of the label Y_s for that entity.

Figure 6 shows the comparison of all three methods. K-NN+PIC3 generally outperforms K-NN-Baseline, and outperforms MAD on two of the four queries. MAD's improvements over K-NN+PIC3 for the two queries comes at the expense of longer query times (refer to Table 2).

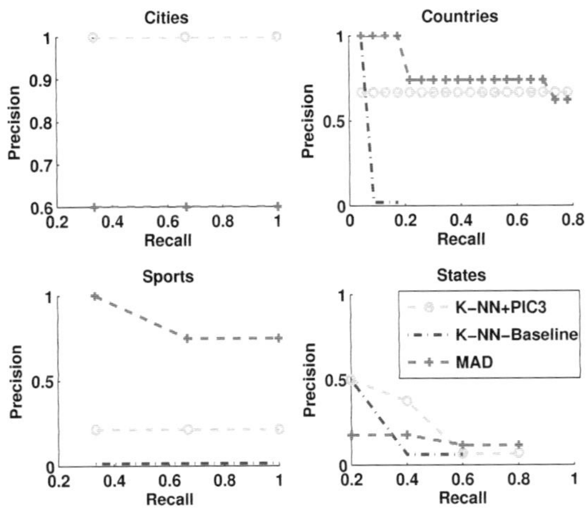

Figure 6: ASIA task : Precision recall curves

5 Conclusion

We presented a novel low-dimensional representation for entities on the Web using Power Iteration Clustering. Our experiments show encouraging results on using this representation for three different tasks : (a) Semi-Supervised Learning, (b) Set Expansion and (c) Automatic Set Instance Acquisition. The experiments show that "this simple representation (PIC3) can go a long way, and can solve different problems in a simpler and faster, if not better way". In future, we would like to use this representation for named-entity disambiguation and unsupervised class-instance pair acquisition, and to explore performance on larger datasets.

Acknowledgments

This work is supported in part by the Intelligence Advanced Research Projects Activity (IARPA) via Air Force Research Laboratory (AFRL) contract number FA8650-10-C-7058. The U.S. Government is authorized to reproduce and distribute reprints for Governmental purposes notwithstanding any copyright annotation thereon. This work is also partially supported by the Google Research Grant.

The views and conclusions contained herein are those of the authors and should not be interpreted as necessarily representing the official policies or endorsements, either expressed or implied, of Google, IARPA, AFRL, or the U.S. Government.

References

Balasubramanyan, R., Lin, F., and Cohen, W. W. (2010). Node clustering in graphs: An empirical study. Workshop on Networks Across Disciplines in Theory and Applications, NIPS.

Carlson, A., Betteridge, J., Wang, R. C., Hruschka, Jr., E. R., and Mitchell, T. M. (2010). Coupled semi-supervised learning for information extraction. In *WSDM*. `http://rtw.ml.cmu.edu/rtw/`.

Dalvi, B., Callan, J., and Cohen, W. (2010). Entity list completion using set expansion techniques. In *Proceedings of the Nineteenth Text REtrieval Conference*.

Dalvi, B., Cohen, W., and Callan, J. (2012). Websets: Extracting sets of entities from the web using unsupervised information extraction. In *WSDM*. datasets : `http://rtw.ml.cmu.edu/wk/WebSets/wsdm_2012_online/index.html`.

Lin, F. and Cohen, W. W. (2010a). Power iteration clustering. In *Proceedings of International Conference on Machine Learning*, ICML'10.

Lin, F. and Cohen, W. W. (2010b). A very fast method for clustering big text datasets. ECAI.

Talukdar, P. and Crammer, K. (2009). New regularized algorithms for transductive learning. In *European Conference on Machine Learning (ECML-PKDD)*.

Talukdar, P. P., Ives, Z. G., and Pereira, F. (2010). Automatically incorporating new sources in keyword search-based data integration. In *Proceedings of the 2010 international conference on Management of data*, SIGMOD '10.

Talukdar, P. P., Reisinger, J., Paşca, M., Ravichandran, D., Bhagat, R., and Pereira, F. (2008). Weakly-supervised acquisition of labeled class instances using graph random walks. In *EMNLP*.

Wang, R. C. and Cohen, W. W. (2009a). Automatic set instance extraction using the web. In *ACL*.

Wang, R. C. and Cohen, W. W. (2009b). Character-level analysis of semi-structured documents for set expansion. In *EMNLP*.

Unsupervised Content Discovery from Concise Summaries

Horacio Saggion
Universitat Pompeu Fabra
Department of Information and Communication Technologies
TALN Group
C/Tanger 122 - Campus de la Comunicación
Barcelona - 08018
Spain

Abstract

Domain adaptation is a time consuming and costly procedure calling for the development of algorithms and tools to facilitate its automation. This paper presents an unsupervised algorithm able to learn the main concepts in event summaries. The method takes as input a set of domain summaries annotated with shallow linguistic information and produces a domain template. We demonstrate the viability of the method by applying it to three different domains and two languages. We have evaluated the generated templates against human templates obtaining encouraging results.

1 Introduction

Our research is concerned with the development of techniques for knowledge induction in the field of text summarization. Our goal is to automatically induce the necessary knowledge for the generation of concise event summaries such as the one shown in Figure 1. This kind of summaries, which can be found on the Web and in text collections, contain key information of the events they describe. Previous work in the area of text summarization (DeJong, 1982; Oakes and Paice, 2001; Saggion and Lapalme, 2002) addressed the problem of generating this type of concise summaries from texts, relying on information extraction and text generation techniques. These approaches were difficult to port to new domains and languages because of the efforts needed for modelling the underlying event template structure. In this paper we propose a method for learning the main concepts in domain summaries in an unsupervised iterative procedure. The proposed algorithm takes a set of unannotated summaries in a given domain and produces auto-annotated summaries which can be used for training information extraction and text generation systems. Domain adaptation is essential for text summarization and information extraction, and the last two decades have seen a plethora of methods for supervised, semi-supervised, and unsupervised learning from texts.

> **2001 August 24**: **Air Transat Flight 236** runs out of **fuel** over **the Atlantic Ocean** and makes **an emergency landing** in **the Azores**. Upon landing some of **the tires** blow out, causing **a fire** that is extinguished by **emergency personnel** on **the ground**. None of **the 304 people** on **board the Airbus A330-200** were seriously injured.

Figure 1: Summary in the aviation domain annotated with chunks

For example, in (Li et al., 2010) clustering is applied to generate templates for specific entity types (actors, companies, etc.) and patterns are automatically produced that describe the information in the templates. In (Chambers and Jurafsky, 2009) narrative schemas are induced from corpora using coreference relations between participants in texts. Transformation-based learning is used in (Saggion, 2011) to induce templates and rules for non-extractive summary generation. Paraphrase templates containing concepts and typical strings were induced from comparable sentences in (Barzilay and Lee, 2003) using multi-sentence alignment to discover "variable" and fixed structures. Linguistic patterns were applied to huge amounts of non-annotated pre-classified texts in (Riloff, 1996) to bootstrap information extraction patterns. Similarly, semi-supervised or unsupervised methods have been used to learn question/answering patterns (Ravichandran and Hovy, 2002) or text schemas (Bunescu and Mooney, 2007). One current paradigm to learn from raw data is open information extraction (Downey et al., 2004; Banko, 2009), which without any prior knowledge aims at discovering all possible relations between pairs of entities occurring in text. Our work tries to learn the main concepts making up the template structure in domain summaries, similar to (Chambers and Jurafsky, 2011). However, we do not rely on any source of external knowledge (i.e. WordNet) to do so.

This paper presents an iterative-learning algorithm which is able to identify the key components of event summaries. We will show that the algorithm can induce template-like representations in various domains and languages. The rest of the paper is organized in the following way: In Section 2 we introduce the dataset we are using for our experiments and describe how we have prepated it for experimentation. Then, in Section 3 we provide an overview of our concept induction learnig algorithm while in Section 4 we explain how we have instantiated the algorithm for the experiments presented in this paper. Section 5 describe the experiments and results obtained and Section 6 discusses our approach comparing it with past research. Finally, in Section 7 we close the paper with conclusions and future work.

2 Data and Data Preparation

The dataset used for this study – part of the CONCISUS corpus (Saggion and Szasz, 2012) – consists of a set of 250 summaries in Spanish and English for three different domains: aviation accidents, rail accidents, and earthquakes. This dataset makes it possible to compare the performance of learning procedures across languages and domains. Based on commonsense, a human annotator developed an annotation schema per domain to describe in a template-like representation the essential elements (i.e., slots) of each event. For example, for the aviation accident domain these essential elements were: the date of the accident, the number of victims, the airline, the aircraft, the location of the accident, the flight number, the origin and destination of the flight, etc. The dataset was then annotated following the schema using the GATE annotation tool. The human annotations are used for evaluation of the concept discovery algorithm. Each document in the dataset was automatically annotated using tools for each language. We relied on basic processing steps to identify sentences, words and word-roots, parts of speech, noun-chunks, and named entities using the GATE system for English (Maynard et al., 2002) and TreeTagger for Spanish (Schmid, 1995).

Algorithm 1 Iterative Learning Algorithm: Main

```
Given: C: Corpus of Summaries Annotated with Chunks
Returns: LIST: A list of concepts discovered by the algorithm
begin
LIST ← ∅;
while (EXIST_CONCEPTS_TO_LEARN) do
    CONCEPT ← LEAN_CONCEPT(C);
    if (not FILTER_CONCEPT(CONCEPT)) then
        LIST ← LIST ∪ CONCEPT;
    end if
    REMOVE_USED_CHUNKS(C);
end while
end
```

3 Learning Algorithm

The method is designed to learn the conceptual information in the summaries by extension (i.e., the set of strings that make up the concept in a given corpus) and by intension (i.e., an algorithm able to recognise the concept members in new documents in the domain) (Buitelaar and Magnini, 2005). Concept extensions identified by our method in the English summaries in the aviation domain are listed in Table 3. Each summary in the corpus can be seen as a sequence of strings and chunks as shown in Figure 1 (named entities and noun chunks are shown in boldface and they may overlap). The procedure to learn a concept in the corpus of summaries is given in pseudocode in Algorithm 2 which is repeatedly invoked by a main algorithm to learn all concepts (Algorithm 1).

The idea of the algorithm is rather simple, at each iteration a document is selected for learning, and from this document a single chunk (i.e., a noun chunk or a named entity) available for learning is selected as a seed example of a hypothetical concept (the concept is given a unique name at each itera-

Concept	Extension
1	Boeign 737-400; Boeign 777-200ER; Airbus 300; ...
2	August 16; December 20; February 12; ...
3	Colombia; Algiers; Brazil; Marseille; ...
4	102; 107; 145; 130; ...
5	Flight 243; Flight 1549; Flight 1907; ...
6	1988; 1994; 2001; ...

Table 1: Concepts Discovered in the Aviation Domain. They correspond (in order) to the type of aircraft, date of the incident, place of the accident, number of victims, flight number, and year of the accident.

Algorithm 2 Iterative Learning Algorithm: Learn Concept

```
 1: Given: C: Corpus of summaries automatically annotated with
    named entities and chunks
 2: Returns: CONCEPT: A concept by extension and a trained algo-
    rithm to discover instances of the concept in text
 3: begin
 4: DOC ← SELECT_DOCUMENT(C);
 5: DOC ← ANNOTATE_WITH_TARGET(DOC);
 6: REST ← C \ {DOC};
 7: TRAINSET ← {DOC};
 8: CONTINUE ← true;
 9: while ((EXIST_DOCUMENTS_TO_LEARN) AND CON-
    TINUE) do
10:    TRAIN(CLASSIFIER,TRAINSET);
11:    APPLY(CLASSIFIER,REST);
12:    if (DOCUMENT_LEANED(REST)) then
13:       BESTDOC ← SELECT_BEST(REST);
14:       TRAINSET ← TRAINSET ∪ {BESTDOC};
15:       REST ← REST \ {BESTDOC};
16:       CLEAN(REST);
17:    else
18:       CONTINUE ← false;
19:    end if
20: end while
21: CONCEPT ←< EXTENSION(TRAINSET); CLASSIFIER >;
22: return CONCEPT;
23: end
```

tion). The document is annotated with this seed as a target concept and a classifier is trained using this document. The trained classifier is then applied to the rest of the documents to identify instances of the hypothetical concept. If the classifier is unsuccessful in identifying new instances, then the chunk used in the current iteration is discarded from the learning process, but if the classifier is successful and able to identify instances of the hypothetical concept, then the "best" annotated document is selected and added to the training set. The classifier is re-trained using the new added document and the process is repeated until no more instances can be identified. A hypothetical concept is kept only if there is enough support for it across the set of documents. The main procedure calls the basic algorithms a number of times while there are concepts to be learnt (or all chunks have been used). The stopping criteria is the number of concepts which could possibly be learnt, an estimation of which is the average number of chunks in a document.

4 Algorithm Instantiation

Experiments were carried out per domain and language to assess the suitability of the algorithm to the conceptual learning task. A number of points in Algorithm 2 need clarification: the selection of a document in line 4 of the algorithm can be carried out using different informed procedures; for the experiments described here we decided to select the document with more available hypotheses, i.e., the document with more chunks. For the selection of a chunk to start the learning procedure in line 5 of the algorithm we select the next available chunk in text order. The classifier we used in line 10 of the algorithm is instantiated to Support Vector Machines (SVMs) which are distributed with the GATE system (Li et al., 2004). The features we use for representing the instance to be learnt are very superficial for these experiments: lemmas, parts-of-speech tags, orthography, and named entity types of the words surrounding the target concept to be learnt. The SVMs provide as output a class together with a probability which is essential to our method. We use this probability for selecting the best document in line 13 of the algorithm: the instance predicted with the highest probability is located and the document where this instance occurs is returned as "best document". In case no instances are learned (e.g., *else* in line 17), the iteration ends returning the extension learnt so far. Concerning Algorithm 1: in line 5 (the *while*) we use as stopping criteria for the maximum number of concepts to learn the average number of chunks in the corpus. In line 7, the FILTER_CONCEPT function evaluates the concept, keeping it only if two criteria are met: (i) there are not "too many" repetitions of a string in the discovered concept and (ii) the discovered concept covers a reasonable number of documents. With criteria (i) we filter out a concept which contains repeated strings: a concept could be formed simply by grouping together all repeated phrases in the set of documents (i.e. "the earthquake" or "the accident" or "the plane"). While these phrases could be relevant in the target domain they do not constitute a key concept in our interpretation. Strings which are repeated in the concept extension are more like the "backbone structure" of the summaries in the domain. In our experiments both criteria are experimental variables and we vary them from 10% to 100% at 20% intervals. In Section 5 we will present results for the best configurations.

5 Experiments and Results

In order to evaluate the discovered concepts we have treated learning as information extraction. In order to evaluate them in this context we first need to map each learnt concept onto one of the human concepts. The mapping, which is based on the concept extension, is straightforward: a discovered concept is mapped onto the human concept with which it has a majority of string matches. Note that we match the discovered text offsets in the analysed documents and not only the identified strings. In order to evaluate the matching procedure we have used precision, recall, and f-score measures comparing the automatic concept with the human concept. Note that we use a lenient procedure – counting as correct strings those with a partial match. This is justified since discovering the exact boundaries of a concept instance is a very difficult task. Table 2 shows some examples of the human annotated instances and related discovered one. It can be appreciated that the learnt concepts have a reasonable match degree with the human annotated ones.

Table 3 gives information extraction results per domain and language for the best configuration of the algorithm. The best scores are generally obtained when coverage is set to 10% of the number of summaries, except for the learning of conceptual information in Spanish for the earthquake domain where the system performs better for 10% summary coverage. The parameter controlling string repetition in the concept extension should be kept small. The obtained results are quite satisfactory considering the small dataset and the limited use of linguistic resources during learning. These results compare favorably to cross-validation results obtained using supervised machine learning techniques (Saggion and Szasz, 2011). Learning from the earthquake domain appears to be more challenging given the more verbose characteristics of these texts. Even though space restricions prevent us from showing all evaluation results, in Table 4 we present detailed results for the two domains and languages. Note that the concepts listed constitute the slots of the induced domain template.

Annotated Instance	**Discovered Instance**
PMTair (Airline)	PMTair Flight
Boeing 777-200ER (TypeOfAircraft)	Boeing 777
the Margalla Hills northest of Islamabad (Place)	Margalla
transporte de mercancias (TypeOfTrain)	mercancias
29 abril 1997 (DateOfAccident)	29 abril

Table 2: Examples of Concept Extensions Partially Matched

Spanish			
Domain (% rep, % cov)	**Prec.**	**Rec.**	**F**
Aviation Accident (10%, 10%)	0.53	0.57	0.60
Rail Accident (10%, 10%)	0.66	0.67	0.66
Earthquake (10%, 30%)	0.41	0.30	0.35
English			
Domain	**Prec.**	**Rec.**	**F**
Aviation Accident (10%, 10%)	0.67	0.64	0.66
Rail Accident (30%, 10%)	0.52	0.33	0.44
Earthquake (10%, 10%)	0.40	0.19	0.26

Table 3: Performance in terms of Precision, Recall, and F-Score per Domain and Language. % rep and % cov are the repetition and coverage parameters used.

6 Discussion

Similar to active learning information extraction techniques (Ciravegna and Wilks, 2003), the concept discovery algorithm presented here is inspired by techniques like learning by reading, where unfamiliar expressions in one document can be "explained" by association to expressions in similar

English - Aviation Accidents			
Concept	**Precision**	**Recall**	**F-score**
Airline	0.90	0.90	0.90
DateOfAccident	0.90	0.93	0.92
FlightNumber	0.91	0.94	0.92
NumberOfVictims	0.41	0.30	0.35
Place	0.34	0.54	0.42
TypeOfAccident	0.42	0.76	0.54
TypeOfAircraft	0.73	0.75	0.74
Year	0.94	0.97	0.95
All	0.67	0.64	0.66
Spanish - Train Accidents			
Concept	**Precision**	**Recall**	**F-score**
DateOfAccident	1.00	1.00	1.00
NumberOfVictims	0.97	0.91	0.94
Place	0.43	0.76	0.55
Survivors	0.55	0.96	0.70
TypeOfAccident	0.74	0.63	0.68
TypeOfTrain	0.35	0.30	0.32
All	0.66	0.67	0.66
Spanish - Earthquakes			
Concept	**Precision**	**Recall**	**F-score**
Country	0.53	0.36	0.43
DateOfEarthquake	0.96	0.94	0.95
Fatalities	0.37	0.28	0.32
Magnitude	0.54	0.32	0.40
Region	0.16	0.56	0.25
All	0.35	0.35	0.35

Table 4: Learning Evaluation in the Train and Aviation Accident and Earthquake Domains (Spanish and English Dataset)

document contexts. However, and unlike active learning, human intervention is unnecessary in our approach. Although the algorithm achieves reasonably lenient performance, strict (hard) evaluation indicates that in each experimental condition performance drops when a strict match is required. This is expected given the difficulty of finding the right instance boundaries based only on automatic chunking information. For this reason, we intend to carry out additional experiments based on richer domain independent features from a syntactic parser. We have identified a number of reasons why some concept instances can not be correctly associated with their concepts. In the aviation domain, for example, numeric expressions constitute the extensions of different concepts including: number of victims, crew members, and number of survivors; it is a rather common feature in the aviation domain to include these different concepts together in one sentence, making their "separation" complicated. Same explanations apply to other tested domains: for example locations playing the role of origin and destination of a given train or airplace are also sometimes confused. Our work demonstrates the possibility of learning conceptual information in several domains and languages, while previous work (Chambers and Jurafsky, 2011) has addressed sets of related domains (e.g., MUC-4 templates) in English. Learning *full conceptualizations* from raw data is a daunting and difficult enterprise (Biemann, 2005). Here, we provide a short-cut by proposing a method able to learn the essential concepts of a domain by relying on summaries which are freely available on the Web. Our method is able to produce conceptualizations from a few documents in each domain and language unlike recent open domain information extraction which requires massive amount of texts for relation learning (Banko, 2009). Our algorithm has a reasonable computational complexity, unlike alignment-based or clustering-based approaches (Barzilay and Lee, 2003), which are computationally expensive.

7 Conclusions and Outlook

Domain adaptation is a time consuming and costly procedure calling for the development of algorithms and tools to facilitate its automation. In this paper we have presented a novel algorithm for learning information content in event summaries. The approach is fully unsupervised and based on the application of an iterative algorithm which grows a concept extension step-by-step. We have also proposed an instantiation of the algorithm and demonstrated its applicability to learning conceptual information in three different domains and two languages. We have obtained encouraging results, with the procedure able to model the main conceptual information in the summaries with lenient F-scores ranging from 0.25 to 0.66 F-scores depending on the language and domain. There are, however, a number of avenues that should be further explored such as the use of a richer document representation based on syntactic information and the development of additional procedures to improve instance boundary recognition.

Acknowledgements

We are grateful to the Advanced Research Fellowship RYC-2009-04291 from Programa Ramón y Cajal 2009, Ministerio de Economía y Competitividad, Secretaría de Estado de Investigación, Desarrollo e Innovación, Spain. We thank Biljana Drndarevic who helped proofreading the paper.

References

M. Banko. 2009. *Open Information Extraction for the Web*. Ph.D. thesis, University of Washington.

R. Barzilay and L. Lee. 2003. Learning to paraphrase: an unsupervised approach using multiple-sequence alignment. In *Proceedings of the 2003 Conference of the North American Chapter of the Association for Computational Linguistics on Human Language Technology - Volume 1*, NAACL '03, pages 16–23, Stroudsburg, PA, USA. Association for Computational Linguistics.

C. Biemann. 2005. Ontology Learning from Text: A Survey of Methods. *LDV Forum*, 20(2):75–93.

P. Buitelaar and B. Magnini. 2005. Ontology learning from text: An overview. In *In Paul Buitelaar, P., Cimiano, P., Magnini B. (Eds.), Ontology Learning from Text: Methods, Applications and Evaluation*, pages 3–12. IOS Press.

R.C. Bunescu and R.J. Mooney. 2007. Learning to extract relations from the web using minimal supervision. In *ACL*.

N. Chambers and D. Jurafsky. 2009. Unsupervised learning of narrative schemas and their participants. In *ACL/AFNLP*, pages 602–610.

N. Chambers and D. Jurafsky. 2011. Template-Based Information Extraction without the Templates. In *ACL*, pages 976–986.

F. Ciravegna and Y. Wilks. 2003. Designing Adaptive Information Extraction for the Semantic Web in Amilcare. In S. Handschuh and S. Staab, editors, *Annotation for the Semantic Web*. IOS Press, Amsterdam.

G. DeJong. 1982. An Overview of the FRUMP System. In W.G. Lehnert and M.H. Ringle, editors, *Strategies for Natural Language Processing*, pages 149–176. Lawrence Erlbaum Associates, Publishers.

D. Downey, O. Etzioni, S. Soderland, and D. S. Weld. 2004. Learning Text Patterns for Web Information Extraction and Assessment. In *Proceedings of AAAI 2004 Workshop on Adaptive Text Extraction and Mining (ATEM'04)*.

Y. Li, K. Bontcheva, and H. Cunningham. 2004. An SVM Based Learning Algorithm for Information Extraction. Machine Learning Workshop, Sheffield.

P. Li, J. Jiang, and Y. Wang. 2010. Generating Templates of Entity Summaries with an Entity-Aspect Model and Pattern Mining. In *Proceedings of ACL*, Uppsala. ACL.

D. Maynard, V. Tablan, H. Cunningham, C. Ursu, H. Saggion, K. Bontcheva, and Y. Wilks. 2002. Architectural Elements of Language Engineering Robustness. *Journal of Natural Language Engineering – Special Issue on Robust Methods in Analysis of Natural Language Data*, 8(2/3):257–274.

Michael P. Oakes and Chris D. Paice. 2001. Term extraction for automatic abstracting. In D. Bourigault, C. Jacquemin, and M-C. L'Homme, editors, *Recent Advances in Computational Terminology*, volume 2 of *Natural Language Processing*, chapter 17, pages 353–370. John Benjamins Publishing Company.

D. Ravichandran and E. Hovy. 2002. Learning surface text patterns for a question answering system. In *ACL*, pages 41–47.

E. Riloff. 1996. Automatically generating extraction patterns from untagged text. *Proceedings of the Thirteenth Annual Conference on Artificial Intelligence*, pages 1044–1049.

H. Saggion and G. Lapalme. 2002. Generating Indicative-Informative Summaries with SumUM. *Computational Linguistics*, 28:497–526, December.

H. Saggion and S. Szasz. 2011. Multi-domain Cross-lingual Information Extraction from Clean and Noisy Texts. In *Proceedings of the 8th Brazilian Symposium in Information and Human Language Technology*, Cuiabá, Brazil. BCS.

H. Saggion and S. Szasz. 2012. The CONCISUS Corpus of Event Summaries. In *Proceedings of the 8th Language Resources and Evaluation Conference (LREC)*, Istanbul, Turkey. ELDA.

H. Saggion. 2011. Learning predicate insertion rules for document abstracting. In *Lecture Notes in Computer Science*, volume 6609, pages 301–312.

H. Schmid. 1995. Improvements in part-of-speech tagging with an application to german. In *In Proceedings of the ACL SIGDAT-Workshop*, pages 47–50.

Automatic Evaluation of Relation Extraction Systems on Large-scale

Mirko Bronzi †, **Zhaochen Guo** ‡, **Filipe Mesquita** ‡, **Denilson Barbosa** ‡, **Paolo Merialdo** †

†Università degli Studi Roma Tre
Via della Vasca Navale, 79
Rome, Italy
{bronzi,merialdo}@dia.uniroma3.it

‡University of Alberta
2-32 Athabasca Hall
Edmonton, Canada
{zhaochen,mesquita,denilson}@ualberta.ca

Abstract

The extraction of relations between named entities from natural language text is a long-standing challenge in information extraction, especially in large-scale. A major challenge for the advancement of this research field has been the lack of meaningful evaluation frameworks based on realistic-sized corpora. In this paper we propose a framework for large-scale evaluation of relation extraction systems based on an automatic annotator that uses a public online database and a large web corpus.

1 Introduction

It is envisioned that in the future, the main source of structured data to build knowledge bases will be automatically extracted from natural language sources (Doan et al., 2009). One promising technique towards this goal is Relation Extraction (RE): the task of identifying relations among named entities (e.g., people, organizations and geo-political entities) from natural language text. Traditionally, RE systems required each target relation to be given as input along with a set of examples (Brin, 1998; Agichtein and Gravano, 2000; Zelenko et al., 2003). A new paradigm termed *Open RE* (Banko and Etzioni, 2008) has recently emerged to cope with the scenario where the number of target relations is too large or even unknown. Open RE systems try to extract every relation described in the text, as opposed to focusing on a few relations (Zhu et al., 2009; Banko and Etzioni, 2008; Hasegawa et al., 2004; Rosenfeld and Feldman, 2007; Chen et al., 2005; Mesquita et al., 2010; Fader et al., 2011).

One challenge in advancing the state-of-the-art in open RE (or any other field for that matter) is having meaningful and fair ways of evaluating and comparing different systems. This is particularly difficult when it comes to evaluating the *recall* of such systems, as that requires one to enumerate all relations described in a corpus.

In order to scale, a method for evaluation of open RE must have no human involvement. One way to automatically produce a benchmark is to use an existing database as ground truth (Agichtein and Gravano, 2000; Mintz et al., 2009; Mesquita et al., 2010) . Although a step in the right direction, this approach limits the evaluation to those relations that are present in the database. Another shortcoming is that the database does not provide "true" recall, since it often contains many more facts (for the relations it holds) than described in the corpus.

Measuring true precision and recall In this paper we discuss an automatic method to estimate true precision and recall of open RE systems. We propose the use of an automatic annotator: a system capable of verifying whether or not a fact was correctly extracted. This is done by leveraging external sources of data and text, which are not available to the systems being evaluated. The external database used in this work is Freebase, a curated online database maintained by an active community. In addition to the external database, our automatic annotator leverages Pointwise Mutual Information (PMI) (Turney, 2001) from the web. PMI has been widely accepted to measure the confidence score of an extraction (Etzioni et al., 2005). We show that

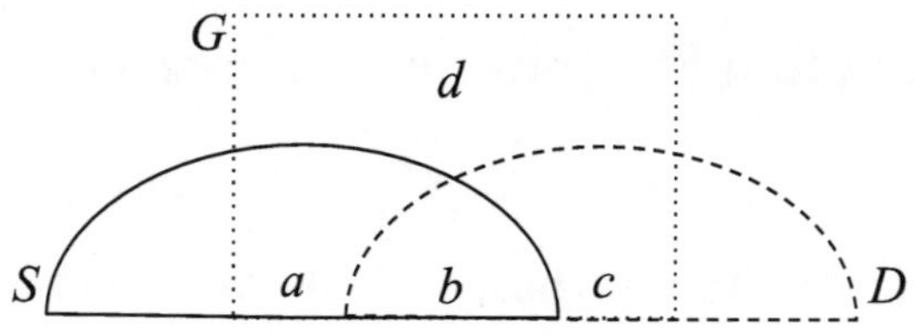

Figure 1: Venn diagram showing the interaction between an external database D (Freebase), the ground truth G and a system output S.

PMI is also useful to evaluate systems automatically.

Using our method, we compare two state-of-the-art open RE systems, ReVerb (Fader et al., 2011) and SONEX (Mesquita et al., 2010), applied to the same corpus, namely the New York Times Corpus (Sandhaus, 2008).

2 Evaluation Methodology

We now describe how our method measures both true precision and true recall, using a database and the web (as a large external text corpus). A *fact* is a triple $f_i = \langle e_1, r, e_2 \rangle$ associating entities e_1 and e_2 via relation r. We measure precision by assessing how many of the facts produced by the system have been correctly extracted. A fact is said to be *correct* if (1) we can find the fact in the database or (2) we can detect a statistically significant association between e_1, e_2 and r on the web. To measure recall, we estimate the size of the ground truth (i.e., the collection of *all* facts described in the corpus).

2.1 Interactions between the system, database and ground truth

Now, we discuss our method to evaluate open RE systems. Given a corpus annotated with named entities, an open RE system must produce a set of facts $S = \{f_1, f_2, \ldots, f_{|S|}\}$. An example of fact is ⟨"Barack Obama","married to","Michelle Obama"⟩. In order to evaluate the precision of S, we partially rely on an external database $D = \{f_1, f_2, \ldots, f_{|D|}\}$. In order to measure recall, we try to estimate the set of facts described in the input corpus. This set corresponds to the ground truth and it is denoted by $G = \{f_1, f_2, \ldots, f_{|G|}\}$.

In Figure 1, we present a Venn diagram that illustrates the interactions between the system output (S), the ground truth (G) and the external database (D). There are four marked regions (a, b, c, d) in this diagram. We need to estimate the size of these regions to measure the true precision and recall of a system. We discuss each marked region as follows.

- a contains correct facts from the system output that are not in the database.
- b is the intersection between the system output and the database ($S \cap D$). We assume that this region is composed by correct facts only, i.e., facts that are in the ground truth. This is because it is unlikely for a fact mistakenly extracted by a system to be found in the database.
- c contains the database facts described in the corpus but not extracted by the system.
- d contains the facts described in the corpus that are not in the system output nor in the database.

Precision and recall Observe that all true positives are in regions a and b, while all false negatives are in regions c and d. Considering that $|G|$ = $|a| + |b| + |c| + |d|$, we can define precision (P), recall (R) and F-measure (F) as follows.

$$P = \frac{|a| + |b|}{|S|} \qquad R = \frac{|a| + |b|}{|a| + |b| + |c| + |d|}$$

$$F = \frac{2 \cdot P \cdot R}{P + R}$$

The need for the web An evaluation method that relies exclusively on a database can only determine the size of regions b and c. Therefore, in order to compute true precision and recall we need to evaluate those facts that are not in the database. The whole web would be the ideal candidate for this task since it is by far the most comprehensive source of information. In our preliminary experiments, more than 97% of the extractions cannot be evaluated using a database only.

2.2 Estimating precision

To measure precision, we need to estimate the size of the regions a and b.

Using the external database We calculate the size of region b by determining, for each fact $f = \langle e_1, r, e_2 \rangle$ in S, whether f is in D. In our experiments, D corresponds to Freebase, which contains data from many sources, including Wikipedia. Freebase provides Wikipedia ids for many of its entities. Since we perform entity disambiguation with Wikipedia as a preprocessing step, finding e_1 and e_2 in Freebase is trivial.

On the other hand, we are required to match r to a relation in Freebase. We perform this matching by using a widely-used semantic similarity measure proposed by Jiang and Conrath (Jiang and Conrath, 1997). This measure uses a lexical terminology structure (WordNet) with corpus statistics. Given a relation r' in Freebase, we determine the similarity between r and r' by the maximum similarity between the words that compose r and r'. We select the relation r' with maximum similarity with r and consider that $r = r'$ if their similarity score is above a predetermined threshold.

Using the web We estimate $|a|$ by leveraging Pointwise Mutual Information (PMI) on web documents. In particular, we use an adaptation of the PMI-IR (Turney, 2001), which computes PMI using a web search engine. The PMI of a fact $f = \langle e_1, r, e_2 \rangle$ measures the likelihood of observing f, given that we observed e_1 and e_2, i.e,

$$\text{PMI}(e_1, r, e_2) = \frac{Count(e_1 \text{ AND } r \text{ AND } e_2)}{Count(e_1 \text{ AND } e_2)} \quad (1)$$

where $Count(q)$ is the number of documents returned by the query q. PMI values range from 0 (when f is not observed) to 1 (when f is observed for every occurrence of the pair e_1 and e_2). We use the PMI function to determine whether a fact was correctly extracted. The underlying intuition is that facts with high (relative) frequency are more likely to be correct.

There are different ways one can estimate the result of the $Count(\cdot)$ function. One may use the hit counts of a web search engine, such as Google or Bing. Another option is to use a local search engine, such as *Lucene*[1], on a large sample of the web, such as the ClueWeb09 corpus.

[1]http://lucene.apache.org/

We consider two versions of the PMI function, which differ by how their queries are defined. Equation 1 presents the CLASSIC version, which uses the AND operator. This simple approach is efficient but ignores the locality of query elements. It is known that query elements close to each other are more likely to be related than those sparsely distributed throughout the document. The second version of PMI, called PROXIMITY, relies on proximity queries, which consider the locality aspect. In this version, queries are of the form "e_1 NEAR:X r NEAR:X e_2", where X is the maximum number of words between the query elements. In Figure 2 we see an example of proximity query.

We deem a fact as correct if its PMI value is above a threshold t, determined experimentally [2] . By calculating the PMI of extracted facts that are not in the region b, we are able to estimate $|a|$. With both $|a|$ and $|b|$, we estimate the precision of the system.

2.3 Estimating recall

To provide a trustworthy estimation of recall, we need to estimate the size of regions c and d. We produce a superset G' of the ground truth G ($G' \supseteq G$). Note that G' contains real facts (G) as well as wrongly generated facts ($G' \setminus G$). We approximate G by removing these wrong facts, either exploiting the external database and the PMI function.

One way to produce G' is to perform a Cartesian product of all possible entities and relations. Let $E = \{e_1, e_2, \ldots, e_m\}$ be the set of entities and $R = \{r_1, r_2, \ldots, r_n\}$ be set of relations found in the input corpus. The superset of G produced by Cartesian product is $G' = E \times R \times E$. For example, the facts extracted from the sentence "Barack Obama is visiting Rome to attend the G8 Summit" are presented in Figure 3, where the correct facts are highlighted. The shortcoming of this approach is the huge size of the resulting G'. Even so, we remove many incorrect facts thanks to heuristics; e.g., we do not consider entities from different sentences.

Once G' is produced, we estimate $|G \cap D| = |b| + |c|$ by looking for facts in G' that match a fact in the database D, as before. Once we have $|b|$ and $|G \cap D|$, we can estimate $|c| = |G \cap D| - |b|$. By applying

[2]Threshold t is domain-independent, as shown by other important works such as (Hearst, 1992; Banko et al., 2007; Banko and Etzioni, 2008).

1	2	3	4	5	6	7	8
Valerie Jarrett	was	appointed	as	senior	advisor	by	Barack Obama

Figure 2: A sentence matching the query "(Valerie Jarrett) NEAR:4 (advisor) NEAR:4 (Barack Obama)". Grey words represent matching terms, while white words are noise.

e_1	r	e_2
Barack Obama	**visit**	**Rome**
Barack Obama	visit	G8 Summit
Barack Obama	attend	Rome
Barack Obama	**attend**	**G8 Summit**
Rome	visit	G8 Summit
Rome	attend	G8 Summit

Figure 3: Facts produced for the superset G' for "Barack Obama is visiting Rome to attend the G8 Summit". Facts in the ground truth G are highlighted in bold.

Annotators	Agreement
$H_0 - H_1$	80.8%
$H_1 - H_2$	80.3%
$H_0 - H_2$	78.0%
$A - H_0$	71.9%
$A - H_1$	68.8%
$A - H_2$	72.8%
$A - H_{12}$	75.9%

Table 1: Agreement between human and automatic annotators.

the PMI of the facts not in the database ($G' \setminus D$) we can determine $|G \setminus D|$. Finally, we can estimate $|d| = |G \setminus D| - |a|$. Now that we have estimated the sizes of regions a, b, c and d, we can determine the true recall of the system.

2.4 PMI Effectiveness

To measure PMI effectiveness, we compare the results of our evaluation system (A) and a human (H_0) over a set of 558 facts. To this end, we defined the agreement between A and H_0 as follows.

$$\text{Agreement} = \frac{\text{Number of facts where } A = H_0}{\text{Number of facts}}$$

Our system achieved an agreement of 73% with respect to the human evaluation; the agreement increases up to 80% if we consider only popular facts. This is a well-known property of PMI: when dealing with small hit count numbers, the PMI function is very sensible to changes, amplifying the effect of errors.

We also compare how distant the agreement achieved with the automatic annotator (A) is from the agreement between humans. For this experiment, we asked two additional volunteers (H_1 and H_2) to evaluate the set of 558 facts as before. For a more reliable measurement we created an additional annotator (H_{12}) by selecting the facts where H_1 and H_2 agreed. We also include the human annotations (H_0) from the previous experiment.

Table 1 shows the agreement between humans and the automatic annotator. While the agreement between humans varies between 78% and 81%, the agreement between human and automatic annotators varies between 69% and 73%. These results show that our automatic annotator is promising and could potentially achieve human levels of agreement with little improvement. In addition, the agreement with the more reliable annotator H_{12} is quite high at 76%.

2.5 The Difference Between Extracting and Evaluating Relations

The tasks of extracting relations from a corpus (e.g., New York Times) and evaluating relations using a corpus (e.g., the web) are virtually the same. However, we stress how an evaluation process is performed in an easier scenario, thus more effective.

In order to measure precision, we judge a fact as correct or wrong by looking for mentions in the external sources. This process is easier than extracting a fact: first, we already know the fact we are looking for; second, this fact is probably going to be replicated many times in several different ways, and so easy to spot. This is not true for a generic extraction process, where the fact may be published only once and in a particular difficult form.

For measuring recall, our evaluation system has both to generate and validate facts; as a consequence, it has to perform as a real extraction system. Even so, our system still performs in a easier scenario: in fact, to materialize the extracted data, we randomly generate facts, and then we filter out the ones that are not replicated anywhere else. Note that our system can hardly be used as an extraction system: we only validate facts already published somewhere else, i.e., we do not generate any new information, that is the main goal of an extraction system; moreover, we require several additional information sources.

3 Comparing ReVerb and SONEX

We now use our evaluation method to compare two open RE systems: ReVerb and SONEX. The input corpus for this comparison is the New York Times corpus, composed by 1.8 million documents.

ReVerb (Fader et al., 2011) extracts relational phrases using rules over part-of-speech tags and noun-phrase chunks. It also employs a logistic regression classifier to produce a confidence score for each extracted fact; an extracted fact is only included in the output if above a user-defined threshold. SONEX (Mesquita et al., 2010) tries to find sets of entity pairs that share the same relation by clustering them. SONEX uses a hierarchical agglomerative clustering algorithm (Manning et al., 2008).

3.1 Results

We run ReVerb with five different confidence thresholds (0.2, 0.4, 0.6, 0.8, 0.95) and report the output with highest F-measure (0.2 in our case). SONEX uses a user-defined threshold to stop the agglomerative clustering. We try five different thresholds (0.1, 0.2, 0.3, 0.4, 0.5) and report the output with highest F-measure (0.4 in our case). For each run, we randomly select 10 thousand facts from the output of each system. These are used to estimate the sizes of regions a and b. We also randomly select 40 thousand facts from G' to estimate the sizes of c and d.

Reverb produced about 2.6 million facts, while SONEX produced over 3.2 million facts. We found about 63 million facts in G', the superset of the ground truth G. Table 2 presents the size of all regions for ReVerb and SONEX. Note that Freebase (regions b and c) plays a minor role in this estimation when compared to PMI (regions a and d): more than 97% of the ground truth is defined by using PMI. This behaviour can be explained by the small number of facts with two entities with a corresponding entry in Wikipedia: 1.6% for ReVerb, 0.9% for SONEX, 1.7% for G'. The importance of the external database may be higher for other corpora (e.g., Wikipedia) better covered by the database (e.g., Freebase).

Systems	a	b	c	d	S	D	G'
ReVerb	77	3	41	1,944	2,643	3,926	62,930
SONEX	259	4	40	1,763	3,288	3,926	62,930

Table 2: The size of all regions for ReVerb and SONEX, in thousands of facts.

Systems	Precision	Recall	F-measure
ReVerb	3.1%	3.9%	3.4%
SONEX	8.0%	12.8%	9.8%

Table 3: Performance results for ReVerb and SONEX.

Table 3 shows the precision, recall and F-measure for ReVerb and SONEX. Observe that SONEX achieves more than double the precision and recall presented by ReVerb; however both systems presented low results. These results not only illustrate but also quantify the challenges of dealing with large corpora. Moreover, they underscore the pressing need for more robust and effective open RE tools. Finally, they yield a vast amount of incorrect extractions, which are in turn an invaluable source of open problems in this field.

4 Conclusion and Future Work

This paper introduces the first automatic method for large-scale evaluations of open RE systems that estimates true precision *and* recall. Our method scales to realistic-sized corpora with million of documents, instead of the few hundreds of previous evaluations.

Our contributions indicate that a fully automatic annotator can indeed be used to provide a fair and direct evaluation of competing open RE systems. Moreover, we stress how an automatic evaluation tool represents an invaluable resource in aiding and speeding-up the development process of open RE systems, by removing the tedious and error-prone task of manual evaluation.

References

Eugene Agichtein and Luis Gravano. 2000. Snowball: extracting relations from large plain-text collections. In *Proceedings of the ACM Conference on Digital libraries*, pages 85–94. ACM.

Michele Banko and Oren Etzioni. 2008. The tradeoffs between open and traditional relation extraction. In *Proceedings of the Annual Meeting of the ACL*, pages 28–36, Columbus, Ohio, June. Association for Computational Linguistics.

Michele Banko, Michael J. Cafarella, Stephen Soderland, Matthew Broadhead, and Oren Etzioni. 2007. Open information extraction from the Web. In *Proceedings of the International Joint Conference on Artificial Intelligence*, pages 2670–2676.

Sergey Brin. 1998. Extracting patterns and relations from the world wide web. In *The World Wide Web and Databases, International Workshop*, pages 172–183.

Jinxiu Chen, Donghong Ji, Chew Lim Tan, and Zhengyu Niu. 2005. Unsupervised feature selection for relation extraction. In *Proceedings of the International Joint Conference on Natural Language Processing*. Springer.

A. Doan, J. F. Naughton, A. Baid, X. Chai, F. Chen, T. Chen, E. Chu, P. Derose, B. Gao, C. Gokhale, J. Huang, W. Shen, and B. Vuong. 2009. The Case for a Structured Approach to Managing Unstructured Data. In *Proc. CIDR*.

Oren Etzioni, Michael J. Cafarella, Doug Downey, Ana-Maria Popescu, Tal Shaked, Stephen Soderland, Daniel S. Weld, and Alexander Yates. 2005. Unsupervised named-entity extraction from the web: An experimental study. *Artif. Intell.*, 165(1):91–134.

Anthony Fader, Stephen Soderland, and Oren Etzioni. 2011. Identifying Relations for Open Information Extraction. In *EMNLP*.

Takaaki Hasegawa, Satoshi Sekine, and Ralph Grishman. 2004. Discovering relations among named entities from large corpora. In *Proceedings of the Annual Meeting of the ACL*, page 415. Association for Computational Linguistics.

Marti A. Hearst. 1992. Automatic acquisition of hyponyms from large text corpora. In *In Proceedings of the 14th International Conference on Computational Linguistics*, pages 539–545.

Jay J Jiang and David W Conrath. 1997. Semantic similarity based on corpus statistics and lexical taxonomy. *Computational Linguistics*, cmp-lg/970(Rocling X):15.

Christopher D. Manning, Prabhakar Raghavan, and Hinrich Schütze. 2008. *Introduction to Information Retrieval*. Cambridge University Press, 1 edition, July.

Filipe Mesquita, Yuval Merhav, and Denilson Barbosa. 2010. Extracting information networks from the blogosphere: State-of-the-art and challenges. In *Proceedings of the Fourth AAAI Conference on Weblogs and Social Media (ICWSM), Data Challenge Workshop*.

Mike Mintz, Steven Bills, Rion Snow, and Daniel Jurafsky. 2009. Distant supervision for relation extraction without labeled data. In *ACL-IJCNLP '09: Proceedings of the Joint Conference of the 47th Annual Meeting of the ACL and the 4th International Joint Conference on Natural Language Processing of the AFNLP: Volume 2*, pages 1003–1011, Morristown, NJ, USA. Association for Computational Linguistics.

Benjamin Rosenfeld and Ronen Feldman. 2007. Clustering for unsupervised relation identification. In *Proceedings of the ACM Conference on Information and Knowledge Management*, pages 411–418. ACM.

Evan Sandhaus. 2008. The new york times annotated corpus. `http://ldc.upenn.edu/Catalog/docs/LDC2008T19`.

Peter D. Turney. 2001. Mining the web for synonyms: Pmi-ir versus lsa on toefl. In *Proceedings of the 12th European Conference on Machine Learning*, EMCL '01, pages 491–502, London, UK. Springer-Verlag.

Dmitry Zelenko, Chinatsu Aone, and Anthony Richardella. 2003. Kernel methods for relation extraction. *J. Mach. Learn. Res.*, 3:1083–1106.

Jun Zhu, Zaiqing Nie, Xiaojiang Liu, Bo Zhang, and Ji-Rong Wen. 2009. Statsnowball: a statistical approach to extracting entity relationships. In *Proceedings of the International Conference on World Wide Web*, pages 101–110. ACM.

Relabeling Distantly Supervised Training Data for Temporal Knowledge Base Population

Suzanne Tamang and Heng Ji
Computer Science Department and Linguistics Department
Graduate Center and Queens College, City University of New York
New York, NY 10016, USA
stamang@gc.cuny.edu, hengji@cs.qc.cuny.edu

Abstract

We enhance a temporal knowledge base population system to improve the quality of distantly supervised training data and identify a minimal feature set for classification. The approach uses multi-class logistic regression to eliminate individual features based on the strength of their association with a temporal label followed by semi-supervised relabeling using a subset of human annotations and lasso regression. As implemented in this work, our technique improves performance and results in notably less computational cost than a parallel system trained on the full feature set.

1 Introduction

Temporal slot filling (TSF) is a special case of Knowledge Base Population (KBP) that seeks to automatically populate temporal attributes or *slots* for people and organizations that occur in national and international newswire sources, and less formal digital publications such as forums or blogs. Typical facts in a knowledge base (KB) contains are attributes for people such as *title*, *residence*, or *spouse* and for organizations, *top employees*, or *members*. We describe work that extends traditional KBP in that not only are relations extracted, but the time for which the relation is valid is also populated, requiring a automated system to construct a timeline for time dependent slot fills.

For many new learning tasks such as TSF, the lack of annotated data presents significant challenges for building classifiers. Distant supervision is a learning paradigm that exploits known relations to extract contexts from a large document collection and automatically labels them accordingly. The distance supervision assumption is that whenever two entities that are known to participate in a relation appear in the same context, this context is likely to express the relation. By extracting many such contexts, different ways of expressing the same relation will be captured and a general model may be abstracted by applying machine learning methods to the annotated data.

Although the distance supervision assumption is generally true, it is considered a weak labeling approach. Recent work in relation extraction has reported challenges using Freebase to distantly supervise training data derived from news documents (Riedel et al., 2010) and TAC's standard slot-filling task (Surdeanu et al., 2010). While extending this framework to TSF, we encounter additional challenges: (1) time normalization results can result in additional errors that proliferate in consequent pipeline steps, (2) Web data is more likely to contradict Freebase facts, and (3) the size of the feature set required to express the rich contexts for a large set of temporal instances can be prohibitively large to learn supervised models efficiently.

To address the challenges associated with noisy, heuristically labeled Web data for training a classifier to detect temporal relations, we improve the accuracy of distantly supervised training data using a semi-supervised relabeling approach, and identify a minimal feature set for classifying temporal instances. The rest of this paper is structured as follows. Section 2 discusses the CUNY TSF system. Section 3 describes our enhancements and how they were implemented in our experiments. Section 4 presents the experimental results and Section 6 concludes the paper and sketches our future work.

2 Task and System Overview

The temporal KBP slot filling task posed by NIST Text Analysis Conference (TAC) (Ji et al., 2010; Ji and Grisham, 2011) uses a collection of Wikipedia infoboxes as a rudimentary knowledge representation that is gradually populated as new information is extracted from a document collection. This source corpus consists of over one million documents that have been collected from a variety of national and international newswire sources and less formal digital publications. The CUNY TSF system shown in 2 ran several parallel submissions, two that varied only in how the classifier is trained. The methods used to develop the system are described in more detail in previous work (Li et al., 2012).

In order to obtain a large amount of data to train a classifier for labeling temporal instances, we extended a general distance supervision framework for relation extraction (Mintz et al., 2009) and modify the assumption to consider the value of a temporal expression that additionally cooccurs. That is, for a known query, q, attribute, a, and time range, $[t_{begin}, t_{end}]$, sentences in a corpus where q,a, and a temporal expression t co-occur can be automatically labeled with the classes *start, end, hold, range* or *irrelevant* for training purposes using a mapping based on the following heuristic rules and on the value of t:

$$coocur_{q,a,t} = \begin{cases} t = t_{begin}, & start \\ t = t_{end}, & end \\ t_{begin} > t < t_{end}, & hold \\ t = t_{begin} \wedge t_{end}, & range \\ (t < t_{begin}) \vee (t > t_{end}), & irr. \end{cases}$$

As indicated in Figure 2, the system begins with a regular slot filling component to extract slot fills for the given query. Then, document retrieval is performed based on the query and attribute indicated in Freebase. The next step, sentence retrieval, considers the time expression indicated in Freebase, namely that the sentence should include the query, slot fills, as well as candidate time expressions. The remaining processing can be decomposed into two problems: (1) the classification of any temporal expression in the extracted query and slot fill contexts; and (2) temporal aggregation to form a temporal tuple for each query's slot fills. The motivation for this work was to improve classification performance by improving the quality of that data used to generate the classification model.

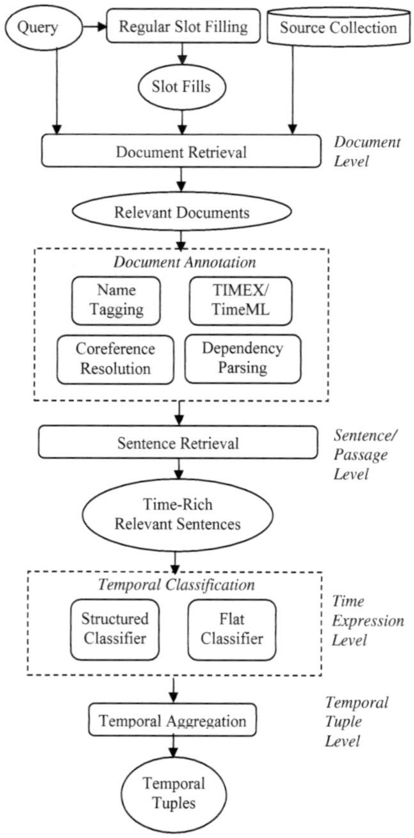

Figure 1: CUNY Temporal KBP System

3 Methods

Table 3 compares the number of temporal relations identified by a human annotator using the TAC KBP corpus with what we were able to retrieve from the Web without human intervention. We can see that our automatic method has obtained much larger training data (more than 40,000 instances). The major advantage of using additional Web data to retrieve candidate temporal instances is the diversity of contexts that can be obtained. For example, expressions captured by this larger data set included common patterns as well less common phrases and

Category	Type	Total	Start	End	Holds	Range	Others
Spouse	Manual	28	10	3	15	0	9
	Automatic	**10,196**	**2,463**	**716**	**1,705**	**182**	**5,130**
Title	Manual	461	69	42	318	2	30
	Automatic	**14,983**	**2,229**	**501**	**7,989**	**275**	**3,989**
Employment	Manual	592	111	67	272	6	146
	Automatic	**17,315**	**3,888**	**965**	**5,833**	**403**	**6,226**
Residence	Manual	91	2	9	79	0	1
	Automatic	**4,168**	**930**	**240**	**727**	**18**	**2,253**

Table 1: Number of human and distantly supervised training instances by dataset

implied information. We used a variety of lexical and syntactic features after document annotation and sentence retrieval to generate a feature set for supervised learning.

3.1 Relabeling

The temporal class labels, *start, end, hold, range* and *irrelevant*, are used to inform the final aggregation that is done for each entity in the KB. In order improve the accuracy and of the training instances and incorporate local context that distance supervision does not capture, we used *self-training*, a semi-supervised learning method that has been used to label data for tasks such as parsing (Mcclosky et al., 2006). Using a small set of human annotations, or *seed* examples, we iteratively labels the partitioned unlabeled set, retaining only the confident labels for retraining the classifier in each round. However, the size of the training dataset resulted in a prohibitively large, sparse feature space. We perform two step in order to generate a more parsimonious classification model that can be used for self-training: (1) *feature elimination* to identify a minimal set of model features, followed by (2) *relabeling* using the reduced feature set and a lasso regression classifier.

Feature elimination: First, for each of the M features in the set $F = \{f_1, ...f_M\}$ extracted from the training data we test the independence of each feature given each class label, inserting only those features that meet a threshold p-value into the minimal feature set F'. Although this approach tests each feature uniquely, many of the features already express conjunctive combinations of tokens.

Self-training: To relabel the instances using the reduced feature set F', we annotated a small set of training data by hand and used lasso (least absolute shrinkage and selection operator) regression, which has the benefit of shrinking the coefficients of features towards zero so that only the subset of features with the strongest effects are incorporated into the classifier (Ng, 2004; Li et al., 2005). The shrinkage parameter ($s > 0$) is tuned using cross-validation. For a collection of N training instances, $D = \{(x_1, y_1), ..., (x_N, y_N)\}$, of d dimensions the lasso coefficients $\hat{\beta}$ are calculated as follows:

$$\hat{\beta}^{lasso} = \arg\min_\beta \left\{ \sum_{i=1}^{N} (y_i - \beta_0 - \sum_{j=1}^{d} \beta_j x_{ij})^2 \right\}$$

$$\text{subject to: } \Sigma_{j=1}^{d} |\beta_j| \leq s$$

Lasso regression limits the expression of extraneous information and as a result provides additional feature selection properties. The lasso minimizes the residual sum of squares with the constraint that the absolute value of the regression coefficients must be less than a constant, s, that functions as a tuning parameter and is used for shrinkage. When s is large enough, there is no effect on the solution, but when it shrinks it has the effect of reducing some model coefficients close or equal to zero. We used cross-validation to determine the best values for s in our experiments.

In our experiments, we used .005%-.101% of training instances from distant supervision data as the initial labeling seeds for self-training. We used the agreement between classification results for two different values of s, the regularization parameter for the model. As the new data portion is labeled, those retained for retraining are instances for which there is an agreement reached by multiple classifiers.

4 Results

Figure 2 presents the performance of our system on the full TSF task, before and after applying feature selection and re-labeling techniques. The F1 measure for the system that used relabeled training data and the reduced feature space for classification of training instances reported a top F1 measure, slightly improving the overall performance (F-measure from 22.56% to 22.77%). Experimental results on development results have also shown that the F-measure gain on each slot type correlates (.978) with the number of seed instances used in self-training based re-labeling. The most dramatic improvements are obtained for the `per:spouse` slot (7.12% absolute F-Measure gain) which also came the closest to that of human performance.

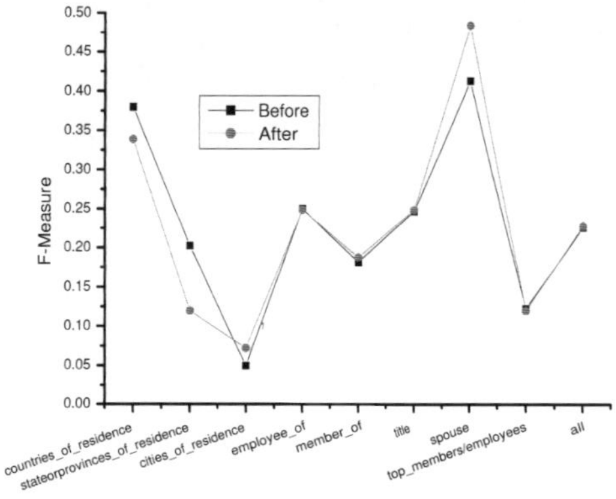

Figure 2: Impact of feature selection and relabeling

To more closely examine the effects of relabeling on classification, we compared the accuracy of the labels before and after relabeling for the spouse slot type using development data. Since the set of all instances would entail considerable work for a human annotator, we selected 1000 instances at random, eliminating all instances where the labels agreed between the two systems and were left with 83% of all labeled training data. Then, for those instances remaining, a human annotator assigned a *start*, *end*, *hold*, *range* or *irrelevant* label that was used as a gold standard. Figure 3 shows the distribution of labels. Compared with human annotation or after relabeling, the system without relabeling shows a notably higher proportion of irrelevant labels and relatively few range labels. Table 2 further details performance pre-post relabeling, reporting the precision, recall.

5 Discussion

The lack of training data for supervised learning is a bottleneck to improving automated KBP systems and distant supervision offers an attractive approach to expediting the labeling of training data at low cost. Not surprisingly, using heuristics to label temporal instances leads to the introduction of erroneous annotations. Some common causes of error are: coreference results match the wrong named entities in a document, temporal expressions are normalized incorrectly, temporal information with different granularities has to be compared (e.g., we know John married Mary in 1997, but not the exact day and month. Should the time expression September 3, 1997 be labeled *start*?), and information offered by the KB is incorrect or contradictory with information found on the Web documents.

Label	Precision	Recall
Start	.27-.64	.60-.60
End	.10-.55	.29-.50
Hold	.30-.24	.66-.62
Range	0-.64	0-.56

Table 2: Pre-post relabeling preformance

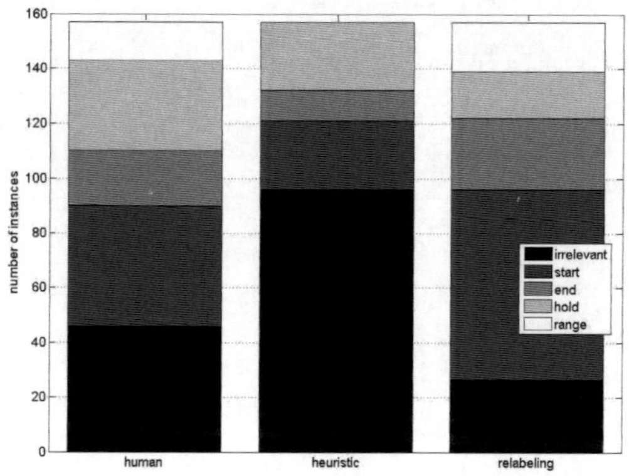

Figure 3: Distribution of class labels

To address these challenges, we develop a simple but effective techniques to relabel temporal instances. Noise is a major obstacle when extending distant supervision to more complex tasks than traditional IE, and our techniques focuses on refining the feature set so that more meaningful features are expressed, and spurious features are removed, or ignored. We perform two steps: using multi-class logistic regression as the basis for eliminating features followed by relabeling with a lasso regression which has additional feature selection properties.

Feature reduction: reasons to perform variable selection include addressing the curse-of-dimensionality, interpretability of the model, and reducing the cost of storing, and processing the predictive variables. We were motivated by the need to provide a more succinct classification model for self-training. Some slots generated over 100,000 features from the training data, and high dimensionality and sparsity was associated with the feature space. Feature reduction with multi-class logistic regression was most dramatic in first development system, which was also the noisiest, averaging 96.2% feature elimination. The classifiers trained on our final system showed an average of 89% feature reduction for the temporal slots, resulting in a more parsimonious classification model.

Relabeling: the procedure described in this work resulted in slightly increased performance on the TSF task. Temporal labels are initially assigned using distant supervision assumptions, which in some cases result in inaccurate labels that could be better informed by local context. For example, the temporal instance below was returned by distant supervision given the query *Jon Voight*, the slot value for the spouse, *Marcheline Bertrand*, and the relevant date range, 1971-1978. Caps are used to show the normalization with the substituted text in brackets:

> "According to former babysitter late mother TARGET ATTRIBUTE [Marcheline Bertrand] virtually abandoned her baby daughter after a painful TARGET DATE [1976] split from husband TARGET_ENTITY [Jon Voight]."

Since the date 1976 is between the range indicated by Freebase it was labeled a target date, and distance supervision heuristics assigned a *hold* label, indicating that the relation was true for 1976, but that it was not the beginning or end. However, the context supports the labeling of this instance more accurately labeled as the *end* of the spouse relation.

Similarly, the following sentence has a date detected that was within the valid range and was also mislabeled, this time as *irrelevant*:

> "TARGET ATTRIBUTE [Shirley] has one daughter, 54, with her TARGET ENTITY [Parker], who she split from in TARGET DATE [1982]."

In this example, a different date was indicated for the *end* of the relation spouse in Freebase. Although supporting text can be used to infer the end of a relation, the simplicity of the distant supervision causes it to fail in this case. Relabeling provided the correct assignment in both of these examples, and it ability to correctly label the instances is likely due to a strong association of the feature 'split_from' with the *end* label.

6 Conclusion

To address the challenges associated with noisy, heuristically labeled Web data for training a classifier to detect the temporal relations, we develop a method with several important characteristics. First, it achieves state-of-the-art performance for TSF, slightly improving on a parallel system that was trained on the full feature set without relabeling. Second, it dramatically reduces the size of the feature space used for labeling temporal instances. Lastly, it can be used to identify which model features are more significant for predicting temporal aspects of a query attribute relation.

Our future work will continue to develop techniques for addressing the challenges posed by extending distant supervision to new types of IE tasks, and the refinement of our techniques. Specifically, it is still unclear how the number of seed instances for semi-supervised relabeling impacts TSF performance and why slot level performance is variable when the number of seed examples is similar. Also, we used a random set of seed examples for self-training and it is possible that learning from certain types of instances may prove more beneficial and that more iterations in the self-training process may continue to improve the accuracy of training labels and overall system performance.

7 Acknowledgements

This work was supported by the U.S. Army Research Laboratory under Cooperative Agreement No. W911NF- 09-2-0053 (NS-CTA), the U.S. NSF CAREER Award under Grant IIS-0953149, the U.S. NSF EAGER Award under Grant No. IIS-1144111, the U.S. DARPA Broad Operational Language Translations program and PSC-CUNY Research Program. The views and conclusions contained in this document are those of the authors and should not be interpreted as representing the official policies, either expressed or implied, of the U.S. Government. The U.S. Government is authorized to reproduce and distribute reprints for Government purposes notwithstanding any copyright notation here on.

References

Qi Li and Javier Artiles and Taylor Cassidy and Heng Ji. 2012. Combining Flat and Structured Approaches for Temporal Slot Filling or: How Much to Compress? *Lecture Notes in Computer Science*, 2012.

Heng Ji and Ralph Grishman. 2011. Knowledge Base Population: Successful Approaches and Challenges. *Proc. of ACL2011*, June:1148–1158.

Heng Ji and Ralph Grishman and Hoa Trang Dang. 2011. An Overview of the TAC2011 Knowledge Base Population Track. *Proc. Text Analytics Conference (TAC2011)*, 2011.

Heng Ji and Ralph Grishman and Hoa Trang Dang and Kira Griffitt and Joe Ellis. 2010. An Overview of the TAC2010 Knowledge Base Population Track. Proceedings of the Third Text Analysis Conference, November, 2010.

Mihai Surdeanu and David McClosky and Julie Tibshirani and John Bauer and Angel Chang and Valentin Spitkovsky and Christopher Manning. 2010. A Simple Distant Supervision Approach for the TAC-KBP Slot Filling Task. Proceedings of the Third Text Analysis Conference, November, 2010.

Sebastian Riedel and Limin Yao and Andrew McCallum. 2010. Modeling Relations and Their Mentions without Labeled Text. ECML/PKDD, (3),2010:148–163.

David Mcclosky and Eugene Charniak and Mark Johnson. 2006. Effective self-training for parsing. In Proc. N. American ACL (NAACL), 2006:152–159.

Andrew Y. Ng. 2004. Feature selection, L1 vs. L2 regularization, and rotational invariance. In ICML, 2004.

Fan Li and Yiming Yang and Eric P. Xing. 2006. From Lasso regression to Feature vector machine. NIPS, 2005.

Mike Mintz and Steven Bills and Rion Snow and Daniel Jurafsky 2009. Distant supervision for relation extraction without labeled data. ACL/AFNLP, 2009:1003–1011.

Web Based Collection and Comparison of Cognitive Properties in English and Chinese

Bin Li[1,2] Jiajun Chen[1] Yingjie Zhang[1]
[1.] State Key Lab for Novel Software Technology
Nanjing University
[2.] Research Center of Language and Informatics
Nanjing Normal University
Nanjing, PR China
{lib;chenjj;zhangyj}@nlp.nju.edu.cn

Abstract

Cognitive properties of words are very useful in figurative language understanding, language acquisition and translation. To overcome the subjectivity and low efficiency in manual construction of such database, we propose a web-based method for automatic collection and analysis of cognitive properties. The method employs simile templates to query the search engines. With the help of a bilingual dictionary, the method is able to collect tens of thousands of "vehicle-adjective" items of high quality. Frequencies are then used to obtain the common and independent cognitive properties automatically. The method can be extended conveniently to other languages to construct multi-lingual cognitive property knowledgebase.

1 Introduction

Cognitive Linguistics focuses on the cognitive and metaphorical usage in language. For example, In English the "pig" is fat, dirty and lazy, etc. But it is not the case in other languages. As in Chinese, 猪 (pinyin: zhu, means pig) is fat, lazy and happy, but not dirty. Different cultural backgrounds lead to differences in everyday cognitive knowledge (Lakoff 1980). Therefore it is beneficial for literature translation, cross language retrieval and language acquisition to compare the cognitive properties of words across languages. Traditionally, this kind of knowledge is generally possessed by experienced translators. In this article, we propose a method to collect the knowledge from the web automatically. It also makes a comparison between the obtained results with a traditional bilingual dictionary.

2 Related Work

To collect the cognitive properties by hand is considered as both labour intensive and subjective. Therefore the researchers have sorted to corpus and search engine for help. Kintsch(2000) collects the noun-adjective pairs like "pig-fat" using the Latent Semantic Analysis(LSA) method on a large corpora. Roncero(2006) considers the simile sentences which contain the specific metaphor property like "as adjective as noun". Veale(2007) collects a large scale of English similes by querying the nouns and adjectives in WordNet from Google to construct the English lexical metaphor knowledgebase "sardonicus", which contains about 10,000 items of "noun vehicle-adjective property". In a similar way, Jia(2009) collects Chinese similes from Chinese search engine Baidu. A total number of about 20,000 "noun vehicle-adjective property" items were acquired.

Querying search engines is an efficient way to collect "noun-adjective" items. However, all the previous works are monolingual and do not use the frequencies of the items. Therefore, we want to extend the research to multi-languages and use frequency for the comparison of cognitive properties.

3 Construction of the Bilingual Cognitive Property Knowledgebase

Just like Veale(2007) and Jia(2009), we use specific simile templates to collect English and Chinese "noun vehicle-adjective property" items by querying the search engines and then construct the Chinese-English bilingual lexical cognitive property knowledgebase.

The words in WordNet and HowNet are used for querying the search engines. For English, the adjectives in WordNet are used. For Chinese, the words are taken from HowNet.

3.1 Lexical Resources

WordNet 3.0 is a widely used lexical resource, which contains 21,479 adjectives and 117,798 nouns(Miller 1990). It supplies plenty words for collecting English similes.

HowNet is a structured Chinese-English lexical semantic resource(Dong 2006). Different from WordNet, it defines the meaning of a word by a set of structured semantic features, named "sememes". About 2200 sememes are used to define 95000 Chinese words and 85000 English words In HowNet(ver. 2007). For example, the noun 猪(pig) and 笨(stupid) are defined as follows.

猪-pig, noun：{livestock|牲畜}

笨-stupid, adjective：{foolish|愚}

3.2 English Item Collection

We used the 21,479 adjectives in WordNet to fill in the simile template "as ADJ as". When querying Google, 3 limitations are set in advanced search to refine the search results: exact phrase, English language and up to 100 results for each query. We do not use the nouns in WordNet, but the template will supply thousands of nouns where querying Google. Thus, a number of 585,300 types (1,054,982 tokens) of "as…as…" items are gathered from Google. To trim the great number of nonsense, noisy and erroneous items, Veale(2007) manually checks the returned results. It is accurate but takes too much time. We introduce a simple trick for the purpose, which uses the dictionary for filtering. Nouns and adjectives in HowNet are taken to filter the "noun-adjective" items. Then, 27,331 types (87,529 tokens) of "noun-adjective" items are left, covering 6,319 nouns and 4,100 adjectives. Table 1 gives the top 10 most frequent items with their frequencies.

The item "blood-red" is the most frequent one in English. The frequency can tell the salience of the cognitive properties of nouns. Nevertheless, the frequencies we got are not exactly the frequency of the items on the web. They only show the statistical situation in the collected items.

TABLE 1. Top10 most frequent vehicle-adjective items in English

ID	VEHICLE	ADJ	FREQ
1	blood	red	628
2	twilight	gay	466
3	grass	perennial	413
4	ice	cold	392
5	mustard	keen	385
6	snow	white	340
7	sea	boundless	314
8	feather	light	289
9	night	black	280
10	hell	mad	254

The frequency of "blood-red" is over 100, because it also occurs in returned results of other words. Ideally, it is better to use the simile template "as ADJ as NOUN" for the parings of 21,479 adjectives multiple 117,798 nouns. But the limitation of the frequency to query search engines makes it impossible to finish the collecting work within a short time.

3.3 Chinese Item Collection

For Chinese, there are more simile templates. Three templates "像(as)+NOUN+一样(same)", "像(as)+VERB+一样(same)", "像(as)+一样(same)+ADJ" are adopted and are filled with the 51020 nouns, 27901 verbs and 12252 adjectives from HowNet to query Baidu(www.baidu.com). Verbs are also considered, because some of them may function grammatically as nouns in English. For example, "呼吸(breath)" is a verb in Chinese, but it may serve as a noun phrase in certain contexts, and one of its cognitive properties extracted from Baidu is "自然(natural)". It tells people's experience in breathing. We submit 91173 queries to Baidu, with configurations set to 100 returned results for each query. Totally, 1,258,430 types (5,637,500 tokens) of "vehicle-adjective" items are gathered. Then, nouns and adjectives in HowNet are used to filter these items, leaving only 24,240 items. The web database of the Chinese filtered items is already available for search at `http://nlp.nju.edu.cn/lib/cog/ccb_nju.php`. Table 2 shows the top 10 most frequent items with their frequencies.

TABLE 2. Top10 most frequent vehicle-adjective items in Chinese

ID	VEHICLE	ADJ	FREQ
1	苹果 apple	时尚 fashionable	1445
2	呼吸 breath	自然 natural	758
3	晨曦 sun rise	朝气蓬勃 spirited	750
4	纸 paper	薄 thin	660
5	雨点 rain drop	密集 dense	557
6	自由 freedom	美丽 beautiful	543
7	雪 snow	白 white	521
8	花儿 flower	美丽 beautiful	497
9	妖精 spirit	温柔 gentle	466
10	大海 sea	深 deep	402

It is surprising to see that "apple" has taken the first place on the web media in China. And "snow-white" occurs in the top10 place in both languages. In next section, we will compare the cognitive properties based on the collection works done on Google and Baidu.

4 Bilingual Comparison

Previous sections have already done some comparison by showing the most frequent items in English and Chinese. In this section, we continue to find the common parts and differences in cognitive properties.

4.1 Common vehicles and properties

We can compare the common vehicles and properties in English and Chinese. By consulting HowNet, 3,106 types of bilingual "vehicle-property" items are gathered, including 1,500 English items and 2,254 Chinese items. They cover only about 10% of all items in each language.

Table 3 shows the top 10 most frequent bilingual items. We can see that people in different cultures share many same properties of things, such as "snow-white", "blood-red". However, the "fox-sly" is somewhat strange and interesting, for the animal is not as smart as man or monkey, but is considered sly. About 90% of the "vehicle-adjective" items do not have their corresponding items in the other language. But it does not necessarily mean that the two languages share few common parts. Too many words miss their translations only due to the size of the bilingual dictionary HowNet. For example, "snazzy" and "popular" are not translated to "时尚" or "时髦" in HowNet. Thus, "apple" does not appear in the bilingual common items. So a larger bilingual dictionary is necessary in further researches. However, no matter how large the dictionary is, it may still encounter the difficulty to find all the translation word pairs.

TABLE 3. Top10 most frequent vehicle-adjective pairs in English and Chinese

ENG VEHICLE	ENG ADJ	ENG FREQ	CHS VEHI-CLE	CHS ADJ	CHS FREQ
snow	white	340	雪	白	521
blood	red	628	血	红	227
paper	thin	132	纸	薄	660
ice	cold	392	冰	冷	256
feather	light	289	羽毛	轻	111
honey	sweet	55	蜜	甜	324
sea	bound-less	314	大海	广阔	63
steel	strong	64	钢铁	硬	194
fox	cunning	88	狐狸	狡猾	166
fox	sly	85	狐狸	狡猾	166

4.2 Dependent vehicles and properties

As can be seen below, the "vehicle-property" items depend on culture backgrounds.

TABLE 4. Top10 most frequent dependent vehicle -adjective pairs in English and Chinese

ENG VEH	ENG ADJ	ENG FRQ	CHS VEH	CHS ADJ	CHS FRQ
twilight	gay	466	苹果 apple	时尚 fashionable	1445
grass	peren-nial	413	呼吸 breath	自然 natural	758
mustard	keen	385	晨曦 sun rise	朝气蓬勃 spirited	750
hell	mad	323	雨点 rain drop	密集 dense	557
life	large	288	自由 freedom	美丽 beautiful	543
punch	pleased	254	妖精 spirit	温柔 gentle	466
beetroot	red	240	阳光 sunlight	灿烂 resplendent	386
hatter	mad	226	天神 deity	美丽 beautiful	341
school children	cruel	209	天使 angle	美丽 beautiful	337
moun-tain	im-mova-ble	100	裁判员 referee	狠 ruthless	300

Most of the items are dependent on their language and culture. Table 4 shows the top10 most frequent independent items in English and Chinese, But when a bilingual dictionary is used, some items are wrong like"苹果-时尚"and "天使-美丽", as HowNet does not give good translations. With the bilingual cognitive properties, we can see the cognitive property differences among languages in a quick and convenient fashion. It will supply useful information for a literature translator or a second language learner. Here is a detailed example of the common and dependent properties of translation word pairs "山" and "mountain". The two concepts share 8 common properties and differ in more properties as shown in table 5.

TABLE 5. The Cognitive Properties of "山-mountain" in Chinese and English with frequencies

CHS-Dependent	山 VS. mountain		ENG-Dependent
高 high-196	Common Properties		immovable-100
高耸 high-149	CHS	ENG	dignified-4
深重 deep&heavy-85	沉重-153	heavy-7	determined-3
多 many-50	重-37	heavy-7	hyaloid-3
高大 high-27	稳重-34	heavy-7	insensate-2
执着 persistence-26	大-31	big-2	bottleful-2
平静 calm-9	沉稳-24	heavy-7	earthbound-1
坚实 stable-9	坚定-8	staunch-1	foggy-1
挺拔 upright-9	伟岸-7	stalwart-1	phrasal-1
坚忍不拔 fortitudinous-8	坚强-6	staunch1	nonliving-1
崇高 sublimity-6			converse-1
…			…

In English, the most important property of mountain is "immovable" while it is "high" in Chinese. [1] The contrast is very useful in cross language teaching and communications. The automatic comparison is not very precise yet, we need to enlarge the scale of the cognitive property knowledgebase.

5 Conclusion and Future Work

Cognitive properties of words are very meaningful and useful but are not given in the traditional dictionaries. To overcome the difficulty in manual collecting, tagging and comparing of the cognitive properties in different languages, we employ search engines and bilingual dictionaries to construct an English-Chinese cognitive property knowledgebank. With the frequencies of the "vehicle-adjective" items, it is fast and convenient to see the language common and dependent properties of the word-pairs, which have translation relations. Using HowNet, we've already seen that most of the "vehicle-adjective" items are language dependent. Thus, the knowledgebank is very helpful to literature translators, language learners and machine translations.

In the future, we are to find better ways to collect more "vehicle-adjective" items from search engines and to use larger bilingual dictionaries to refine the common parts of English and Chinese cognitive properties. With more multi-lingual dictionaries, we are also able to deal with more languages under different cultures.

Acknowledgments

We are grateful for the comments of the anonymous reviewers. This work was supported in part by National Social Science Fund of China under contract 10CYY021, 11CYY030, State Key Lab. for Novel Software Technology under contract KFKT2011B03, China PostDoc Fund under contract 2012M510178, Jiangsu PostDoc Fund under contract 1101065C.

References

Dong, Z. D. & Dong, Q. 2006. *HowNet and the Computaion of Meaning*. Singapore, World Scientific Press,.

Miller, G. A., R. Beckwith, C. D. Fellbaum, D. Gross, K. Miller. 1990. WordNet: An online lexical database. *Int. J. Lexicograph.* 3, 4:235-244.

Jia Y. X. and Yu S. W. 2009. Instance-based Metaphor Comprehension and Generation. *Computer Science*, 36(3):138-41.

Kintsch, W. 2000. Metaphor comprehension: A computational theory. *Psychonomic Bulletin & Review*, volumn7: 257-66.

Lakoff, G. & Johnson. M. 1980. *Metaphors We Live by*. Chicago: The University of Chicago Press.

Roncero, C., Kennedy, J. M., and Smyth, R. 2006. Similes on the internet have explanations. *Psychonomic Bulletin and Review*, 13(1).

Veale, T. & Hao, Y. F. 2007. Learning to Understand Figurative Language: From Similes to Metaphors to Irony. *Proceedings of CogSci 2007*, Nashville, USA.

[1] The item "mountain-high" does not exist in our collection but appears in Google. Because it is hard to get the item only using the template "as adjective as".

Population of a Knowledge Base for News Metadata from Unstructured Text and Web Data

Rosa Stern
Univ. Paris 7, Sorbonne Paris Cité, France
INRIA-Alpage, Paris, France
AFP-Medialab, Paris, France
rosa.stern@afp.com

Benoît Sagot
INRIA-Alpage, Paris, France
benoit.sagot@inria.fr

Abstract

We present a practical use case of knowledge base (KB) population at the French news agency AFP. The target KB instances are entities relevant for news production and content enrichment. In order to acquire uniquely identified entities over news wires, i.e. textual data, and integrate the resulting KB in the Linked Data framework, a series of data models need to be aligned: Web data resources are harvested for creating a wide coverage entity database, which is in turn used to link entities to their mentions in French news wires. Finally, the extracted entities are selected for instantiation in the target KB. We describe our methodology along with the resources created and used for the target KB population.

1 An Entity Extraction Methodology for Knowledge Base Population

Current research conducted at the French news agency AFP focuses on the acquisition and storage of knowledge, particularly entities, relevant for the news production and usable as metadata for content enrichment. This objective sets off the need for a dedicated knowledge base (KB) relying on a light-weight ontology of entities mappable to the Linked Data framework. Identification of entities such as persons, organizations and geopolitical entities (GPEs)[1] in unstructured textual data, news wires in French in our case, underlie the construction and enrichment of such a KB.

This specific need is met by the KB *population task*, now well defined within the annual TAC dedicated track (Ji et al., 2011). KB population indeed relies on the ability to link entity mentions in textual data to a KB entry (*entity linking subtask*, henceforth EL),[2] which follows pioneer work in entity disambiguation (Bunescu and Pasca, 2006; Cucerzan, 2007). In a similar way to systems described in Dredze et al. (2010) and Ji & Grishman (2011), we conduct EL over AFP news wires in order to obtain relevant entities meant to populate the target KB, adapting these techniques to French data. This linking process is based on Web data extraction for both coverage and the purpose of Linked Data integration, which has become a widely explored trend in news management and publishing projects, such as the ones conducted by the BBC (Kobilarov et al., 2009) or the New York Times (NYT).

Compared to other KB population settings, this knowledge acquisition process is done throughout a sequence of resources and extraction steps rather than in a cyclic way. Instead of considering one KB as both an entity resource and the target of the population task, the target KB (AFP *Metadata Ontology*, henceforth AMO) is viewed as initially empty and progressively augmented with entity instances. This is because the use intended for AMO does not rely on exhaustivity, but on a relevant set of entities mentioned in the daily news production. This set is not fixed *a priori* and must be regularly updated in order to maintain a reflection of entities' emergence in the news domain. For instance, not all cities in the world

[1] These entity types are the usual focus of Information Extraction systems and are defined among others by the ACE entity recognition task (Doddington et al., 2004).

[2] The consequent *slot filling subtask* associates these entries to attributes and relations to other entities.

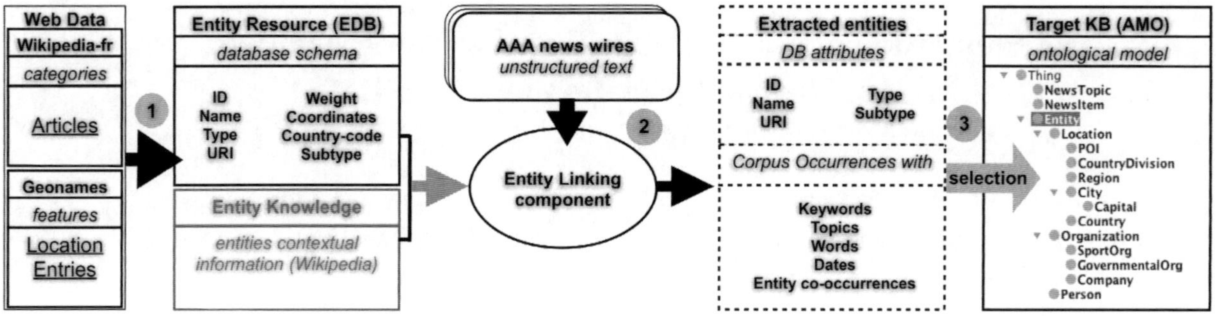

Figure 1: Overview of entity extraction and KB population process

need be instanciated in AMO, but the city *Fukushima* should become an entry as soon as its part in major events is stated in news wires. The relevant entity set can then be matched to new entries and updates in parallel documentation resources maintained at the AFP. The KB population process is broken down into several layers of data extraction and alignment, as sketched in Figure 1:

Step 1 The models of GeoNames and Wikipedia are mapped to a unified entity model; extraction from these Web datasets based on this mapping result in an entity database named Aleda, whose schema is presented in section 2, along with its alignement with Wikipedia and GeoNames data models.

Step 2 The Aleda database obtained in Step 1 provides entities for the linking step, where entity mentions in news wires are aligned with entries from Aleda. This process, along with the use of a joint resource for entity knowledge access, is described in section 3. EL in our particular task also targets the identification of new entities (i.e. absent from Aleda) and attempts to deal with the problem of possible named entity recognition errors in queries made to the system.

Step 3 The resulting entities aligned in Aleda must be anchored in the target KB, *via* instantiation of the adequate ontological class. Contextual information gathered during the entity extraction and linking process can be used at this point (section 4).

2 Entity Extraction from Web Data

Step 1 in our architecture is based on two Web datasets: the geographical database GeoNames brings together millions of location identifiers with associated information; Wikipedia is a wide coverage resource for entities, with continuous updates and article creations for entities involved in current events. The creation of a large-scale and unified entity resource is achieved by defining a database schema dedicated to entity representation, and by aligning both Wikipedia's and GeoNames' model with it. The schema considers *Person, Organization* and *GPE* as types of entries. The building of Aleda therefore relies on the identification of Wikipedia's and GeoNames' entries to which one of these types can be assigned.

Wikipedia Exploiting Wikipedia as a large-scale entity resource has been the focus of numerous efforts, such as (Balasuriya et al., 2009; Charton and Torres-Moreno, 2010). Each Wikipedia article, referring to an entity, concept or notion, is referenced under a number of *categories*, often fine-grained and specific. A hierarchical or ontological organization of these categories can be inferred (Syed et al., 2008) but a given article is not anchored in a generic conceptual class such as an entity type in a straightforward fashion. The present model alignment thus consists in a mapping from Wikipedia categories to one of the target entity types. Each article mapped to one of these types leads to adding a corresponding entity in Aleda. The selection and typing process of articles as entities makes use of heuristics based on articles' categories and *infoboxes* and is achieved as follows.

Around 100 of the most frequent infobox templates are retrieved from the articles' structure and manually associated with an entity type (e.g., the *Politician* template is typed as Person). All articles associated with one of these templates (23% of the French Wikipedia) are assigned the same type. The categories associated with these typed articles are then considered: a category appearing mostly in articles of a given type is associated with it. 20,328 categories are thus typed (e.g., all articles with an infobox and tagged by a category such as *Born in ** have been assigned the type *Person*, which is therefore associated to this category). An article is selected as referring to an entity by assigning the type with maximal category association to it. If no type can be assigned (when no categories were associated with any type), an article's infobox whose template has been typed can provide the information. If the article has no such infobox, no entity is derived from it. Aleda's schema is filled with attribute values extracted from each selected article: the columns URI, name, weight are mapped to the article's URL, the normalized name inferred from the article's title and the article's length,[3] respectively. A joint table furthermore groups possible *variants* or *labels* for each entity; these are inferred from Wikipedia's redirection and disambiguation pages, which provide aliases for article titles. For person names, additional variants are automatically generated, by identifying the first, possible middle and last names.

GeoNames The model alignment from GeoNames is fairly straightforward since all its entries are locations. However this database is huge and present some noisy aspects, which we aim at avoiding by limiting the extraction to entities considered relevant for news content enrichment in French. Only GPEs such as countries, cities or country divisions were selected, based on the GeoNames *feature* provided. Heuristics are then designed for further selection: all GPEs in France are retained, as well as all non-French GPEs with more than 200 inhabitants. Aleda's schema is filled with values provided by GeoNames for each selected GPE: the columns URI, name, weight, subtype, country-code and coordinates are mapped to the GeoNames' entity URL, *name*, number of inhabitants, *feature* (such as P.PPL for populated place), ISO country code and coordinates, respectively. The joint variants table is filled with GeoNames' labels indicated as French or without language indication.

A unified entity resource of persons, organizations and GPEs[4] is obtained, with 832,452 uniquely identified entities (33%, 62% and 5% of type *Person, GPE* and *Organization*, respectively), associated with 1,673,202 variants.[5]

3 Text-Entity Alignment: Entity Linking

3.1 Methodology for Entity Linking

The knowledge acquisition step, crucial for the target KB population, consists in entity extraction from a corpus of AFP news wires. This is done by aligning detected entity mentions in news wires with entries the Aleda database introduced in 2. This linking component is based on the learning of a similarity model between entity attributes, including contextual ones, and a mention in a given document. It is challenging particularly because of name variation and ambiguity, which can prevent an accurate entity identification. The named entity recognition (NER) module first detects entity mentions, along with a possible type, which become queries for the candidates selection among the database entries. The entry with the highest similarity w.r.t. the mention and the document is chosen. This similarity is computed in a way comparable to a number of linking systems (described and evaluated in Dredze et al. (2010) and Ji & Grishman (2011)) and using the following features:

Surface similarity The candidate's name and labels, available in the entity database, are compared to the mention (exact, partial, null string match).

Candidate attributes The other candidate's attributes available in Aleda, such as its weight (or popularity) and its country-code, can be indicators in cases of ambiguity.

Contextual similarity Entity contextual knowledge (associated to the entity resource for the linking component in fig. 1) is made available from the corpus of Wikipedia articles. In each article, entity mentions (identified by hyperlinks) are surrounded with information such as the article's categories (i), the most salient words of the article's text (ii) and the co-occurring entities in the article (iii). As news items are indexed *via* keywords and topics from AFP's controlled vocabulary lists, (i) are mapped to the document keywords and topics; (ii) and (iii) are

[3]This value is seen as a weight in the extend that an article size can indicate the popularity of an entity relatively to others, particularly in cases of homonymy.

[4]GPEs extracted from both GeoNames and Wikipedia are listed and associated by an *owl:sameAs* relation.

[5]A comparison with the NLGbAse resource (Charton and Torres-Moreno, 2010), which has similar objectives, can be found in (Sagot and Stern, 2012). Aleda is freely available at `gforge.inria.fr/frs/download.php/30598/`

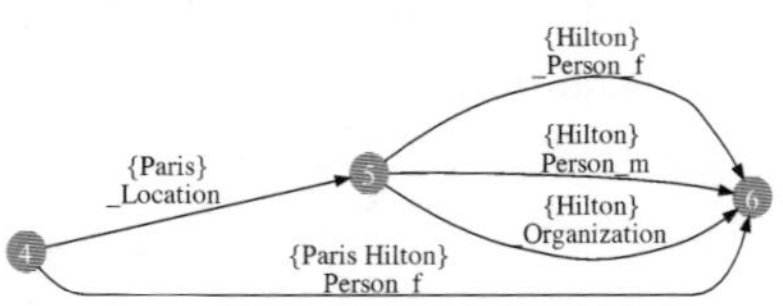

Figure 2: SXPipe/NP output for the segment *Paris Hilton*

compared to the document's salient words and entity mentions, respectively.

The candidate maximizing the similarity is selected as the mention linking. However, this selection should not occur for every query, since (i) a number of entities mentioned in news wires don't have a corresponding Aleda entry and (ii) the automatic NER can return a number of *false mentions*. In the case of (i), the *out-of-base* entity (NIL) should be output as a linking result; in (ii), the mention should be discarded and indicate a *not-an-entity* reading (NAE) rather than give rise to a false link; for the latter eventuality, features indicating ambiguities with the common lexicon are added to the feature set. These cases are part of the training examples and are taken into account in the prediction by including the NIL and NAE candidates in the ranking process.

3.2 Experiments and Evaluation

Experiments and evaluation are conducted over a manually annotated corpus of 96 news items, dated May-June 2009, where each entity mention's boundaries and Aleda ID, if relevant, are indicated. Mentions referring to entities absent from Aleda are identified by a normalized name. The corpus includes 1,476 entity mentions, referring to 610 distinct entities among which 28% are absent from Aleda. The corpus is also annotated with the NER system SXPipe/NP[6] to add examples of false matches to the linking model. More precisely, the NER is applied without complete disambiguation: a number of typing and segmentation alternatives are not resolved at this level, but rather passed to the linking module. The underlying idea is to leave final entity recognition decisions to a level where knowledge and semantic information about entities are available. Figure 2 illustrates this ambiguity preservation, where SXPipe/NP builds possible readings of a text segment in terms of entity mentions.

In each reading built by the NER module, each mention (gold or not) is associated with a set of candidates: all Aleda entries for which the mention is a possible variant, as well as NIL and NAE instances. All mention/candidate pairs are assigned a class, positive for correct links and negative for wrong ones, and form the training set for the linking model. A pair consisting in a false mention and the NAE candidate is for instance labeled as positive. The training examples are fed to a maximum entropy classifier[7] with a 10-fold cross-validation. Based on the resulting model, each pair is then ranked according to the *score* assigned by the classifier, which amounts to a pointwise ranking strategy. Once mentions are locally linked to the top-ranked candidates in all readings, the latter must in turn be ranked in order to finally disambiguate the current text segment. This ranking is done by assigning to each reading the score of its top-ranked candidate or, when the reading contains a sequence of mentions, the minimum of all top-ranked candidates' scores.

On the evaluation data, the system obtains encouraging results of linking accuracy (A) over the set of correctly detected entities (NER columns), compared to the top TAC-KB population evaluation results over English data with only correct entity mentions (table 1). The overall task, i.e. of joint entity recognition and linking, is also measured and is not comparable to equivalent work to the best of our knowledge. Results show that the system's ability to detect false entity mentions should be considerably improved, but filters out some NER noise, which could not be the case in a mere sequential system where all detected mentions would be equally handled by the linking module.

Conducted over a corpus of ≈ 400,000 news items of 2009 and 2010 on 16 news topics such as *Politics, Economy* or *Culture*, the EL step results in a set of 46,616 distinct identified entities (35%, 50% and 15% of GPEs, persons and organizations), along with information retrieved from Aleda. Moreover, each entity is associated with new information gathered at each of its occurrence in the extraction corpus. Hence the most frequent association of entities with news features (see *Extracted entities* in fig. 1) augment the extraction list with useful knowledge for further integration.

[6] `http://alpage.inria.fr/~sagot/sxpipe.html`

[7] Megam: `http://www.cs.utah.edu/~hal/megam/`

	NER			EL	Joint NER+EL			
	P	R	F	A (all/NILs)	P	R	F	NAE
AFP (French)	0.849	0.768	0.806	0.871/0.597	0.740	0.669	0.702	33%
Top TAC-KBP (English)	-	-	-	0.821/0.891	-	-	-	-

Table 1: NER, linking and joint results

4 Target KB Population and Enrichment

The entities identified during the previous step are made available for the target KB population. Given the specialized use intended for AMO in further content enrichment, a high precision rate is expected w.r.t. its instances, which requires a phase of human intervention. However this process should not come down to a time costly and off-putting task, and should rely on concrete and systematic validation criteria. The extracted entities are presented to domain specialists in order to assess their relevance w.r.t. the KB. This judgement can leverage various type of information, including the usage of entities in the extraction corpus. Each entity is submitted to validation with its Wikipedia or GeoNames URL, which allows for an unambiguous verification of its identity on the Web. Furthermore, candidates are submitted in reverse frequency order: the mention rate of an entity over a given period can by itself indicate its relevance for a KB integration.[8] The validation of less frequent entities can rely in a greater extend on contextual information derived from news features: news topics, keywords, salient words and co-occurring entities can indicate the level of contribution of a given entity to the domain, and therefore its usefulness as a KB instance for further content enrichment. Moreover, the news publication dates collected for each occurrence allow to visualize an entity salience in a given period of time, and can indicate its emergence as an important news actor at certain event peaks.

Following this process, 5,759 relevant entities were selected. Their concrete integration in AMO consists in an automatic instantiation within the underlying ontological model (see AMO in fig. 1). The adequate AMO *Entity* subclass is determined by a straightforward mapping from Aleda entity types to AMO *Entity* subclasses. Finer subclasses, such as *Location/POI* (*point of interest*) can be instantiated based on GeoNames *features* associated with the entity (e.g., locations with the GeoNames *museum* feature are mapped to the *POI* subclass). The instantiation process also considers useful information available on entities: Aleda attributes - the entity normalized name or its geographical coordinates -, are represented in the form of an *owl:dataProperty*. Knowledge elements extracted from the corpus, such as the news topic with which the entity is most mentioned, give rise to *owl:objectProperties* (whose domain and range are the considered entity and an adequate instance of the ontology, e.g. the *Politics* instance of the *NewsTopic* class).

When the process described in section 3 is repeated over new data, i.e. over the daily news flow, and along with regular updates of the Aleda to take into account new entries, the entities presented to validation can either be new w.r.t. AMO or already present as an instance. In the latter case, the additional information linked to the entity should be merged with the adequate existing node. Automatically identifying the adequate existing instance can be achieved by entity resolution techniques, such as systematic comparison of attribute values. In the case of a new entity, a new instance should be created as described above. This illustrates the challenge of dynamic enrichment of resources, comparable to the automatic detection of neologisms in the general language for lexical resources. This aspect of the KB population is intended to be at the center of further developments of our architecture.

In order to integrate AMO in the Linked Data (LD) framework, we applied entity resolution *via* URIs matches with existing LD datasets: all instances defining a Wikipedia URL could be linked to the equivalent DBpedia resource; 20% of AMO instances after the initial population were linked to the NYT data, thus making AMO a suitable resource for content enrichment and Web publishing in the news domain.

[8]Roughly 20% of the distinct entities constitute 80% of the total occurrences in corpus (more than 4 million mentions); hence examining most frequent entities quickly allows for an initial population with the most prominent instances.

References

D. Balasuriya, N. Ringland, J. Nothman, T. Murphy, and J. R. Curran. 2009. Named entity recognition in wikipedia. In *People's Web '09: Proceedings of the 2009 Workshop on The People's Web Meets NLP*, 10–18, Suntec, Singapour.

R. Bunescu and M. Pasca. 2006 Using encyclopedic knowledge for named entity disambiguation. In *Proceeding of EACL*, 6:9–16, Trento, Italy.

E. Charton and J.M. Torres-Moreno. 2010. Nlgbase: a free linguistic resource for natural language processing systems. In *Proceedings of LREC 2010*, Valletta, Malta.

S. Cucerzan. 2007. Large-scale named entity disambiguation based on Wikipedia data. In *Proceedings of EMNLP-CoNLL*, 708–716, Prague, Czech Republic.

G. Doddington, A. Mitchell, M. Przybocki, L. Ramshaw, S. Strassel and R. Weischedel. 2004 The Automatic Content Extraction (ACE) Program–Tasks, Data, and Evaluation. In *Proceedings of LREC 2004*, 4:837–840, Lisbon, Portugal

M. Dredze, P. McNamee, D. Rao, A. Gerber, and T. Finin. 2010. Entity Disambiguation for Knowledge Base Population. In *Proceedings of the 23rd International Conference on Computational Linguistics*, Beijing, China.

H. Ji and R. Grishman. 2011. Knowledge Base Population: Successful Approaches and Challenges. In *Proceedings of the Annual Meeting of the Association of Computational Linguistics*, Portland (OR), USA.

H. Ji, R. Grishman and H. Trang Dang. 2011. An Overview of the TAC2011 Knowledge Base Population Track. In *Proceedings of Text Analysis Conference (TAC2011)*,

G. Kobilarov, T. Scott, Y. Raimond, S. Oliver, C. Sizemore, M. Smethurst, C. Bizer and R. Lee. 2009. Media Meets Semantic Web - How the BBC Uses DBpedia and Linked Data to Make Connections. In *The Semantic Web: Research and Applications*, Springer.

B. Sagot and R. Stern. 2011. Aleda, a free large-scale entity database for French. In *Proceedings of LREC 2012*, Istanbul, Turkey.

Z. Syed, T. Finin and A. Joshi. 2008. Wikipedia as an ontology for describing documents. In *Proceedings of the Second International Conference on Weblogs and Social Media*, 136–144, Seattle (WA), USA.

DBpedia. `http://dbpedia.org/`

GeoNames. Web database:
`http://www.geonames.org/`
Downloadable data:
`http://download.geonames.org/export/dump/`

NYT. The New York Times Linked Data Web site: `http://data.nytimes.com/`

Wikipedia. French Wikipedia (XML version): `http://dumps.wikimedia.org/frwiki/`

Real-time Population of Knowledge Bases: Opportunities and Challenges

Ndapandula Nakashole, Gerhard Weikum
Max Planck Institute for Informatics
Saarbrücken, Germany
{nnakasho,weikum}@mpi-inf.mpg.de

Abstract

Dynamic content is a frequently accessed part of the Web. However, most information extraction approaches are batch-oriented, thus not effective for gathering rapidly changing data. This paper proposes a model for fact extraction in real-time. Our model addresses the difficult challenges that timely fact extraction on frequently updated data entails. We point out a naive solution to the main research question and justify the choices we make in the model we propose.

1 Introduction

Motivation. Dynamic content is an important part of the Web, it accounts for a substantial amount of Web traffic. For example, much time is spent reading news, blogs and user comments in social media. To extract meaningful relational facts from text, several approaches have emerged (Dalvi 2009; Etzioni 2008; Weikum 2009). These approaches aim to construct large knowledge bases of facts. However, most knowledge bases are built in a batch-oriented manner. Facts are extracted from a snapshot of a corpus and some weeks or months later, another round of facts are extracted from a new snapshot. This process is repeated at irregular and long intervals resulting in incomplete and partly stale knowledge bases. If knowledge bases were updated in-sync with Web changes, time spent examining long Web articles for facts would be reduced significantly.

Current Web information extraction systems rely on snapshots such as the ClueWeb09 crawl[1] (Fader 2011; Nakashole 2011) which is now three years old. The NELL system (Carlson 2010) follows a "never-ending" extraction model with the extraction process going on 24 hours a day. However NELL's focus is on language learning by iterating mostly on the same ClueWeb09 corpus. Our focus is on capturing the latest information enriching it into the form of relational facts. Web-based news aggregators such as Google News and Yahoo! News present up-to-date information from various news sources. However, news aggregators present headlines and short text snippets. Our focus is on presenting this information as relational facts that can facilitate relational queries spanning new and historical data.

Challenges. Timely knowledge extraction from frequently updated sources entails a number of challenges:

1. **Relation Discovery:** We need to discover and maintain a *dynamically evolving open set of relations*. This needs to go beyond common relations such as "bornIn" or "headquateredIn". For example, major knowledge bases lack potentially interesting relations like "firedFrom" or "hasGoddaughter". For completeness, we need to automatically discover such relations. Furthermore, we may occasionally pick up completely new relations, such as the new notion of a person "unfriending" another person in an online community. The TextRunner/Reverb project has addressed this challenge to some extent(Banko 2007; Fader 2011) , but the output has the form of verbal phrases, rather than typed relations and it is computed in a batch-oriented manner.

[1] lemurproject.org/clueweb09.php/

2. **Dynamic Entity Recognition:** We need to map noun phrases in text to entities in a dictionary of entities provided by knowledge bases. For example, when we encounter the noun phrase "Jeff Dean", we need to map it to the correct entity, which can either be the Google engineer or the rock musician. However, knowledge bases are incomplete in the entities they contain, due to newly emerging entities and entities in the long tail. For example, Jeff Dean the Google engineer, does not have a Wikipedia page, and thus is missing in Wikipedia-derived knowledge bases. We need to recognize and handle out-of-knowledg-base entities as they emerge.

3. **Extraction under Time Constraints:** Due to the need for timely extraction, our extraction methods need to produce results under *time constraints*. We discuss ideas for optimizing execution time.

Our goal is to design a model for fact extraction that adequately addresses these three main challenges.

Overview. Section 2 presents a naive baseline and points out its shortcomings. Section 3 gives an overview of our approach. Sections 4 and 5 describe our solutions for generating open sets of relations and entities. Section 6 describes our proposal for dealing with time constraints. Finally, Section 7 concludes.

2 Naive Approach

One straightforward approach that embodies the concepts of open sets of relations and entities, is to greedily extract all pairs of noun phrases co-occurring within a sentence. Each such extracted co-occurrence would then be considered to be a relational facts. However, this results meaningless facts. More importantly, even for the facts that are supposed to be meaningful, they do not exhibit real semantics. Figure 1 is a screenshot of a prototype where we applied this approach to the ClueWeb corpus. From Figure 1, we can spot meaningless patterns which should not be extracted (see marked lines). We can also spot patterns that can benefit from having semantics associated with them. Such

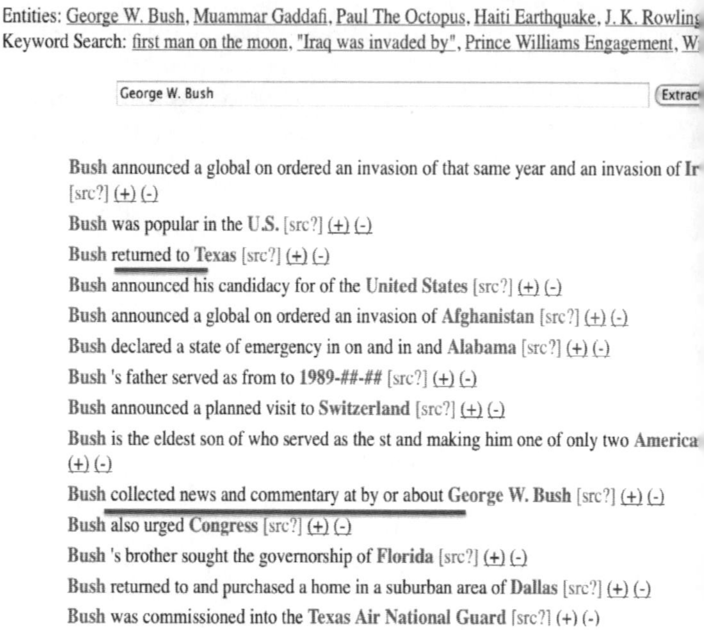

Figure 1: Noisy triples obtained from naive approach

semantics would indicate what the pattern actually means. For example, synonymy semantics could indicate that "return to" is the same as "traveled to, trip to, ...", and typing semantics could reveal that it is a pattern that applies to a person and a location. Such lexical semantics would be useful for both a user looking at the data, and also for an application using the data.

TextRunner/Reverb has developed a method for reducing noise by aggregating and cleaning the resulting triples, in a linguistic and statistical manner. However, they do not address the issue of semantics, for example, there are no synonyms or type constraints provided. We aim for an approch which provides semantics.

3 Overview of our Approach

Our main idea is that *semantic types* are crucial for discovering an open set of relations of high quality and for recognizing out-of-knowledge-base entities. Semantic types or classes are available in many knowledge bases. For example, Wikipedia assigns entities to categories (e.g., Jeff Dean is in the categories "living people, rock musicians, ..."), YAGO

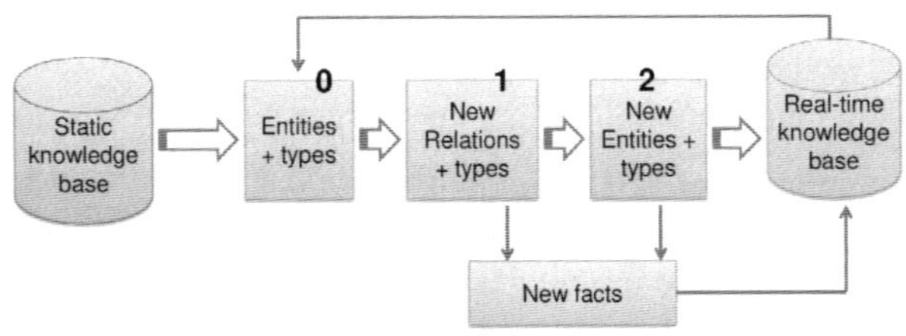

Figure 2: Architectural overview of our approach

(Suchanek 2007) assigns entities to Wordnet classes, Freebase (Bollacker 2008) assigns entities to its own set of categories.

Starting with a static knowledge base consisting of entities and their semantic types, we can generate relations in the form of phrases associated with type signatures. For example, we could generate a relation ⟨*actor*⟩ *'s character in* ⟨*movie*⟩. The types indicate the kinds of entities that can stand in the relation expressed by the phrase. Having typed phrases helps to remove many noisy facts by automatically disqualifying entities whose types do not agree with phrase types. Additionally, for out-of-knowledge-base entities we can leverage the phrases they co-occur with to infer types for new entities. In the simplest case, we can assume that for all pairs of entities X and Y occurring with the phrase "'s character in", X is an actor and Y is a movie. We elaborate later on the limitations of this assumption. Figure 2 illustrates the overall approach.

4 Open Set of Relations

In order to generate a large comprehensive set of relations, we developed methods for automatically mining relations from text corpora. We define a relation as a pattern which frequently occurs with entities of the same type, this results in *semantically-typed patterns*, example relations are: ⟨*actor*⟩ *'s character in* ⟨*movie*⟩ and ⟨*comedian*⟩ *parodied* ⟨*person*⟩. We say that each pattern has a type signature; for example for the latter, the type signature is: *comedian* × *person*.

Requiring that the patterns have type signatures provides a number of benefits: First we add semantics to our patterns; second we prune noisy patterns; third, we can infer types for previously unseen entities. For further semantics of a our relations, we arrange them into groups of synonymous patterns and into a hierarchy of subsumptions where general patterns subsume more specific ones. For example, the relation ⟨*person*⟩ *met* ⟨*person*⟩ subsumes the relation ⟨*person*⟩ *married* ⟨*person*⟩. A full description of the relation mining algorithm is beyond the scope of this paper.

5 Open Set of Entities

Having mined a large collection of semantically-typed patterns, we now discuss the open set of entities. Patterns require that entities have types which satisfy the type signatures. However, if an entity is new, its types are not known at the time of extraction. To prevent missing out on the facts pertaining to new entities, we need to deduce types for new entities. We propose to align new entities along the type signatures of patterns by inferring entity types from the type signatures. One approach would be based on the following hypothesis: For a given pattern such as ⟨*actor*⟩*'s character in* ⟨*movie*⟩, we can conclude that an entity pair (X, Y), occurring with the pattern in text, implies that X and Y are of the types actor and movie, respectively. However, directly inferring the types from the semantically-typed patterns would lead to many false positives due to the following problems:

- **Polysemy of Syntax.** The same lexico-syntactic pattern can have different type signatures. For example, the following are three different patterns: ⟨*singer*⟩ *released* ⟨*album*⟩, ⟨*music_band*⟩ *released* ⟨*album*⟩, ⟨*country*⟩ *released* ⟨*prisoner*⟩. For an entity pair (X, Y) occurring with this pattern, X can be one of three different types (singer, music_band, country) and Y can be one of two different types (album, prisoner).

- **Incorrect Paths between Entities.** Path tracing between entities is a larger limitation which emerges when a pair of entities occurring in the same sentence do not stand in a relation. This arises more prominently in long sentences. Deep linguistic processing such as dependency parsing facilitates correct path finding between entity pairs. However, due to time limitations in a real-time setting, deep linguistic parsing would be a throughput bottleneck. For example, consider the sentence: *Liskov graduated from Stanford and obtained her PhD degree from MIT.*, In this sentence, there is no relationship between Stanford and MIT, however we may erroneously extract: *[Stanford] obtained her PhD degree from [MIT]*. If Stanford were an unknown entity and we had a semantically-typed pattern which says people obtain PhDs from institutions, then we would wrongly infer that Stanford is a person.

We propose to jointly tackle the polysemy and incorrect-path limitations. Our approach aims to solve the optimization problem: which types are most likely valid for a new entity X, given that X occurs with patterns associated with different type signatures. The features over which to optimize include: relative frequencies that X occurs in placeholders of different types, specificity of patterns to different types, and type disjointness constraints which state, for example, that a university cannot be a person. This optimization problem can be formulated as an integer linear program.

6 Constrained Response Times

Online algorithms have to be responsive and return results within a timeframe that users are willing to tolerate. The extraction process is time-consuming, as we have to perform a range of expensive functions, such as named-entity tagging, entity disambiguation and entity-type inference for new entities. For this reason, we avoid using an online algorithm that performs information extraction at query time. Instead we propose a *continuous background processing model*. This approach processes a stream of in-coming documents. The stream provider can be a Web crawler or RSS feeds. Extraction is performed on the stream of documents one *time-slice (e.g., an hour)* at a time. The time-slice is a time window where data is accumulated before extraction is executed.

Document filtering. Within a given time-slice we can process all the documents. However, not all documents contain any meaningful relational facts which express relations in our *open set of relations*. We can therefore filter out documents that are not promising. A natural filtering approach is to build an index on the documents and use the patterns as queries on the index. If none of the queries return a non-empty result for a given document, then we discard the document. Building an index as a filter can speed up overall execution time.

Another dimension for filtering is the topic focus of a given stream. We imagine a customizable stream, whereby the general topic of interest can be picked, much like in news aggregators. For example, consider a stream following music-related news. This setting does not require that we find facts about sports. Because our patterns are typed, we can filter out all documents which do not contain music-specific patterns.

Execution time optimization. There is a lot of redundancy on the Web. Therefore, for a given time-slice, we might not need to process all the documents to get high recall. It could be that processing 10% of the documents already gives us 80% fact recall but at a much lower execution time compared to processing all documents. So there is a trade-off between execution time and recall. We would assume that each time-slice has a target recall value T_{recall}, $0 < T_{recall} \leq 1$. We can then estimate the number of documents we need to process to achieve the target recall (Ipeirotis 2006).

7 Conclusions

In this paper, we discussed ongoing research on timely fact extraction from frequently changing data. We have described a model that uses semantically-typed patterns for relations, infers entity types for new entities from the semantically-typed patterns, and follows a continuous background processing model which removes extraction from query time. We envision a scalable system capable of discovering new entities and relations as they emerge in data under time constraints. We believe our model contains key ingredients toward this goal. We are investigating our model further and developing a system that embodies these ideas.

References

Enrique Alfonseca, Marius Pasca, Enrique Robledo-Arnuncio: Acquisition of instance attributes via labeled and related instances. SIGIR 2010

Michele Banko, Michael J. Cafarella, Stephen Soderland, Matthew Broadhead, Oren Etzioni: Open Information Extraction from the Web. IJCAI 2007

Kurt D. Bollacker, Colin Evans, Praveen Paritosh, Tim Sturge, Jamie Taylor: Freebase: a collaboratively created graph database for structuring human knowledge. SIGMOD Conference 2008, data at `http://freebase.com`

Michael J. Cafarella, Alon Y. Halevy, Nodira Khoussainova: Data Integration for the Relational Web. PVLDB 2(1): 1090-1101 (2009)

Andrew Carlson, Justin Betteridge, Bryan Kisiel, Burr Settles, Estevam R. Hruschka Jr., Tom M. Mitchell. Toward an Architecture for Never-Ending Language Learning. AAAI 2010.

Timothy Chklovski, Patrick Pantel: VerbOcean: Mining the Web for Fine-Grained Semantic Verb Relations. EMNLP 2004

N.N. Dalvi, R. Kumar, B. Pang, R. Ramakrishnan, A. Tomkins, P. Bohannon, S. Keerthi, S. Merugu: A web of concepts. PODS 2009

O. Etzioni, M. Banko, S. Soderland, D.S. Weld: Open information extraction from the web. Commun. ACM 51(12), 2008

Anthony Fader, Stephen Soderland, Oren Etzioni: Identifying Relations for Open Information Extraction. EMNLP 2011.

Panagiotis G. Ipeirotis, Eugene Agichtein, Pranay Jain, Luis Gravano To search or to crawl?: towards a query optimizer for text-centric tasks. SIGMOD 2006

Ndapandula Nakashole, Martin Theobald, Gerhard Weikum: Scalable Knowledge Harvesting with High Precision and High Recall. WSDM 2011

Fabian M. Suchanek, Gjergji Kasneci, Gerhard Weikum: YAGO: a Core of Semantic Knowledge. WWW 2007

G. Weikum, G. Kasneci, M. Ramanath, F.M. Suchanek: Database and information-retrieval methods for knowledge discovery. Commun. ACM 52(4), 2009

Limin Yao, Aria Haghighi, Sebastian Riedel, Andrew McCallum: Structured Relation Discovery using Generative Models. EMNLP 2011

Adding Distributional Semantics to Knowledge Base Entities through Web-scale Entity Linking

Matthew Gardner
Carnegie Mellon University
5000 Forbes Avenue
Pittsburgh, PA 15213, USA
mg1@cs.cmu.edu

Abstract

Web-scale knowledge bases typically consist entirely of predicates over entities. However, the distributional properties of how those entities appear in text are equally important aspects of knowledge. If noun phrases mapped unambiguously to knowledge base entities, adding this knowledge would simply require counting. The many-to-many relationship between noun phrase mentions and knowledge base entities makes adding distributional knowledge about entities difficult. In this paper, we argue that this information should be explicitly included in web-scale knowledge bases. We propose a generative model that learns these distributional semantics by performing entity linking on the web, and we give some preliminary results that point to its usefulness.

1 Introduction

Recent work in automatically creating web-scale knowledge bases (like YAGO, Freebase, and NELL) has focused on extracting properties of concepts and entities that can be expressed as n-ary relations (Suchanek et al., 2007; Bollacker et al., 2008; Carlson et al., 2010b). Examples might be Athlete(`Michael Jordan 1`), Professor(`Michael Jordan 2`), PlaysForTeam(`Michael Jordan 1`, `Chicago Bulls`), and UniversityFaculty(`UC Berkeley`, `Michael Jordan 2`). The task of the knowledge extraction algorithm is to find new instances of these relations given some training examples, perhaps while jointly determining the set of relevant entities.

While these knowledge extraction approaches have focused on relational knowledge, knowing how `UC Berkeley` appears distributionally in text is also an important aspect of the entity that is potentially useful in a variety of tasks. For example, Peñas and Hovy (2010) showed that a collection of distributional knowledge about football entities helped in interpreting noun compounds like "Young touchdown pass." Haghighi and Klein (2010) used distributional information about entity types to achieve state-of-the-art coreference resolution results. It has long been known that word sense disambiguation and other tasks are best solved with distributional information (Firth, 1957), yet this information is lacking in web-scale knowledge bases.

The primary reason that distributional information has not been included in web-scale knowledge bases is the inherent ambiguity of noun phrases. Knowledge bases typically aim to collect facts about entities, not about noun phrases, but distributional information is only easily obtained for noun phrases. In order to add distributional semantics to knowledge base entities, we must perform *entity linking*, determining which entity any particular noun phrase in a document refers to, at web scale.

We suggest that distributional semantics should be included explicitly in web-scale knowledge bases, and we propose a generative model of entity linking that learns these semantics from the web. This would both enrich the representation of entities in these knowledge bases and produce better data for further relational learning. In the next section, we frame this idea in the context of prior work. In Section 3, we describe a model that learns distributional semantics for the set of entities in a knowledge base in the context of an entity linking task. Finally, in Section 4 we conclude.

2 Related Work

Our work builds off of a few related ideas. First, Haghighi and Klein (2010) presented a coreference resolution system that had at its core a set of distributional semantics over entity types very similar to what we propose. For each of a set of entity types (like Person, Organization, and Location) and each of a set of properties (like "proper head," "common head," "subject of verb"), they have a distribution over values for that property. People are thus more likely to have "Steve" or "John" as noun modifiers, while Organizations are more likely to have "Corp." as proper heads.

Their system learned these distributions in a semi-supervised fashion, given a few seed examples to their otherwise unsupervised coreference model. Their system did not, however, have any notion of global *entities*; they had global *types* whose parameters were shared across document-specific entities. Every time they saw the noun phrase "Barack Obama" in a new document, for example, they created a new entity of type "Person" for the mentions in the document. Even though they did not model individual entities, their system achieved state-of-the-art coreference resolution results. We believe that their modeling of distributional semantics was key to the performance of their model, and we draw from those ideas in this paper.

Our proposal is also very similar to ideas presented by Hovy (2011). Hovy describes a "new kind of lexicon" containing both relational information traditionally contained in knowledge bases and distributional information very similar to that used in Haghighi and Klein's coreference model. Each item in this "new lexicon" is represented as a set of distributions over feature values. The lexical entry for "dog," for example, might contain a feature "name," with "Spot" and "Lassie" receiving high weight, and a feature "agent-of," with highly probable values "eat," "run," and "bark." While Hovy has presented this vision of a new lexicon, he has left as open questions how to actually construct it, and how compositionality, dependence, and logical operators can function efficiently in such a complex system.

Peñas and Hovy (2010) have shown how a very small instance of a similar kind of lexicon can perform well at interpreting noun compounds, but they needed to resort to a severely restricted domain in order to overcome the challenges of constructing the lexicon. Because they only looked at a small set of news articles about football, they could accurately assume that all mentions of the word "Young" referred to a single entity, the former San Francisco 49ers quarterback. At web scale, such assumptions quickly break down.

There has been much recent work in distantly supervised relation extraction, using facts from a knowledge base to determine which sentences in a corpus express certain relations in order to build relation classifiers (Hoffmann et al., 2011; Riedel et al., 2010; Mintz et al., 2009). This work depends on first performing entity linking, finding sentences which contain pairs of knowledge base entities. Typically, this linking has been a simple string-matching heuristic, a noisy alignment that throws away a lot of useful information. Using coreference resolution after a noisy alignment can help to mitigate this issue (Gabbard et al., 2011), but it is still mostly a heuristic matching. A benefit of our approach to adding distributional semantics to web-scale knowledge bases is that in the process we will create a large entity-disambiguated corpus that can be used for further relational learning.

3 Entity Linking

We add distributional semantics to knowledge base entities through performing entity linking. Specifically, given a knowledge base and a collection of dependency parsed documents, entity linking maps each noun phrase in the document collection to an entity in the knowledge base, or labels it as unknown (a deficiency we will address in future work). Our model does this by learning distributions over dependency link types and values for each entity in the knowledge base. These distributions are both the features that we use for entity linking and the distributional semantics we aim to include in the knowledge base.

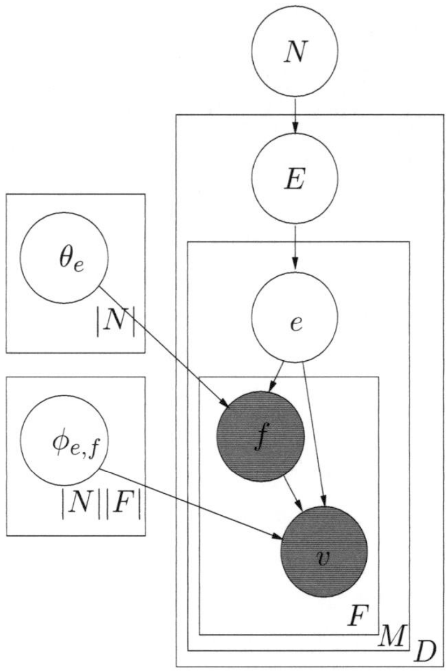

Figure 1: Graphical model for entity linking.

3.1 Model Structure

The model we propose is similar in structure to hierarchical models like latent Dirichlet allocation (Blei et al., 2003) or hierarchical Dirichlet processes (Teh et al., 2006). Instead of the "topics" of those models, we have entities (i.e., one "topic" in the model for every entity in the knowledge base, plus one "unknown" topic), and instead of modeling individual words, we model entity mentions in the document.

The generative story of the model is as follows. First, given a set of entities from a knowledge base, fix a Dirichlet prior N over them, and draw a set of multinomial parameters $\phi_{e,f}$ and θ_e for each entity from a set of Dirichlet priors α and β. Next, for each of D documents, draw a multinomial distribution over entities E appearing in that document from N. Then for each of M mentions in the document, draw from E an entity e to which that mention refers. Given the entity e, draw a set of F feature types f from θ_e. For each feature type f, draw a feature value v from the distribution $\phi_{e,f}$ corresponding to the entity e and the feature type f. This model is shown graphically in Figure 1.

We chose a generative model with multinomial distributions instead of other options because we want the resultant distributions ϕ and θ to be immediately interpretable and usable in other models, as the intent is that they will be stored as part of the knowledge in the knowledge base. Also, we intend to extend this model to allow for the creation of new entities, a relatively easy extension with a model of this form.

3.2 Features

Here we describe in more detail what we use as the features f in the model. These features and their corresponding parameters ϕ and θ constitute the distributional information that we propose to include in web-scale knowledge bases, and they aim to capture the way knowledge-base entities tend to appear in text.

The features we propose are the set of Stanford dependency labels that attach to the head word of each mention, with the values being its dependents or governors. We also have features for the head word of the mention, whether it is a proper noun, a common noun, or a pronoun. We keep track of the direction of the dependencies by prepending "gov-" to the dependency label if the mention's head word is governed by another word, and we stem verbs. For example, in the sentence "Barack Obama, president of the United States, spoke today in the Rose Garden," the mention "Barack Obama" would have the following features:

Feature	Value
proper-head	Obama
nn	Barack
gov-nsubj	speak
appos	president

When there are deterministically coreferent mentions, as with appositives, we combine the features from both mentions in preprocessing.

We note here also that we use dependency links as features over which to learn distributional semantics because they are the deepest semantic representation that current tools will allow us to use at web scale. We would like to eventually move from dependency links to semantic roles, and to include relations expressed by the sentence or paragraph as features in our model. One possible way of doing that is to use something like ReVerb (Fader et al., 2011), setting its output as the value and an unobserved relation in the knowledge base as the feature type. This would learn distributional information about the textual expression of relations directly, which would also be very useful to have in web-scale knowledge bases.

3.3 Inference

Inference in our model is done approximately in a MapReduce sampling framework. The map tasks sample the entity variables for each mention in a document, sequentially. The entity variables are constrained to either refer to an entity already seen in the document, or to a new entity from the knowledge base (or unknown). Sampling over the entire knowledge base at every step would be intractable, and so when proposing a new entity from the knowledge base we only consider entities that the knowledge base considers possible for the given noun phrase (e.g., NELL has a "CanReferTo" relation mapping noun phrases to concepts (Krishnamurthy and Mitchell, 2011), and Freebase has a similar "alias" relation). Thus the first mention of an entity in a document must be a known alias of the entity, but subsequent mentions can be arbitrary noun phrases (e.g., "the college professor" could not refer to `Michael Jordan 2` until he had been introduced with a noun phrase that the knowledge base knows to be an alias, such as "Michael I. Jordan"). This follows standard journalistic practice and aids the model in constraining the "topics" to refer to actual knowledge base entities.

The reduce tasks reestimate the parameters for each entity by computing a maximum likelihood estimate given the sampled entity mentions from the map tasks. Currently, there is no parameter sharing across entities, though we intend to utilize the structure of the knowledge base to tie parameters across instances of the same category in something akin to a series of nested Dirichlet processes.

While we have not yet run experiments with the model at web scale, it is simple enough that we are confident in its scalability. Singh et al. and Ahmed et al. have shown that similarly structured models can be made to scale to web-sized corpora (Singh et al., 2011; Ahmed et al., 2012).

3.4 Evaluation

Evaluating this model is challenging. We are aiming to link *every noun phrase* in every document to an entity in the knowledge base, a task for which no good dataset exists. It is possible to use Wikipedia articles as labeled mentions (as did Singh et al. (2011)), or the word sense labels in the OntoNotes corpus (Weischedel et al., 2011), though these require a mapping between the knowledge base and Wikipedia entities or OntoNotes senses, respectively. The model also produces a coreference decision which can be evaluated. These evaluation methods are incomplete and indirect, but they are likely the best that can be hoped for without a labor-intensive hand-labeling of large amounts of data.

3.5 Preliminary Results

We do not yet have results from evaluating this model on an entity linking task. However, we do have preliminary distributional information learned from 20,000 New York Times articles about baseball. Some of the distributions learned for the New York Mets baseball team are as follows.

gov-nsubj	gov-poss
had: 0.040	manager: .088
have: 0.035	president: .032
won: 0.028	clubhouse: .024
lost: 0.026	victory: .024
got: 0.018	baseman: .020
scored: 0.015	coach: .019

These distributions themselves are inherently useful for classification tasks—knowing that an entity possesses managers, presidents, basemen and coaches tells us a lot about what kind of entity it is. The learning system for the NELL knowledge base currently uses distributions over noun phrase contexts (a few words on either side) to learn information about its concepts (Carlson et al., 2010a). The results of this model could provide much better data to NELL and other learning systems, giving both more structure (distributions over dependency links instead of windowed contexts) and more refined information (distributions over concepts directly, instead of over noun phrases) than current data sources.

4 Conclusion

We have argued for the inclusion of distributional semantics directly in web-scale knowledge bases. This is more difficult than simple counting because of the inherent ambiguity in the noun phrase to entity mapping. We have presented a model for obtaining this distributional knowledge for knowledge base entities (instead of for ambiguous noun phrases) by performing entity linking at web scale. While producing useful distributional knowledge about entities, this work will also provide much richer data sources to traditional relation extraction algorithms. Though our work is still preliminary and there are challenges to be overcome, the primary purpose of this paper is to argue that this research direction is feasible and worth pursuing. A knowledge base that includes both properties about entities and distributional knowledge of how those entities appear in text is much more useful than a knowledge base containing facts alone.

Acknowledgments

We thank Jayant Krishnamurthy and Tom Mitchell for helpful conversations, the anonymous reviewers for their comments, and the Intel Science and Technology Center on Embedded Computing for financial support.

References

A. Ahmed, M. Aly, J. Gonzalez, S. Narayanamurthy, and A.J. Smola. 2012. Scalable inference in latent variable models. In *Proceedings of the fifth ACM international conference on Web search and data mining*, pages 123–132. ACM.

David M. Blei, Andrew Y. Ng, and Michael I Jordan. 2003. Latent dirichlet allocation. *Journal of Machine Learning Research*, 3:993–1022.

K. Bollacker, C. Evans, P. Paritosh, T. Sturge, and J. Taylor. 2008. Freebase: a collaboratively created graph database for structuring human knowledge. In *Proceedings of the 2008 ACM SIGMOD international conference on Management of data*, pages 1247–1250. ACM.

A. Carlson, J. Betteridge, R.C. Wang, E.R. Hruschka Jr, and T.M. Mitchell. 2010a. Coupled semi-supervised learning for information extraction. In *Proceedings of the third ACM international conference on Web search and data mining*, pages 101–110. ACM.

Andrew Carlson, Justin Betteridge, Bryan Kisiel, Burr Settles, Estevam R. Hruschka Jr., and Tom M. Mitchell. 2010b. Toward an architecture for never-ending language learning. In *Proceedings of the Twenty-Fourth Conference on Artificial Intelligence (AAAI 2010)*.

A. Fader, S. Soderland, and O. Etzioni. 2011. Identifying relations for open information extraction. In *Proceedings of the Conference on Empirical Methods in Natural Language Processing*, pages 1535–1545. Association for Computational Linguistics.

J.R. Firth, 1957. *A synopsis of linguistic theory 1930–1955*, pages 1–32. Philological Society, Oxford.

R. Gabbard, M. Freedman, and R. Weischedel. 2011. Coreference for learning to extract relations: yes, virginia, coreference matters. In *Proceedings of the 49th Annual Meeting of the Association for Computational Linguistics: Human Language Technologies: short papers-Volume 2*, pages 288–293. Association for Computational Linguistics.

A. Haghighi and D. Klein. 2010. Coreference resolution in a modular, entity-centered model. In *Proceedings of the 48th Annual Meeting of the Association for Computational Linguistics: Human Language Technologies*, pages 385–393. Association for Computational Linguistics.

R. Hoffmann, C. Zhang, X. Ling, L. Zettlemoyer, and D.S. Weld. 2011. Knowledge-based weak supervision for information extraction of overlapping relations. In *Proceedings of the 49th Annual Meeting of the Association for Computational Linguistics: Human Language Technologies-Volume 1*, pages 541–550. Association for Computational Linguistics.

E.H. Hovy. 2011. Toward a new semantics: Merging propositional and distributional information. Presentation at Carnegie Mellon University.

J. Krishnamurthy and T.M. Mitchell. 2011. Which noun phrases denote which concepts? In *Proceedings of the 49th Annual Meeting of the Association for Computational Linguistics: Human Language Technologies*, volume 1, pages 570–580.

M. Mintz, S. Bills, R. Snow, and D. Jurafsky. 2009. Distant supervision for relation extraction without labeled data. In *Proceedings of the 47th Annual Meeting of the Association for Computational Linguistics*, pages 1003–1011. Association for Computational Linguistics.

A. Peñas and E. Hovy. 2010. Filling knowledge gaps in text for machine reading. In *Proceedings of the 23rd International Conference on Computational Linguistics: Posters*, pages 979–987. Association for Computational Linguistics.

S. Riedel, L. Yao, and A. McCallum. 2010. Modeling relations and their mentions without labeled text. *Machine Learning and Knowledge Discovery in Databases*, pages 148–163.

S. Singh, A. Subramanya, F. Pereira, and A. McCallum. 2011. Large-scale crossdocument coreference using distributed inference and hierarchical models. *Association for Computational Linguistics: Human Language Technologies (ACL HLT)*.

F.M. Suchanek, G. Kasneci, and G. Weikum. 2007. Yago: a core of semantic knowledge. In *Proceedings of the 16th international conference on World Wide Web*, pages 697–706. ACM.

Y.W. Teh, M.I. Jordan, M.J. Beal, and D.M. Blei. 2006. Hierarchical Dirichlet processes. *Journal of the American Statistical Association*, 101(476):1566–1581.

R. Weischedel, M. Palmer, M. Marcus, E. Hovy, S. Pradhan, L. Ramshaw, N. Xue, A. Taylor, J. Kaufman, M. Franchini, et al. 2011. Ontonotes release 4.0. Linguistic Data Consortium.

KRAKEN: N-ary Facts in Open Information Extraction

Alan Akbik **Alexander Löser**
Technische Univeristät Berlin
Databases and Information Systems Group
Einsteinufer 17, 10587 Berlin, Germany
alan.akbik@tu-berlin.de, aloeser@cs.tu-berlin.de

Abstract

Current techniques for Open Information Extraction (OIE) focus on the extraction of binary facts and suffer significant quality loss for the task of extracting higher order N-ary facts. This quality loss may not only affect the correctness, but also the completeness of an extracted fact. We present KRAKEN, an OIE system specifically designed to capture N-ary facts, as well as the results of an experimental study on extracting facts from Web text in which we examine the issue of fact completeness. Our preliminary experiments indicate that KRAKEN is a high precision OIE approach that captures more facts per sentence at greater completeness than existing OIE approaches, but is vulnerable to noisy and ungrammatical text.

1 Introduction

For the task of fact extraction from billions of Web pages the method of Open Information Extraction (OIE) (Fader et al., 2011) trains domain-independent extractors. This important characteristic enables a potential application of OIE for even very large corpora, such as the Web. Existing approaches for OIE, such as REVERB (Fader et al., 2011), WOE (Wu and Weld, 2010) or WANDERLUST (Akbik and Bross, 2009) focus on the extraction of binary facts, e.g. facts that consist of only two arguments, as well as a fact phrase which denotes the nature of the relationship between the arguments. However, a recent analysis of OIE based on Semantic Role Labeling (Christensen et al., 2011) revealed that N-ary facts (facts that connect more than two arguments) were present in 40% of surveyed English sentences. Worse, the analyses performed in (Fader et al., 2011) and (Akbik and Bross, 2009) show that incorrect handling of N-ary facts leads to extraction errors, such as incomplete, uninformative or erroneous facts. Our first example illustrates the case of *a significant information loss*:

a) *In the 2002 film Bubba Ho-tep, Elvis lives in a nursing home.*
REVERB: LivesIn(Elvis, nursing home)

In this case, the OIE system ignores the significant contextual information in the argument *the 2002 film Bubba Ho-tep*, which denotes the domain in which the fact LivesIn(Elvis, nursing home) is true. As a result, and by itself, the extracted fact is false. The next example shows a binary fact from a sentence that de-facto expresses an N-ary fact.

b) *Elvis moved to Memphis in 1948.*
REVERB: MovedTo(Elvis, Memphis)
WANDERLUST: MovedIn(Elvis, 1948)

Contrary to the previous example, the OIE systems extracted two binary facts that are *not false, but incomplete*, as the interaction between all three entities in this sentence can only be adequately modeled using an ternary fact. The fact MovedIn(Elvis, 1948) for example misses an important aspect, namely the *location* Elvis moved to in 1948. Therefore, each of these two facts is an example of important, but not crucial information loss.

Unfortunately, current OIE systems are not designed to capture the complete set of arguments for each fact phrase within a sentence and to link arguments into an N-ary fact. We view intra-sentence fact completeness as a major measure of data quality. Following existing work from (Galhardas et al., 2001) complete factual data is a key for advanced data cleansing tasks, such as fact de-duplication, object resolution across N-ary facts, semantic fact interpretation and corpus wide fact aggregation. Therefore we argue that complete facts may serve a human reader or an advanced data cleansing approach as additional clue for interpreting and validating the fact. In order to investigate the need and feasibility for N-ary OIE we have performed the following, the results of which we present in this paper:

1. We introduce the OIE system KRAKEN, which has been built *specifically* for capturing complete facts from sentences and is capable of extracing unary, binary and higher order N-ary facts.

2. We examine intra sentence fact correctness (true/false) and fact completeness for KRAKEN and REVERB on the corpus of (Fader et al., 2011).

In the rest of the paper we review earlier work and outline KRAKEN, our method for extracting N-ary facts and contextual information. Next, we describe our experiments and end with conclusions.

2 KRAKEN

We introduce KRAKEN, an N-ary OIE fact extraction system for facts of arbitrary arity.

2.1 Previous Work

Binary-OIE: Our previous system WANDERLUST (Akbik and Bross, 2009) operates using a typed dependency-style grammar representation called Link Grammar. The system traverses paths of typed dependencies (referred to as linkpaths) to find pairs of arguments connected by a valid grammatical relationship. We identified a set of 46 common linkpaths that can be used for fact extraction. Later, the authors (Wu and Weld, 2010) trained extractors in a system called WOE, one using only shallow syntactic features and one (called WOEPARSE) that also uses typed dependencies as features. The latter system learned more than 15.000 patterns over typed dependencies. In their evaluation they showed that using deep syntactic parsing improves the precision of their system, however at a high cost in extraction speed. The OIE system REVERB (Fader et al., 2011) by contrast uses a fast shallow syntax parser for labeling sentences and applies syntactic and a lexical constraints for identifying binary facts. However, the shallow syntactic analysis limits the capability of REVERB of extracting higher order N-ary facts.

Higher order fact extraction for Wikipedia: In previous work on higher order fact extraction, the focus was placed on specific types of arguments. The authors of (Hoffart et al., 2011) for example extract temporal, spatial and category information from Wikipedia info boxes. (Weikum et al., 2011) and (Ling and Weld, 2010) focused on N-ary fact types from English sentences that contain at least one temporal argument. In contrast, KRAKEN extracts N-ary facts with arbitrary argument types.

path	head of
`nsubj-↓`	subject
`nsubjpass-↓`	subject (passive)
`rcmod-↑,appos-↑`	subject (relative clause)
`partmod-↑-nsubj-↓`	subject
`dobj-↓`	object
`prep-↓, pobj-↓`	object
`prep-↓, npadvmod-↓`	object
`advmod-↓`	context (usually modal)
`tmod-↑`	context (temporal)
`parataxis-↓,nsubj-↓`	context
`ccomp-↓,nsubj-↓`	context

Table 1: Common type-paths and the type of argument head they find.

2.2 Algorithm Outline

KRAKEN expects as input a Stanford dependency parsed sentence, in which two words are *linked* if connected via a typed dependency. Each typed dependency has a *type* denoting the grammatical nature of the link, and is directed, either upward (from child to parent) or downward (from parent to child). Given such a parse, KRAKEN executes the following three steps:

1. Fact phrase detection: The system identifies a fact phrase as a chain of verbs, modifiers and/or prepositions, linked by any of the following types: `aux`, `cop`, `xcomp`, `acomp`, `prt` or `auxpass`. Examples of such chains are *has been known* or *claims to be*. A detected fact phrase may consist of only one word if it is POS-tagged as verb and not linked with any of the aforementioned types.

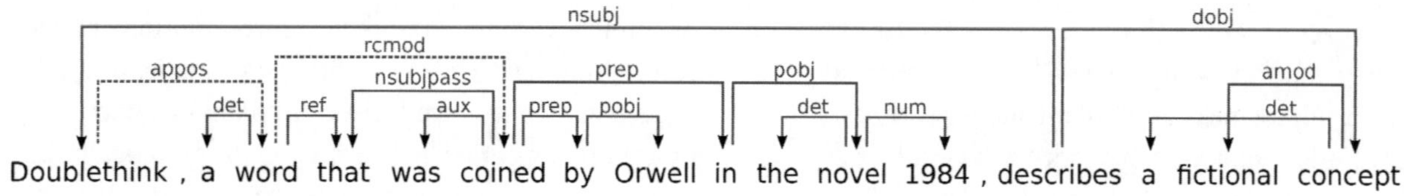

Figure 1: Example of a sentence in Stanford typed dependency formalism. One fact phrase is *was coined*. Using the type-path `rcmod-↑-appos-↑`, the subject the *Doublethink* is found, the path is highlighted in dotted lines. Using `prep-↓`, `pobj-↓`, two arguments are found: *Orwell* and *the novel 1984*. One N-ary fact for this sentence is WasCoined(Doublethink, (by) Orwell, (in) the novel 1984). The other is Describes(Doublethink, fictional concept).

2. Detection of argument heads: Next, for each word of a fact phrase, KRAKEN attempts to find heads of arguments using *type-paths* as listed in Table 1. Each type-path indicates one or more links, as well as the direction of each link, to follow to find an argument head. For example, the type-path `subj-↓` indicates that if one downward link of type `subj` exists, then the target of that link is an argument head. Figure 1 illustrates an example. At the end of this step, KRAKEN returns all found argument heads for the fact phrase.

3. Detection of full arguments: KRAKEN recursively follows all downward links from the argument head to get the full argument, excluding any links that were part of the type-path to the argument head. The combination of the detected fact phrase from step 1 and these full arguments form the fact. If a fact phrase has at least one argument, the system extracts it as a fact.

The ruleset was generated by joining the linkpaths reported in (Akbik and Bross, 2009) that contain at least one overlapping entity and one overlapping verb, and exchanging the underlying grammatical formalism with Stanford typed dependencies[1], resulting in a verb-centric and human-readable ruleset.

3 Preliminary Experimental Study

We compare REVERB, the state-of-the-art in binary fact extraction, with KRAKEN, in order to measure the effect of using N-ary fact extraction over purely binary extractors on overall precision and completeness. Additionally, we test in how far using an IE approach based on deep syntactic parsing can be used for sentences from the Web, which have a higher chance of being ungrammatical or noisy.

[1]http://nlp.stanford.edu/software/dependencies

3.1 Experimental Setup

Data set: We use the data set from (Fader et al., 2011) which consists of 500 sentences sampled from the Web using Yahoo's random link service.[2] The sentences were labeled both with facts found with KRAKEN and the current version of REVERB.[3] We then paired facts for the same sentence that overlap in at least one of the fact phrase words, in order to present to the judges two different versions of the same fact - often one binary (REVERB) and one N-ary (KRAKEN).

Measurements/Instructions: Given a sentence and a fact (or fact-pair), we asked two human judges to label each fact as either 1) true and complete, 2) true and incomplete, or 3) false. *True and incomplete facts* either lack contextual information in the form of arguments that were present in the sentence, or contain underspecified arguments, but are nevertheless valid statements in themselves (see our examples in Section 1). In previous evaluations, such

[2]http://random.yahoo.com/bin/ryl

[3]available at http://reverb.cs.washington.edu/

	KRAKEN	REVERB		
sentences	500	500		
skipped	155	**0**		
elapsed time	319.067ms	**13.147ms**		
min. confidence	-	0	0.1	0.2
total facts	572	**736**	528	457
per sentence	**1.66**	1.47	1.06	0.91
true, complete	**308**	166	146	127
true, incomplete	**81**	256	193	162
false	183	314	189	**168**
precision	**0.68**	0.61	0.64	0.63
completeness	**0.79**	0.39	0.43	0.44

Table 2: The results of the comparative evaluation. KRAKEN nearly doubles the amount of recognized complete and true facts.

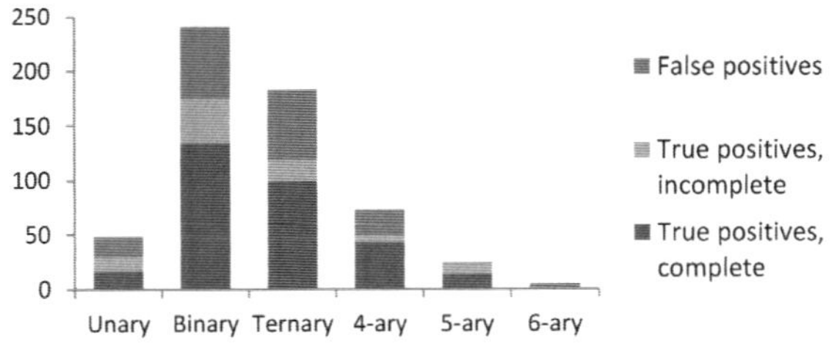

Figure 2: Distribution of arity of facts found by KRAKEN and their correctness.

facts have been counted as true. We distinguish them from *true and complete facts* that capture all relevant arguments as given by the sentence they were extracted from. We measured an inter-annotator agreement of 87%, differently evaluated facts were discussed by the judges and resolved. Most disagreement was caused by facts with underspecified arguments, labeled as false by one judge and as true and incomplete by the other.

3.2 Evaluation Results and Discussion

KRAKEN extracts higher order N-ary facts. Table 2 show results for KRAKEN and REVERB. We measured results for REVERB with different confidence thresholds. In all measurements, we observe a significantly higher number of true and complete facts for KRAKEN, as well as both a higher overall precision and number of facts extracted per sentence. The *completeness*, measured as the ratio of complete facts over all true facts, is also significantly higher for KRAKEN. Figure 2 breaks down the fact arity. KRAKEN performs particularly well for binary, ternary and 4-ary facts, which are also most common. We conclude that even though our ruleset was generated on a different domain (Wikipedia text), it generalizes well to the Web domain.

Dependency parsing of Web text. One major drawback of the settings we used is our (possibly too crude) heuristic for detecting erroneous dependency parses: We set KRAKEN to extract facts from all sentences in which the dependency parse does not contain the typed dependency `dep`, which indicates unclear grammatical relationships. A total of 155 sentences - 31% of the overall evaluation set - were skipped as a consequence. Also, the elapsed time of the fact extraction process was more than one order of magnitude longer than REVERB, possibly limiting the ability of the system to scale to very large collections of documents.

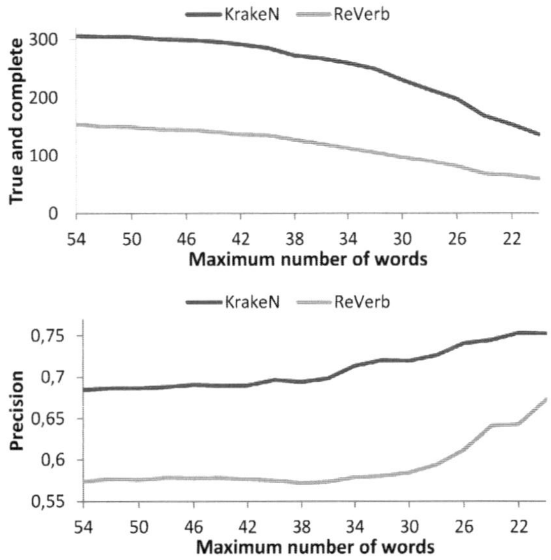

Figure 3: Impact of limiting the maximum sentence length on precision and the number of true positives.

Measurements over different sentence lengths. When limiting the maximum number of words allowed per sentence, we note modest gains in precision and losses in complete positives in both systems, see Figure 3. KRAKEN performs well even on long sentences, extracting more true and complete positives at a high precision.

Lessons learned. Based on these observations, we reach the conclusion that given the 'right portion' of sentences from a collection such as the Web, our method for N-ary OIE can be very effective, extracting more complete facts with a high precision and fact-per-sentence rate. Sentences that are well suited for our algorithm must fulfill the following *desiderata*: 1) They are noise free and grammatically correct, so there is a high chance for a correct parse. 2) They are fact-rich, so that processing resources are wisely used.

4 Summary and Future Work

Current OIE systems do not perform well for the task of higher order N-ary fact extraction. We presented KRAKEN, an algorithm that finds these facts with high precision, completeness, and fact-per-sentence rate. However, we also note that relying on a dependency parser comes at the cost of speed and recall, as many sentences were skipped due to our heuristic of detecting erroneous parses.

Future work focuses on scaling the system up for use on a large Web corpus and increasing the system's recall. To achieve this, we will work on a first step of identifying grammatical and fact-rich sentences before applying dependency parsing in a second step, filtering out all sentences that do not meet the desiderata stated in Section 3. We intend to evaluate using very fast dependency parsers, some more than two orders of magnitude faster than the Stanford parser (Cer et al., 2010), one prominent example of which is the MALTparser (Nivre et al., 2007).

Additionally, we will examine more data-driven approaches for identifying fact phrases and arguments in order to maximize the system's recall. We intend to use such an approach to train KRAKEN for use on other languages such as German.

One interesting aspect of future work is the canonicalization of the fact phrases and arguments given very large collections of extracted facts. Unsupervised approaches that make use of redundancy such as (Bollegala et al., 2010) or (Yates and Etzioni, 2007) may help cluster similar fact phrases or arguments. A related possibility is the integration of facts into an existing knowledge base, using methods such as distant supervision (Mintz et al., 2009). We believe that combining OIE with a method for fact phrase canonicalization will allow us to better evaluate the system in terms of precision/recall and usefulness in the future.

Acknowledgements

We would like to thank the anonymous reviewers for their helpful comments.

Alan Akbik received funding from the European Union's Seventh Framework Programme (FP7/2007-2013) under grant agreement no ICT-2009-4-1 270137 'Scalable Preservation Environments' (SCAPE) and Alexander Löser receives funding from the Federal Ministry of Economics and Technology (BMWi) under grant agreement "01MD11014A, 'MIA-Marktplatz für Informationen und Analysen' (MIA)".

References

Alan Akbik and Jürgen Bross. 2009. Wanderlust: Extracting semantic relations from natural language text using dependency grammar patterns. In *1st. Workshop on Semantic Search at 18th. WWWW Conference*.

D.T. Bollegala, Y. Matsuo, and M. Ishizuka. 2010. Relational duality: Unsupervised extraction of semantic relations between entities on the web. In *Proceedings of the 19th international conference on World wide web*, pages 151–160. ACM.

D. Cer, M.C. de Marneffe, D. Jurafsky, and C.D. Manning. 2010. Parsing to stanford dependencies: Tradeoffs between speed and accuracy. In *Proceedings of LREC*, pages 1628–1632.

Janara Christensen, Mausam, Stephen Soderland, and Oren Etzioni. 2011. An analysis of open information extraction based on semantic role labeling. In *K-CAP*, pages 113–120.

Anthony Fader, Stephen Soderland, and Oren Etzioni. 2011. Identifying relations for open information extraction. In *EMNLP*, pages 1535–1545.

Helena Galhardas, Daniela Florescu, Dennis Shasha, Eric Simon, and Cristian-Augustin Saita. 2001. Declarative data cleaning: Language, model, and algorithms. In *VLDB*, pages 371–380.

Johannes Hoffart, Fabian M. Suchanek, Klaus Berberich, Edwin Lewis-Kelham, Gerard de Melo, and Gerhard Weikum. 2011. Yago2: exploring and querying world knowledge in time, space, context, and many languages. In *Proceedings of the 20th international conference companion on World wide web*, WWW '11, pages 229–232, New York, NY, USA. ACM.

Xiao Ling and Daniel S. Weld. 2010. Temporal information extraction. In *24th. AAAI Conference on Artificial Intelligence*.

M. Mintz, S. Bills, R. Snow, and D. Jurafsky. 2009. Distant supervision for relation extraction without labeled data. In *Proceedings of the Joint Conference of the 47th Annual Meeting of the ACL and the 4th International Joint Conference on Natural Language Processing of the AFNLP: Volume 2-Volume 2*, pages 1003–1011. Association for Computational Linguistics.

J. Nivre, J. Hall, J. Nilsson, A. Chanev, G. Eryigit, S. Kübler, S. Marinov, and E. Marsi. 2007. Maltparser: A language-independent system for data-driven dependency parsing. *Natural Language Engineering*, 13(02):95–135.

Gerhard Weikum, Nikos Ntarmos, Marc Spaniol, Peter Triantafillou, András A. Benczúr, Scott Kirkpatrick, Philippe Rigaux, and Mark Williamson. 2011. Longitudinal analytics on web archive data: It's about time! In *CIDR*, pages 199–202.

F. Wu and D.S. Weld. 2010. Open information extraction using wikipedia. In *ACL*, pages 118–127.

A. Yates and O. Etzioni. 2007. Unsupervised resolution of objects and relations on the web. In *Proceedings of NAACL HLT*, pages 121–130.

Structural Linguistics and Unsupervised Information Extraction

Ralph Grishman
Dept. of Computer Science
New York University
715 Broadway, 7th floor
New York, NY 10003, USA
grishman@cs.nyu.edu

Abstract

A precondition for extracting information from large text corpora is discovering the information structures underlying the text. Progress in this direction is being made in the form of unsupervised information extraction (IE). We describe recent work in unsupervised relation extraction and compare its goals to those of grammar discovery for science sublanguages. We consider what this work on grammar discovery suggests for future directions in unsupervised IE.

1 Introduction

Vast amounts of information are available in unstructured text form. To make use of this information we need to identify the underlying information structures – the classes of entities and the predicates connecting these entities – and then automatically map the text into these information structures.

Over the past decade there has been a quickening pace of research aimed at automating the process of discovering these structures, both for broad domains (news stories) and for more limited technical domains. This has taken the form of unsupervised methods for entity set creation and relation extraction.

This research has sometimes been presented as an entirely new exploration into discovery procedures for information structures. But in fact there are relevant precedents for such exploration, albeit completely manual, going back at least half a century. An examination of these precedents can give us some insight into the challenges that face us in unsupervised information extraction.

This brief paper will first review some of the relevant work in unsupervised IE; then turn to some of the earlier work on discovery procedures within linguistics; and finally consider what these discovery procedures may suggest for the next steps in automation.

2 Unsupervised IE

The task of unsupervised information extraction involves characterizing the types of arguments that can occur with particular linguistic predicates, and identifying the predicate-argument combinations which convey the same meaning.

Most of the recent work on unsupervised IE has focused on the more tractable problem of unsupervised binary relation extraction (URE). A potential binary relation instance (a 'triple') consists of two *arguments* (typically names or nouns) connected by a *relation phrase*. A text corpus will yield a large number of such triples. The challenge is to group the triples (or a subset of them) into a set of semantically coherent relations – clusters of triples representing approximately the same semantic relationship.

One of the first such efforts was (Hasegawa et al. 2003), which used a corpus of news stories and identified the most common relations between people and companies. They relied on standard predefined named entity tags and a clustering strategy based on a simple similarity metric between relation instances (treating relation phrases as bags of words). Subsequent research has expanded this research along several dimensions.

(Zhang et al. 2005) introduced a more elaborate similarity metric based on similarity of relation phrase constituent structure. However, this direction was not generally pursued; (Yao et al. 2011) used the dependency path between arguments as a feature in their generative model, but most URE systems have treated relation phrases as unanalyzed entities or bags of words.

Several researchers have extended the scope from news reports to the Web, using in particular robust triples extractors such as TextRunner (Banko et al. 2007) and ReVerb (Fader et al. 2011), which capture relation phrases involving verbal predicates. Moving to a nearly unrestricted domain has meant that predefined argument classes would no longer suffice, leading to systems which constructed both entity classes and relation classes. SNE (Kok and Domingos 2008) used entity similarities computed from the set of triples to construct such entity classes concurrently with the construction of relation sets. (Yao et al. 2011) learned fine-grained argument classes based on a predefined set of coarse-grained argument types. Resolver (Yates and Etzioni 2007) identified coreferential names while building relation classes.

Moving to Web-scale discovery also magnified the problem of relation-phrase polysemy, where a phrase has different senses which should be clustered with different sets of triples. This was addressed in WEBRE (Min et al. 2012), which clusters generalized triples (consisting of a relation phrase and two argument classes). WEBRE also uses a larger range of semantic resources to form the argument classes, including hyponymy relations, coordination patterns, and HTML structures.

Most of this work has been applied in the news domain or on Web documents, but there has also been some work on technical domains such as medical records (Rink and Harabagiu 2011).

Closely related to the work on unsupervised IE is the work on collecting paraphrase and inference rules from corpora (e.g., DIRT (Lin and Pantel 2001)) and some of the work on unsupervised semantic parsing (USP), which maps text or syntactically-analyzed text into logical forms. The predicate clusters of USP (Poon and Domingos 2009) capture both syntactic and semantic paraphrases of predicates. However, the work on paraphrase and USP is generally not aimed at creating an inventory of argument classes associated with particular predicates.

All of this work has been done on binary relations.[1] Discovering more general (n-ary) structures is more difficult because in most cases arguments will be optional, complicating the alignment process. (Shinyama and Sekine 2006), who built a system for unsupervised event template construction, addressed this problem in part through two levels of clustering – one level capturing stories about the same event, the second level capturing stories about the same *type* of event. (Chambers and Jurafsky 2011) clustered events to create templates for terrorist events which involve up to four distinct roles.

3 Discovery of Linguistic Structure

Current researchers on unsupervised IE share some goals with the structural linguists of the early and mid 20th century, such as Bloomfield, Saussure, and especially Zellig Harris. "The goal of structural linguistics was to discover a grammar by performing a set of operations on a corpus of data" (Newmeyer 1980, p. 6). Harris in particular pushed this effort in two directions: to discover the relations between sentences and capture them in *transformations*; and to study the grammars of *science sublanguages* (Harris 1968).

A sublanguage is the restricted form of a natural language used within a particular domain, such as medicine or a field of science or engineering. Just as the language as a whole is characterized by word classes (noun, transitive verb) and patterns of combination (noun + transitive verb + noun), the sublanguage is characterized by domain-specific word classes (N_{ion}, $V_{transport}$, N_{cell}) and patterns (N_{ion} + $V_{transport}$ + N_{cell}). Just as a speaker of the language will reject a sequence not matching one of the patterns (Cats eat fish. *but not* Cats fish eat.) so will a speaker of the sublanguage reject a sequence not matching a sublanguage pattern (Potassium enters the cell. *but not* The cell enters potassium.) Intuitively these classes and patterns have semantic content, but Harris asserted they could be characterized on a purely structural basis.

[1] Unsupervised semantic parsing (Poon and Domingos 2009) could in principle handle n-ary relations, although all the examples presented involved binary predicates. USP is also able to handle limited nested structures.

Harris described procedures for discovering the sublanguage grammar from a text corpus. In simplest terms, the word classes would be identified based on shared syntactic contexts, following the distributional hypothesis (Harris 1985; Hirschman et al. 1975). This approach is now a standard one for creating entity classes from a corpus. This will reduce the corpus to a set of word class sequences. The sublanguage grammar can then be created by aligning these sequences, mediated by the transformations of the general language (in other words, one may need to decompose and reorder the sequences using the transformations in order to get the sequences to align).

Fundamental to the sublanguage grammar are the set of elementary or *kernel* sentences, such as N_{ion} $V_{transport}$ N_{cell} ("Potassium enters the cell."). More complex sentences are built by applying a set of *operators*, some of which alter an individual sentence (e.g., passive), some of which combine sentences (e.g., conjunction, substitution). The derivation of a sentence is represented as a tree structure in which the leaves are kernel sentences and the internal nodes are operators. Within the sublanguage, repeating patterns (subtrees) of kernel sentences and operators can be identified. One can distill from these repeating derivational patterns a set of *information formats*, representing the informational constituents being combined (Sager et al. 1987).

Harris applied these methods, by hand but in great detail, to the language of immunology (Harris et al. 1989). Sager and her associates applied them to clinical (medical) narratives as well as some articles from the biomedical literature (Sager et al. 1987).

These sublanguage grammatical patterns really reflect the information structures of the language in this domain – the structures into which we want to transform the text in order to capture its information content. In that sense, they represent the ultimate goal of unsupervised IE.

Typically, they will be much richer structures than are created by current unsupervised relation extraction. For papers on lipid metabolism, for example, 7 levels of structure were identified, including kernel sentences, quantifying operators (rates, concentrations, etc.), causal relations, modal operators, and *metalanguage* relations connecting experimenters to reported results (Sager et al. 1987, p. 226).

Harris focused on narrow sublanguages because the 'semantic' constraints are more sharply drawn in the sublanguage than are seletional constraints in the language as a whole. (They were presumably also more amenable to a comprehensive manual analysis.) If we look at a broader domain, we can still expect multiple levels of information, but not a single overall structure as was possible in analyzing an individual topic.

4 What we can learn

What perspective can Harris's work provide about the future of discovery methods for IE?

First, it can give us some picture of the richer structures we will need to discover in order to adequately represent the information in the text. Current URE systems are limited to capturing a set of relations between (selected classes of) names or nouns. In terms of the hierarchical information structures produced by sublanguage analysis, they are currently focused on the predicates whose arguments are the leaves of the tree (roughly speaking, the kernel sentences).[2] For example, for

The Government reported an increase in China's export of coal.

we would expect a URE to capture

export(China, coal)

which might be able to generalize this to

export(*country*, *commodity*)

but not capture the *report(Government, increase)* or *increase(export)* relations. A more comprehensive approach would also capture these and other relations that arise from modifiers on entities, including quantity and measure phrases and locatives; modifiers on predicates, including negation, aspect, quantity, and temporal information; and higher-order predicates, including sequence and causal relations and verbs of belief and reporting. The modifiers would in many cases yield unary relations; the higher-order predicates would take arguments which are themselves relations and would be generalized to relation sets.[3]

[2] This is not quite true of OpenIE triples extractors, which may incorporate multiple predicates into the relation, such as 'expect a loss' or 'plan to offer'.

[3] Decomposing predicates in this way – treating "report an increase in export" as three linked predicates rather than one – has both advantages and disadvantages in capturing paraphrase – i.e., in grouping equivalent relations. Advantages because paraphrases at a single level may be learned more easily: one doesn't have to learn the equivalence of "began to

A second benefit of studying these precedents from linguistics is that they can suggest some of the steps we may need to enrich our unsupervised IE processing. Current URE systems suffer from cluster recall problems … they fail to group together many triples which should be considered as instances of the same relation. For example, SNE (Kok and Domingos 2008) cites a pairwise recall for relations of 19%, reporting this as a big improvement over earlier systems. In Harris's terms, this corresponds to not being able to align word sequences. This is a reflection in part of the fact that most systems rely primarily or entirely on distributional information to group triples, and this is not sufficient for infrequent relation phrases.[4] Expanding to Web-scale discovery will increase the frequency of particular phrases, thus providing more evidence for clustering, but will also introduce new, complex phrases; the combined 'tail' of infrequent phrases will remain substantial. The relation phrases themselves are for many systems treated as unanalyzed word sequences. In some cases, inflected forms are reduced to base forms or phrases are treated as bags of words to improve matching. A few systems perform dependency analysis and represent the relation phrases as paths in the dependency tree. Even in such cases active objects and passive subjects are typically labeled differently, so the system must learn to align active and passive forms separately for each predicate. (In effect, the alignment is being learned at the wrong level of generality.)

The problem will be more acute when we move to learning hierarchical structures because we will have both verbal and nominalized forms of predicates and would like to identify their equivalence.

Not surprisingly, the alignment process used by Harris is based on a much richer linguistic analysis involving transformationally decomposed sentences. This included regularization of passives, normalization of nominalizations (equating "uptake of potassium by the cell" with "the cell takes up potassium"), treatment of support verbs (reducing "take a walk" to "walk"), and handling of transparent nouns (reducing "I ate a pound of chocolate" to "I ate chocolate." plus a quantity modifier on "chocolate"). Many instances of equivalent sublanguage patterns could be recognized based on such syntactic transformations.

Incorporating such transformations into an NLP pipeline produces of course a slower and more complex analysis process than used by current URE systems, but it will be essential in the long term to get adequate cluster recall – in other words, to unify different relation phrases representing the same semantic relation. Its importance will increase when we move from binary to n-ary structures. Fortunately there has been steady progress in this area over the last two decades, based on increasingly rich representations: starting with the function tags and indexing of Penn TreeBank II, which permitted regularization of passives, relatives, and infinitival subjects; PropBank, which enabled additional regularization of verbal complements (Kingsbury and Palmer 2002), and NomBank (Meyers et al. 2004) and NomLex, which support regularization between verbal and nominal constructs. These regularizations have been captured in systems such as GLARF (Meyers et al. 2009), and fostered by recent CoNLL evaluations (Hajic et al. 2009).

In addition to these transformations which can be implicitly realized through predicate-argument analysis, Harris (1989, pp. 21-23) described several other classes of transformations essential to alignment. One of these is modifier movement: modifiers which may attach to entities or arguments ("In San Diego, the weather is sunny." vs. "The weather in San Diego is sunny."). If we had a two-level representation, with both entities and predicates, this would have to be accommodated through the alignment procedure.

There will be serious obstacles to automating the full discovery process. The manual 'mechanical' process is no doubt not as mechanical as Harris would have us believe. Knowledge of the meaning of individual words surely played at least an implicit role in decisions regarding the granularity of word classes, for example. Stability-based clustering (Chen et al. 2005) has been applied to select a suitable granularity for relation clusters but the optimization will be more complex when clustering both entities and relations. Obtaining accurate syntactic structure across multiple domains will

X" and "started Xing" for each verb X. Disadvantages because paraphrases may require aligning a single predicate with two predicates, as in "grow" and "increase in size". Handling both cases may require maintaining both composite and decomposed forms of a relation.

[4] Some systems, such as WEBRE (Min et al. 2012), do use additional semantic resources and are able to achieve better recall.

require adaptive methods (for modifier attachment, for example). However, it should be possible to apply these enhancements – in structural complexity and linguistic matching – *incrementally* starting from current URE systems, thus gradually producing more powerful discovery procedures.

References

Michele Banko, Michael Cafarella, Stephen Soderland, Matt Broadhead, and Oren Etzioni. 2007. Open information extraction from the web. *Proc. 20th Int'l Joint Conf. on Artificial Intelligence.*

Nathanael Chambers and Dan Jurafsky. 2011. Template-Based Information Extraction without the Templates. *Proceedings of ACL 2011.*

Jinxiu Chen, Donghong Ji, Chew Lim Tan, and Zhengyu Niu. 2005. Automatic relation extraction with model order selection and discriminative label identification. *Proc. IJCNLP 2005.*

Jan Hajic, Massimiliano Ciarmita, Richard Johansson, Daisuke Kawahara, Maria Antonia Marti, Lluis Marquez, Adam Meyers, Joakim Nivre, Sebastian Paso, Jan Stepanek, Pavel Stranak, Mihai Surdeanu, Nianwen Xue, and Yi Zhang. 2009. The CoNLL-2009 Shared Task: syntactic and semantic dependencies in multiple languages. *Proc. Thirteenth Conf. on Computational Natural Language Learning (CoNLL)*, Boulder, Colorado.

Zellig Harris. 1968. *Mathematical Structures of Language.* New York: Interscience.

Zellig Harris. 1985. Distributional Structure. *The Philosophy of Linguistics.* New York: Oxford University Press.

Zellig Harris, Michael Gottfried, Thomas Ryckman, Paul Mattcik Jr., Anne Daladier, T.N. Harris and S. Harris. 1989. *The Form of Information in Science: Analysis of an Immunology Sublanguage.* Dordrecht: Kluwer Academic Publishers.

Takaaki Hasegawa, Satoshi Sekine, and Ralph Grishman. 2004. Discovering Relations among Named Entities from Large Corpora. *Proceedings of ACL 2004.*

Lynette Hirschman, Ralph Grishman, and Naomi Sager. Grammatically-based automatic word class formation. 1975. *Information Processing and Management* **11**, 39-57.

P. Kingsbury and Martha Palmer. 2002. From treebank to propbank. *Proc. LREC-2002.*

Stanley Kok and Pedro Domingos. 2008. Extracting Semantic Networks from Text via Relational Clustering. *Proceedings of ECML 2008.*

Dekang Lin and Patrick Pantel. 2001. DIRT - discovery of inference rules from text. *Proc.Seventh ACM SIGKDD International Conf. on Knowledge Discovery and Data Mining.*

Adam Meyers, Ruth Reeves, Catherine Macleod, Rachel Szekely, Veronika Zielinska, Brian Young and Ralph Grishman. 2004. Annotating noun argument structure for NomBank. *Proc. LREC-2004.*

Adam Meyers, Michiko Kosaka, Heng Ji, Nianwen Xue, Mary Harper, Ang Sun, Wei Xu, and Shasha Liao. 2009. Transducing logical relations from automatic and manual GLARF. *Proc. Linguistic Annotation Workshop-III at ACL 2009.*

Bonan Min, Shuming Shi, Ralph Grishman, and Chin-Yew Lin. 2012. Ensemble semantics for large-scale unsupervised relation extraction. Microsoft Technique Report, MSR-TR-2012-51.

Frederick Newmeyer. 1980. *Linguistic Theory in America.* Academic Press, New York.

Hoifung Poon and Pedro Domingos. 2009. Unsupervised semantic parsing. *Proc. 2009 Conf. Empirical Methods in Natural Language Processing.*

Bryan Rink and Sanda Harabagiu. 2011. A generative model for unsupervised discovery of relations and argument classes from clinical texts. *Proc. 2011 Conf. Empirical Methods in Natural Language Processing.*

Naomi Sager, Carol Friedman, and Margaret S. Lyman. 1987. *Medical Language Processing: Computer Management of Narrative Data.* Addison-Wesley, Reading, MA.

Yusuke Shinyama and Satoshi Sekine. 2006. Preemptive Information Extraction using Unrestricted Relation Discovery. *Proc. NAACL 2006.*

Limin Yao, Aria Haghighi, Sebastian Riedel, Andrew McCallum. 2011. Structured Relation Discovery Using Generative Models. *Proc. EMNLP 2011.*

Alexander Yates and Oren Etzioni. 2007. Unsupervised Resolution of Objects and Relations on the Web. *Proc. HLT-NAACL 2007.*

Min Zhang, Jian Su, Danmei Wang, Guodong Zhou, and Chew Lim Tan. 2005. Discovering relations between named entities from a large raw corpus using tree similarity-based clustering. *Proc. Second Int'l Joint Conference on Natural Language Processing (IJCNLP).*

A Context-Aware Approach to Entity Linking

Veselin Stoyanov and **James Mayfield**
HLTCOE
Johns Hopkins University

Tan Xu and **Douglas W. Oard**
University of Maryland
College Park

Dawn Lawrie
Loyola University
in Maryland

Tim Oates and **Tim Finin**
University of Maryland
Baltimore County

Abstract

Entity linking refers to the task of assigning mentions in documents to their corresponding knowledge base entities. Entity linking is a central step in knowledge base population. Current entity linking systems do not explicitly model the discourse context in which the communication occurs. Nevertheless, the notion of shared context is central to the linguistic theory of pragmatics and plays a crucial role in Grice's cooperative communication principle. Furthermore, modeling context facilitates joint resolution of entities, an important problem in entity linking yet to be addressed satisfactorily. This paper describes an approach to context-aware entity linking.

1 Introduction

Given a mention of an entity in a document and a set of known entities in a knowledge base (KB), the *entity linking* task is to find the entity ID of the mentioned entity, or return NIL if the mentioned entity was previously unknown. Entity linking is a key requirement for knowledge base population; without it, accurately extracted attributes and relationships cannot be correctly inserted into an existing KB.

Recent research in entity linking has been driven by shared tasks at a variety of international conferences (Huang et al., 2008; McNamee and Dang, 2009). The TAC Knowledge Base Population track (Ji et al., 2011) provides a representative example. Participants are provided with a knowledge base derived from Wikipedia Infoboxes. Each query comprises a text document and a mention string found in that document. The entity linking system must determine whether the entity referred to by the mention is represented in the KB, and if so, which entity it represents.

State-of-the-art entity linking systems are quite good at linking person names (Ji et al., 2011). They rely on a variety of Machine Learning approaches and may incorporate different external resources such as name Gazetteers (Burman et al., 2011), precompiled estimates of entity popularities (Han and Sun, 2011) and modules trained to recognize name and acronym matches (Zhang et al., 2011).

Two areas are handled less well by current entity linking systems. First, it has been recognized that collective inference over a set of entities can lead to better performance (Cucerzan, 2007; Kulkarni et al., 2009; Hoffart et al., 2011; Ratinov et al., 2011). While the field has begun to move in the direction of collective (or joint) inference, such inference is a computationally hard problem. As a result, current joint inference approaches rely on different heuristics to limit the search space. Thus, collective classification approaches are yet to gain wide acceptance. In fact, only four of the 35 systems that submitted runs to the 2011 TAC KBP task go beyond a single query in a single document. Ji et al. (2011) cite the need for (more) joint inference as one of the avenues for improvement.

The second area not handled well is the notion of discourse context. Grice's principle for collaborative communication postulates that communications should obey certain properties with respect to the context shared between the author and the recipient of the communication (Grice, 1975). For instance, the Maxim of Quantity states that a contribution should be as informative as is required (for the purpose of the exchange), but no more informative than that. Similarly, the Maxim of Manner states that one should avoid ambiguity. Grice's principle is important for entity linking: it argues that communications (e.g., newswire articles) are only possible when the author and the audience share a discourse context, and entity mentions must be unambiguous in this shared context.

The shared discourse context depends on the type of communication, the author, and the intended audience. For newswire with a given readership, there is a broadly shared context, comprising the major personalities and organizations in politics, sports, entertainment, etc. Any entity mentioned that is not part of this broadly shared context will be fully qualified in a news article (e.g., *"Jane Frotzenberry, 42, a plumber from Boaz, Alabama said ... "*). Thus, a system that performs entity linking on newswire needs to maintain a list of entities that are famous at the given time. Less famous entries can be resolved with the help of the extra information that the author provides, as required by the Maxim of Quantity.

The notion of context is all the more important when resolving entities in personal communications such as email. Personal communication often contains unqualified entity mentions. For example, an email from **Ken Lay** to **Jeff Skilling** might mention *Andy* with no other indication that the person mentioned is **Andrew Fastow**. A traditional entity linking system will fail miserably here; the mention *Andy* is simply too ambiguous out of context. Email-specific linkers often rely on access to the communications graph to resolve such mentions. The communications graph is important mainly because it offers a guess at the discourse context shared between the author of a communication and its recipient(s).

We propose a new approach to entity linking that explicitly models the context shared by the participants of a communication. Our context-aware entity linking approach is guided by three principles:

1. *Shared context should be modeled explicitly.* This allows the linker to be easily adapted to new genres, and allows a modular system design that separates context modeling from entity linking.

2. *Most entity linking should be trivial in the shared context.* If the context accurately models the shared assumptions of author and audience, mentions should identify known entities in the context with little ambiguity.

3. *Context facilitates joint inference.* A joint resolution of all entities in a communication must be consistent with a given context. Thus, a resolver must find a context that explains why the particular set of entities are mentioned together. In other words, the discourse context is an extension of the joint resolution of the document's mentions together with additional related entities that are not mentioned in the particular document. Joint context has been recognized as an important notion for collective assignment of a set of mentions (Kulkarni et al., 2009; Ratinov et al., 2011; Hoffart et al., 2011), but previous work has not explicitly modeled the discourse context between the author and recepients of a communication. From a computational point of view the notion of context has two advantages: it limits the number of possibilities that a resolver must consider; and it motivates an efficient iterative joint resolution procedure.

In this paper, we outline a new architecture for context-aware entity linking and discuss our particular implementation. Our system is suitable for both newswire articles and first person communication. We also present some preliminary results.

2 What is a context?

According to linguistic theory, discourse context encompasses the knowledge and beliefs that are shared between the author and the recipient of a communication (Bunt and Black, 2000). This can include objects introduced earlier in the discourse as well as general knowledge that a communication's author can assume the audience possesses.

Representing all knowledge shared between an author and a recipient of a communication is challenging – it requires solving difficult knowledge acquisition and representation problems. We use a more limited notion of context; we define a context to be a weighted set of KB entities. For example, a general *US newswire* context may contain, with high weight, public entities such as **Barack Obama**, **Mitt Romney** and **LeBron James**.

The set of entities that make up a context and their weights should be determined by a number

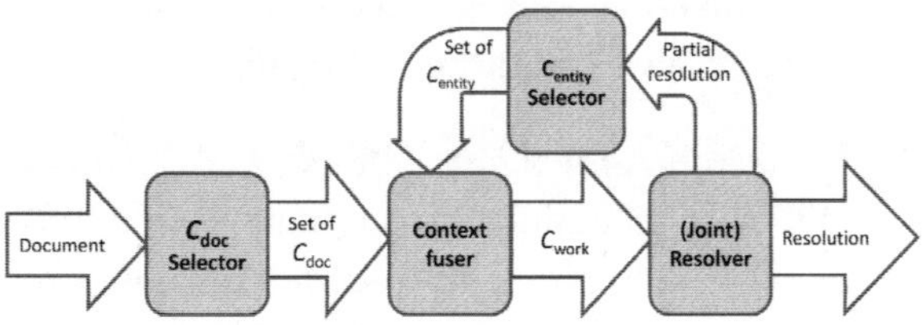

Figure 1: Architecture of our context aware entity linking system.

of factors: the intended audience for a communication (e.g., a typical Westerner vs. a German college student vs. an AKBC-WEKEX 2012 atendee); the time and place of the communication (some entities are only popular over a limited time span); and the topic of the communication (e.g., <u>*Jordan*</u> likely refers to the country when talking about the Middle East; it likely refers to <u>**Michael Jordan**</u> when discussing basketball). Furthermore, the makeup of the context may change as the recipient of communication is provided with more information. For instance, learning that a document talks about <u>**Barack Obama**</u> gives associated entities such as <u>**Joe Biden**</u> and <u>**Michelle Obama**</u> a higher weight.

To accommodate a diverse range of approaches to context, we define a general context-aware architecture that makes few additional assumptions on what contexts can be or how entities can be brought into or re-weighted in the current context. In the next section we describe the general architecture of our system. We then discuss how we generate contexts for newswire and email in Section 4.

3 Context-sensitive Entity Linking Architecture

First we introduce the following terminology to refer to different kinds of context:

- $\mathbf{C}_{work}$ (working context) – the weighted set of entities against which the system is currently resolving mentions. For example, the system may begin with a general context of all prominent entities discussed in the world news. As the system makes decisions about how entities are linked, it may revise the set of entities that are under consideration. The working context can be updated as processing proceeds.

- $\mathbf{C}_{doc}$ (document context) – a context triggered by a particular communication (document). For instance, an article in the New York Times may evoke a particular set of weighted entities. Document contexts can be quite specific; there can be a different document context for each section of the New York Times, for each author, or for each topic of discussion.

- $\mathbf{C}_{entity}$ (entity context) – an entity context refers to the weighted set of entities associated with a particular KB entity. If the system resolves a mention to an entity with high confidence, it updates its working context to include or up-weight these associated entities.

We use *trigger* to refer to a function that given a document or an entity and produces all of the C_{doc}s and C_{entity}s associated with the document or entity respectively. This could be a simple function that keeps an inverted index that associates words with database entities and, for given document, retrieves the entities most associated with the words of the document. It could also be a more sophisticated function that identifies contexts as graph communities and/or observes which entities are often mention together in a corpus of similar communications (e.g., newswire articles). The latter trigger would need either a large corpus of annotated communication or a bootstrapping method to associate entities with communications. Triggers can also associate general contexts with a given source or audience (e.g., a general context associated with the New York Times) or specific contexts associated with the topic of the document (e.g., the IR-based trigger discussed above that associates specific words with each entity and produces a weighted list of matches given the document).

The overall architecture of our context-aware entity linking system is shown in Figure 1. The system processes documents (communications) marked with the mentions that need to be resolved. Processing of a document begins by invoking a collection of *triggers* to produce a set of C_{doc}s associated with the document. Triggers are functions mapping documents to contexts.

The set of selected C_{doc}s is then passed to a context fuser. The fuser unifies individual contexts and produces a single set of entities, which becomes C_{work}. Different algorithms could be used to fuse entities coming from different contexts; we currently use a simple summation of the weights.

The working context is then fed to a resolver. The job of the resolver is to decide for each mention whether there is an entity that represents a good match for that mention. The resolver can produce partial matches (e.g., decide not to match some mentions or match other mentions to more than one entity) in early iterations, but is required to produce a full match at the final iteration.

The partial match produced by the resolver is fed to a C_{entity} selector, which selects a set of entities related to each resolved mention. The selector produces a set of C_{entity}s, which, together with C_{work}, are passed again to the context fuser. This process repeats until either all mentions are resolved to a desired level of confidence or a predefined number of iterations is reached. Upon termination, the algorithm returns an entity match for each mention of the document or *NIL* to indicate that no match exists in the knowledge base.

4 Generating contexts

The success of our approach hinges on the ability to generate and later retrieve effective contexts. Our system currently implements simple context triggers, so most of the triggers discussed in this section are subject of future work. Triggers are tailored to the domain of the communication. We are experimenting with two domains: linking newswire articles to Wikipedia pages and linking names in emails to their corresponding email addresses.

C_{doc} generation. For newswire articles, we currently rely on a single IR-based trigger. This trigger uses Lucene[1] to create an index associating words with Wikipedia entities, based on the content of the Wikipedia page associated with the entity. The trigger then queries the index using the first paragraph in which a given entity is mentioned in the document (e.g., if we want to resolve <u>*Clinton*</u>, our query will be the first paragraph in the document mentioning *Clinton*). Some additional C_{doc} triggers that we plan to implement for this domain include: geographic-, time- and source-specific triggers, and evolutionary triggers that are based on resolutions found in previously processed documents. Note that some of these triggers require a corpus of articles linked to KB entities. We are investigating using bootstrapping and other methods to produce triggers. We also plan to use graph partition algorithms to discover communities in the KB, and use those communities as a source of smoothing (since some entities may be infrequently mentioned).

For email, we currently use three C_{doc} triggers: (D1) an IR-based trigger, that retrieves entities according to the text in emails previously sent or received by the entity; (D2) another IR-based trigger that uses entities in the "from," "to," and "cc" fields of emails relevant to the query email; and (D3) author-specific contexts based on the communication graph. In future work, we plan to use bootstrapping and community detection to expand our email C_{doc} triggers.

C_{entity} generation. For each entity in the KB, its C_{entity} aims to capture a set of related entities. To determine the degree of entity relatedness in newswire, we use a measure based on network distance and textual relatedness (we currently link against Wikipedia, so the text is harvested from the article associated with the entity).

For email, each C_{entity} consists of all one-hop neighbors in the communication graph in which only entity pairs that have exchanged at least one message in each direction are linked.

In future work, we plan to implement E-contexts that use large unsupervised corpora and bootstrapping to determine which entities tend to occur together in documents. Here, again, we plan to use a graph partition algorithm to discover communities and use those for smoothing.

5 Evaluation

Data. We evaluate our newswire system on the data created for the last three TAC entity linking track (McNamee and Dang, 2009; Ji et al., 2010; Ji et al., 2011). This data consists of 6,266 query mentions over 5,962 documents. The KB is formed from the infoboxes of a Wikipedia dump. For email, we use the Enron collection (Klimt and Yang, 2004).

[1] `http://lucene.apache.org`

Ground truth is given by the publicly available set of 470 single-token mentions (in 285 unique emails) that have been manually resolved to email addresses by Elsayed (2009).

Evaluation metrics. We evaluate two components of our system – the working context (C_{work}) and the resolver accuracy. For a working context to be useful for our task, it has to include the gold-standard entities against which mentions in a document are resolved. Thus, we evaluate the working context by its recall, computed as the number of gold-standard entities in the context divided by the total number of entities to be resolved (excluding NILs). Overall system performance is compared on the accuracy of the final resolution of all mentions (including those that are assigned a *NIL* in the gold standard).

Results. Results presented here are preliminary: we currently use simple string-match based resolvers and incorporate only a subset of the contexts that we intend to implement.

On newswire, we rely on a parameter that sets the maximum number of entities returned by the trigger. When we set the parameter to 500, the context recall on non-NIL is 0.735 and the average number of entities per document returned is 452 (some documents return less than the maximum number, 500). When we set the parameter to 5,000, the context recall on non-NIL is 0.829 and the average number of entities is 4,515. We contrast this to the triage mechanism of McNamee et al. (2011), which relies on name and alias matching to obtain all potential entity matches. This mechanism achieves recall of 0.905 on non-NIL with average context size of 52. The set of entities returned by the triage mechanism are much most ambiguity as all of the entities in the set share the same name or alias (or character n-grams found in the mention).

The overall accuracy of the system in the two settings that rely on our document trigger is around 0.6 in both settings (including NILs), while the accuracy of the system using McNamee et al.'s (2011) triage is around 0.3 (including NILs). As discussed above, we currently use a simple rule-based string matching resolver. Additionally, most of the TAC queries ask for one mention per document, so on newswire our system cannot take full advantage of the C_{entity} mechanism. We are working on expanding the query set to include additional unsupervised mentions that are resolved but not scored.

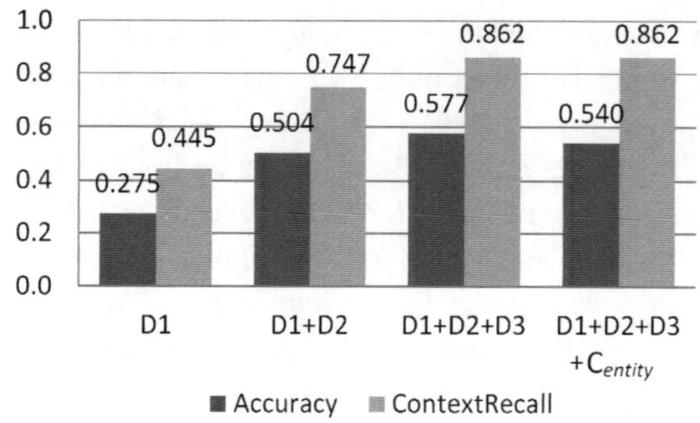

Figure 2: Enron dataset results.

Results for email are shown in Figure 2. We use three different document triggers (described in the previous section). Results show that our simple context fuser effectively leverages multiple C_{doc}s, but a more sophisticated resolver to optimally exploit both C_{doc}s and C_{entity}s is needed.

6 Conclusions

We argue that the notion of discourse context is central to entity linking, and that it facilitates joint inference. We introduce a system that performs context-aware entity linking by building a working context from document and entity contexts. The working context is refined during the course of linking mentions in a communication so that all entities can be linked with high confidence.

References

Harry Bunt and William Black, 2000. *The ABC of computational pragmatics*. MIT Press.

A. Burman, A. Jayapal, S. Kannan, M. Kavilikatta, A. Alhelbawy, L. Derczynski, and R. Gaizauskas. 2011. USFD at KBP 2011: Entity linking, slot filling and temporal bounding. *Proceedings of TAC 2011*.

Silviu Cucerzan. 2007. Large-scale named entity disambiguation based on Wikipedia data. In *Proceedings of EMNLP-CoNLL*, pages 708–716.

Tamer Elsayed. 2009. *Identity resolution in email collections*. Ph.D. thesis, University of Maryland.

Paul Grice. 1975. Logic and conversation. *Syntax and semantics*, 3:41–58.

X. Han and L. Sun. 2011. A generative entity-mention model for linking entities with knowledge base. In *Proceedings of the 49th Annual Meeting of the Association for Computational Linguistics: Human Language Technologies-Volume 1*, pages 945–954.

J. Hoffart, M.A. Yosef, I. Bordino, H. Fürstenau, M. Pinkal, M. Spaniol, B. Taneva, S. Thater, and G. Weikum. 2011. Robust disambiguation of named entities in text. In *Proceedings of EMNLP*, pages 782–792.

Darren Wei Huang, Yue Xu, Andrew Trotman, and Shlomo Geva. 2008. Overview of INEX 2007 Link the Wiki track. In Norbert Fuhr, Jaap Kamps, Mounia Lalmas, and Andrew Trotman, editors, *Focused Access to XML Documents*, pages 373–387. Springer-Verlag, Berlin, Heidelberg.

H. Ji, R. Grishman, H.T. Dang, K. Griffitt, and J. Ellis. 2010. Overview of the TAC 2010 knowledge base population track. *Proceedings of Text Analysis Conference (TAC)*.

H. Ji, R. Grishman, and H.T. Dang. 2011. Overview of the TAC 2011 knowledge base population track. *Proceedings of Text Analysis Conference (TAC)*.

Bryan Klimt and Yiming Yang. 2004. The Enron corpus: A new dataset for email classification research. In *ECML*, pages 217–226.

S. Kulkarni, A. Singh, G. Ramakrishnan, and S. Chakrabarti. 2009. Collective annotation of wikipedia entities in web text. In *Proceedings of ACM SIGKDD*, pages 457–466.

P. McNamee and H.T. Dang. 2009. Overview of the TAC 2009 knowledge base population track. In *Proceedings of Text Analysis Conference (TAC)*.

P. McNamee, J. Mayfield, D.W. Oard, T. Xu, K. Wu, V. Stoyanov, and D. Doermann. 2011. Cross-language entity linking in maryland during a hurricane. In *Proceedings of Text Analysis Conference (TAC)*.

L. Ratinov, D. Downey, M. Anderson, and D. Roth. 2011. Local and global algorithms for disambiguation to wikipedia. In *Proceedings of ACL*.

Wei Zhang, Yan Chuan Sim, Jian Su, and Chew Lim. 2011. Entity linking with effective acronym expansion, instance selection and topic modeling. *Proceedings of IJCAI*.

Evaluating the Quality of a Knowledge Base Populated from Text

James Mayfield
Human Language Technology
Center of Excellence
Johns Hopkins University
james.mayfield@jhuapl.edu

Tim Finin
Computer Science and Electrical Engineering
University of Maryland,
Baltimore County
finin@umbc.edu

Abstract

The steady progress of information extraction systems has been helped by sound methodologies for evaluating their performance in controlled experiments. Annual events like MUC, ACE and TAC have developed evaluation approaches enabling researchers to score and rank their systems relative to reference results. Yet these evaluations have only assessed component technologies needed by a knowledge base population system; none has required the construction of a knowledge base that is then evaluated directly. We describe an approach to the direct evaluation of a knowledge base and an instantiation that will be used in a 2012 TAC Knowledge Base Population track.

1 Introduction

Many activities might fall under the rubric of automatic knowledge base (KB) generation, including information extraction, entity linking, open information extraction and machine reading. The task is broad and challenging: process a large text corpus to extract a KB schema or ontology and populate it with entities, relations and facts. The term *knowledge base population* (KBP) is often used for the narrower task in which we start with a predefined and fixed KB schema or *ontology* and focus on the problem of extracting information from a text corpus to populate the KB with entities, relations and facts using that ontology.

To evaluate progress on such systems, we must answer the question "how do you know that the knowledge base you built is any good?" Before we can say whether an automatically created knowledge base is good, we must first say what a knowledge base is. We define a knowledge base as a combination of four things: a database of facts; a descriptive schema for those facts; a collection of existing background knowledge; and inference capability.

We are concerned in this paper primarily with knowledge bases that use a known schema. Some of the work in open information extraction addresses the question of how a knowledge schema could be derived from text. While this is important work, it nonetheless falls outside the scope of our current inquiry. We seek to assess whether a KB populated according to a known schema accurately encodes the knowledge sources used to create it. These underlying knowledge sources might be structured (e.g., a database), semi-structured (e.g., Wikipedia Infoboxes), or entirely unstructured (e.g., free text). We also do not wish to directly evaluate the breadth or accuracy of the KB's background knowledge. Our proposed approach can be used to evaluate the KB's inferencing ability; however, for the current study, we require that the KB materialize all of the relevant facts it can infer. We also require that the KB justify, where appropriate, the sources (e.g., a document) from which each fact is derived.

Our evaluation approach is characterized by three design decisions. First, we require that KBs be submitted in a simple abstract format that we use to create an equivalent KB in RDF. This gives us a well defined and relatively simple KB that can be tested with mature software tools. Second, instead of assessing the entire KB, the evaluation samples the KB through a set of queries on the RDF KB; each query result is then assessed for correctness. Third, we do not assume an initial set of KB entities with predefined identifiers. We avoid the complexity of aligning entities in the KB and reference model by using the concept of a KB *entry point* specified by an entity mention in an input document.

In the next section we discuss the general problem of KB evaluation and present a concrete proposal for evaluating a KB constructed from text, which will be implemented at the TAC 2012 evaluation.

2 Knowledge Base Evaluation

Mayfield et al. (2008) introduced the problem of direct evaluation of an automatically populated knowledge base and identified six axes along which they might be evaluated: accuracy, usefulness, augmentation, explanation, adaptation and temporal qualification. In this paper we begin by asking the most elementary of those questions: how accurate is a given static knowledge base? Accuracy has two components, which correspond to the ideas of *recall* and *precision* in information retrieval. First, we would like to know whether all of the facts present in or implied by the underlying sources can be retrieved from the KB. Second, are there facts that are not present in or implied by the underlying sources that can nonetheless be retrieved. If all and only the implied facts can be retrieved, we can conclude that the knowledge base accurately reflects those sources. The central tenet of our evaluation approach is that the KB should be judged based on its responses to direct queries about its content. We call such queries *evaluation queries*.

In practice, it will not be possible to examine all of the possible facts that should be present in a knowledge base unless the underlying sources are extremely small. Even for relatively small KBs, a complete comparison for a moderately expressive representation language like OWL DL is a complex task (Papavassiliou et al., 2009). We believe that an approach using sampling of the space of possible queries is therefore a pragmatic necessity.

A central problem in evaluating a KB is aligning the entities in the KB with known ground truth. For example, if we had a reference ground truth KB, we could try to evaluate the created KB by aligning the nodes of the two KBs, then looking for structural differences. Aligning entities is a complex task that, in the worst case, can have exponential complexity in the number of entities involved. Our approach to avoiding this problem is to use known *entry points* into the KB that are defined by a document and an entity mention string. For example, an entry point could be defined as "the entity that is associated with the mention *Bart Simpson* in document DO14." We require that a set of entry points is aligned with the KB by the KB constructor. In practice this is easy if the KB is being constructed from the text that contains the entry point mentions.

Different classes of evaluation queries can assess different capabilities. For example, asking whether two entry points refer to same KB node evaluates coreference resolution (or entity linking if one of the entry points is an existing KB node). Asking facts about the KB node associated with a single entry point evaluates simple slot-filling. More complicated queries that start with one or more entry points can be used to evaluate the overall result of the extraction process involving entity linking, fact extraction, appropriate priors and inference. Note that this approach to KB evaluation is agnostic toward inference. That is, the original KB system may perform sophisticated backward chaining inference or no inference at all; the evaluation mechanism works the same either way.

3 A Specific Proposal

We present a specific proposal for KB evaluation that is both applicable to current research in KB population, and is immediately implementable. The TAC 2012 evaluation will include a *Cold Start Knowledge Base Population* (TAC KBP Web site, 2012). The idea behind this evaluation is to test the ability of systems to extract specific knowledge from text and place it into a KB. The schema for the target KB is specified *a priori*, but the KB is otherwise empty to start. Participant systems will process a document collection, extracting information about entities mentioned in the collection, adding the information to a new KB, and indicating how entry point entities mentioned in the collection correspond to nodes in the KB. In the following subsections, we outline a method for evaluating the TAC task.

3.1 Defining a KB target

We do not want to require that researchers use a particular KB technology to participate in an evaluation experiment. However, until we identify a standard way for a KB to be queried directly, we need to have a common formalism that participants can use to export the KB content to be evaluated, and a common evaluation KB target that can be used during the evaluation by importing the submitted content. The export format should be simple and the target KB system and tools well defined and accessible to researchers.

We have selected RDF (Lassila and Swick, 1998) as the target representation for our evaluation. RDF is a simple yet flexible representation scheme with a well defined syntax and semantics, an expressive ontology layer OWL (Hitzler et al., 2009), a solid query language SPARQL (Prud'Hommeaux and Seaborne, 2008)), and a large collection of open-source and commercial tools that include KB editors, reasoners, databases and interfaces.

The standard semantics for RDF and OWL is grounded in first order logic. Its representation is based on a simple graph model where KB schema as well as instance data are stored as triples. These may seem like severe limitations – we would like to support the evaluation of KB population tasks in which facts can be tagged with certainty measures and that may have extensive provenance data. However, we can exploit RDF's reification mechanism to annotate KB axioms, entities, and relations with the additional metadata. Using reification has its drawbacks: it can make a KB much larger than it need be and slow reasoning and querying. While these issues may be important in developing a production system intended to process large volumes of text and generate huge KBs, they are less problematic in an evaluation context where speed and scaling are not a focus. Moreover, reification offers the flexibility to add more annotation properties in the future.

3.2 Target ontology and submission format

We have developed an OWL ontology corresponding to the KB schema used in the 2011 TAC evaluations that includes classes for person, organization and place entities and properties for each with appropriate domain and range restrictions. For testing, we created a sample corpus of articles about the fictional world of the Simpsons television series and a corresponding reference KB of entities and relationships extracted from it.

Figure 1 shows a portion of one of our test documents, some information representing our test RDF KB about one of the entities (:e12), and one of the annotations that indicates that the mention string "Montgomery Burns" in document D011 was linked

⟨DOC source="..."⟩⟨DOCNO⟩D011⟨/DOCNO⟩⟨TEXT⟩
The Springfield Nuclear Power Plant is a nuclear power plant in Springfield owned by Montgomery Burns. The plant has the monopoly on the city of Springfield's energy supply, and the carelessness of Mr. Burns and the plant's employees (like Homer, who is employed at Sector 7G) ... ⟨ /TEXT⟩⟨ /DOC⟩

:e12 a kbp:PER; kbp:canonical_mention "Montgomery Burns"; kbp:mention "Burns"; kbp:title "Mr.".

[a rdf:Statement; rdf:Subject :e12; rdf:Object "Montgomery Burns"; rdf:Predicate kbp:canonical_mention; rdf:source doc:D011; kbp:probability 1.0].

Figure 1: A sample document and some KB assertions it generates in RDF using the *turtle* serialization.

with :e12 with certainty 1.0. The export format for a participant's KB is kept simple; it consists of a file of tab-separated lines where each line specifies a relation tuple with optional evidence (e.g., a source document ID) and certainty factor values. For example, if a KB links the entity with mention "Montgomery Burns" in document D011 to an instance with local ID :e12 and also determines from document D14 that the entity's age was 104 (with certainty .85), it would export the following two five-tuples.

```
:e12 mention "Montgomery Burns" D011 1.0
:e12 age "104" D014 0.9
```

To simplify the evaluation and avoid potential problems, we restrict the inferencing performed on the submitted KB after its conversion to RDF to a few simple patterns, such as a subset of RDFS entailments (ter Horst, 2005) that follow from the target ontology (e.g., inferring that every *canonical_mention* relation is also a *mention* relation.

3.3 Query-based Knowledge Base Evaluation

We have defined a simplified graph path notation for evaluation queries to make constructing them easier; this notation is then automatically compiled into corresponding SPARQL queries. For example, one pattern starts with an entry point (a mention in a document) and continues with a sequence of properties. The general form of such a path expression is $MDP_1...P_n$ where M is a mention string, D is a document identifier, and each P_i is a property from the target ontology. All of the properties in the path except the final one must go from entities to entities. The final one can have a range that is either an entity or a string. For example, to generate a query for *"The ages of the siblings of the entity mentioned as*

```
SELECT ?CN ?SIBDOC ?A ?ADOC WHERE {
 ?P kbp:mention "Bart Simpson".
 ?P kbp:sibling ?SIB.
 ?SIB kbp:canonical_mention ?CN;
 kbp:age ?A.
 _:x rdf:subject ?P; rdf:predicate kbp:mention; rdf:object "Bart
Simpson"; kbp:source doc:D12.
 _:x rdf:subject ?P; rdf:predicate kbp:sibling; rdf:object ?SIB;
kbp:source doc:SIBDOC.
 _:x rdf:subject ?SIB; rdf:predicate kbp:canonical_mention;
rdf:object ?CN; kbp:source doc:SIBDOC.
 _:x rdf:subject ?SIB; rdf:predicate kbp:age; rdf:object ?A;
kbp:source doc:ADOC.}
```

Figure 2: This SPARQL query generates data that an assessor can use to evaluate the KB.

"Bart Simpson" in document D012" we use the path expression `"Bart Simpson" D012 sibling age`.

The SPARQL query generated for this path expression is shown in Figure 2; when run against a submitted KB, it produces data that will allow the assessor to verify that the KB accurately reflects the supported facts:

sibling mention	sib doc	age	age doc
"Lisa Simpson"	D012	"10"	D008
"Maggie Simpson"	D014	"1"	D014

In general, for each entity in the result, a query produces the canonical mention string for that entity in the supporting document (e.g., support for "Lisa Simpson" as Bart's sister is in D012), while for each slot value (e.g., age:10), the query produces the value (10) and the document that provided evidence for that value (D008). This lets an assessor verify that the correct entities are identified and that there is explicit support for the slot values.

3.4 Metrics

Once SPARQL queries have been designed and run against the knowledge base, the results need to be assessed and scored. Doing so is relatively straightforward; there is a rich history of approaches to assessment and evaluation metrics for similar output that have been widely applied. Two obvious choices are to use binary queries or to use queries that return slot fills. Binary queries such as "is a parent of the 'Bart' mentioned in document D014 the same as a spouse of the 'Homer' mentioned in document D223?" are easy to assess, and can be scored using a single number for accuracy. Queries that return one or more string values for attributes of an entity look very much like slot filling queries. TAC is the latest in a long line of evaluations that have scored slot fills. The standard approach is to view the possible fills as a set, and to calculate precision, recall and F-measure on that set. These numbers are widely understood and intuitively satisfying. For TAC 2012, we will cleave as closely as possible to the measures being used to evaluate the TAC slot-filling task. More details on the assessment and scoring process can be found in the Cold Start 2012 task description (TAC KBP Web site, 2012).

3.5 Errors in the Knowledge Base

One issue with our sampling approach to KB evaluation is ensuring that the collection of sample queries has adequate coverage in at least three dimensions: over a set of error types; over the full range of entities types and their properties; and over the extent of the corpus. Different kinds of errors in the KB will be detected by different sorts of queries. For example, for the TAC KBP task, we have identified the following types of errors:

- Two distinct ground truth entities are conflated.
- A ground truth entity is split into several entities.
- A ground truth entity is missing from the KB.
- A spurious entity is present in the KB.
- A ground truth relation is omitted from the KB.
- A spurious relation is present in the KB.
- An entry point is tied to the wrong KB node.

Some queries can be designed to narrowly target specific error types while others may detect that one or more errors are present but not identify which are the actual culprits. Similarly, attention should be paid to providing queries that test a range of entity types and properties as well as data from documents that represent different genres, sizes, languages, etc.

4 Discussion

The evaluation most similar to our proposal is the one used in the DARPA Machine Reading program (Strassel et al., 2010). In this evaluation, a small document collection of order 10^2 documents is exhaustively annotated to produce a gold standard KB. A submitted KB is evaluated by querying it to produce *all* relations of a given type. While this approach gives excellent insight into a system's operation over the annotated collection, it suffers from requiring a gold standard knowledge base; this both limits the evaluation's ability to scale to larger collections, and raises the issue of how a submitted KB is to be aligned to the gold standard once the collection size is successfully increased.

Sil and Yates (2011) propose an extrinsic evaluation framework that measures the quality of an automatically extracted KB by how much it improves a relation extraction system. While our proposal represents an intrinsic evaluation, it can be easily tailored to a given downstream task by selecting evaluation queries that are directly relevant to that task.

The success of a query-based evaluation approach depends on having an appropriate set of KB queries. They must have good coverage along several dimensions: testing all important information extraction aspects (e.g., entity linking, slot filling, provenance, etc.); fairly sampling the full range of slots; testing for both for both missing and extraneous (false) facts; using a representative set of entry point documents; and anticipating and testing for known or expected system failure modes (e.g., over-merging vs. under-merging entities). Since the queries will not be overly complex, parts of the KB that are not "close to" entry points may not be tested. Our simple path-based scheme for representing queries that are automatically compiled into executable SPARQL queries will probably need to be made more complex for future systems.

Our KB model is quite simple; extending it to evaluate more capable knowledge-base technologies will offer challenges. For example, while we admit certainty values for slot values, we have not yet defined that these actually mean, how they they are handled in queries or how to evaluate them. A simple scheme can also produce ambiguity. For example, if the KB has two slot fills for Homer's children (Bart and Lisa with certainties 0.4 and 0.3) a proper evaluation will also need to also know if the original KB treats these as alternatives or as possible independent values.

Many challenging issues will be raised if we evaluate KBs that represent and exploit indefinite knowledge, which might take the form of Skolem functions, disjunctions or constraints. For example, our ontology may stipulate that every person has exactly one mother and we may read that Patty Bouvier is Bart's mother's sister. But if we know that Patty has two sisters, Marge and Selma, we not know which is Bart's mother but can still identify Bart as Patty's nephew. Knowing that every person has exactly one age (a number), a valid answer to "what are the ages of Homer Simpson's children", might be "Bart's age is 10, Lisa's is 8, and Maggie's age is unknown." This response reveals that the KB knows Homer's has three children even though the age of one has not been populated. A final variation is that a system may not have determined an exact value for a property, but has narrowed its range: reading that Lisa is "too young to vote" in the 2012 U.S. election implies that her age is less than 18.

Future information extraction systems will support many practical features that will need evaluation. Evaluating KBs in which some facts are temporally qualified will add complexity. Our model of provenance is simple and may need to be significantly extended to evaluate systems that represent evidence in a more sophisticated manner, e.g., noting how many documents support a fact and capturing alternative facts that were rejected.

5 Conclusions

While evaluating the quality of an automatically generated knowledge base is an open ended problem, the narrower task of evaluating the results of a knowledge base population task is much easier. This was especially true for the entity linking and slot filling focus of the past TAC KBP tasks, since an initial KB was provided that included not only a schema, but also a fairly complete set of initial entities. This obviated the need for aligning entities between a submitted KB and a reference KB, a major source of evaluation complexity.

Evaluating submissions to the 2012 TAC Cold Start KBP task will be more difficult since the task starts with just a KB schema and no initial entities. We described a general approach to KB evaluation that uses the notion of *KB entry points* specified by mentions in documents to avoid having to align entities between the KB under evaluation and a reference KB. The evaluation can then be done by executing a set of KB queries that sample the results of a submitted KB and generate data to allow a human assessor to evaluate its quality.

References

Hans Chalupsky. 2012. Story-level inference and gap filling to improve machine reading. In *The 25th International FLAIRS Conference*, May.

G. Doddington, A. Mitchell, M. Przybocki, L. Ramshaw, S. Strassel, and R. Weischedel. 2004. The automatic content extraction (ACE) program–tasks, data, and evaluation. In *Proceedings of LREC*, volume 4, pages 837–840. Citeseer.

Oren Etzioni, Michele Banko, Stephen Soderland, and Daniel S. Weld. 2008. Open information extraction from the Web. *Communications of the ACM*, 51(12):68–74, December.

P. Hitzler, M. Krötzsch, B. Parsia, P.F. Patel-Schneider, and S. Rudolph. 2009. OWL 2 web ontology language primer. Technical report.

H. Ji, R. Grishman, H.T. Dang, K. Griffitt, and J. Ellis. 2010. Overview of the TAC 2010 knowledge base population track. In *Proceedings of the Third Text Analysis Conference (TAC 2010)*.

O. Lassila and R.R. Swick. 1998. Resource description framework (RDF) model and syntax specification. Technical report.

James Mayfield, Bonnie J. Dorr, Tim Finin, Douglas W. Oard, and Christine D. Piatko. 2008. Knowledge base evaluation for semantic knowledge discovery. In *Symposium on Semantic Knowledge Discovery, Organization and Use*.

Vicky Papavassiliou, Giorgos Flouris, Irini Fundulaki, Dimitris Kotzinos, and Vassilis Christophides. 2009. On detecting high-level changes in RDF/S KBs. In *International Semantic Web Conference*, pages 473–488.

E Prud'Hommeaux and A. Seaborne. 2008. SPARQL query language for RDF. Technical report, January.

A. Sil, A. Yates, B. St, and M. Ave. 2011. Machine reading between the lines: A simple evaluation framework for extracted knowledge bases. *Proceedings of the Workshop on Information Extraction and Knowledge Acquisition*, pages 37–40, September.

S. Strassel, D. Adams, H. Goldberg, J. Herr, R. Keesing, D. Oblinger, H. Simpson, R. Schrag, and J. Wright. 2010. The DARPA machine reading program-encouraging linguistic and reasoning research with a series of reading tasks. In *International Conference on Language Resources and Evaluation*, May.

TAC KBP Web site. 2012. Cold start knowledge base population at TAC 2012 task description. http://www.nist.gov/tac/2012/KBP/ColdStart/. National Institute of Standards and Technology.

Herman J. ter Horst. 2005. Completeness, decidability and complexity of entailment for RDF Schema and a semantic extension involving the OWL vocabulary. *Journal of Web Semantics*, 3(23):79 – 115.

Dimitris Zeginis, Yannis Tzitzikas, and Vassilis Christophides. 2011. On computing deltas of RDF/S knowledge bases. *ACM Trans. Web*, 5(3):14:1–14:36, July.

Constructing a Textual KB from a Biology TextBook

Peter Clark, Phil Harrison
Vulcan Inc
505 Fifth Ave South
Seattle, WA 98104
{peterc,philipha@vulcan.com}

Niranjan Balasubramanian, Oren Etzioni
Turing Center, Dept CS & Engineering
University of Washington
Seattle, WA 98195
{niranjan,etzioni}@cs.washington.edu

Abstract

As part of our work on building a "knowledgeable textbook" about biology, we are developing a textual question-answering (QA) system that can answer certain classes of biology questions posed by users. In support of that, we are building a "textual KB" - an assembled set of semi-structured assertions based on the book - that can be used to answer users' queries, can be improved using global consistency constraints, and can be potentially validated and corrected by domain experts. Our approach is to view the KB as systematically caching answers from a QA system, and the QA system as assembling answers from the KB, the whole process kickstarted with an initial set of textual extractions from the book text itself. Although this research is only in a preliminary stage, we summarize our progress and lessons learned to date.

1 Introduction

As part of Project Halo (Gunning et al, 2010), we are seeking to build an (iPad based) "knowledgeable textbook" about biology that users can not only browse, but also ask questions to and get reasoned or retrieved answers back. While our previous work has relied on a hand-crafted, formal knowledge base for question-answering, we have a new effort this year to add a textual QA module that will answer some classes of questions using textual retrieval and inference from the book itself. As well as running queries directly against the textbook, we are also constructing a "textual knowledge base" (TKB) of facts extracted from the book, and running queries against those also. The TKB can be thought of as a cache of certain classes of QA pairs, and offers the potential advantages of allowing global constraints to refine/rescore the textual extractions, and of allowing people to review/correct/extend the extracted knowledge in a crowdsourcing style. As a result, we hope that QA performance will be substantially improved compared with querying against the book alone. Although this research is only in a preliminary stage, we summarize our progress and lessons learned to date.

There are four characteristics of our problem that make it somewhat unusual and interesting:

- we have a specific target to capture, namely the knowledge in a specific textbook (although other texts can be used to help in that task)
- the knowledge we want is mainly about concepts (cells, ribosomes, etc.) rather than named entities
- we have a large formal knowledge-base available that covers some of the book's material
- we have a well-defined performance task for evaluation, namely answering questions from students as they read the eBook and do homework

We describe how these characteristics have impacted the design of the system we are constructing.

2 Approach

We are approaching this task by viewing the textual KB as a cache of answers to certain classes of questions, subsequently processed to ensure a degree of overall consistency. Thus tasks of KB construction and question-answering are closely interwoven:

- The KB is a cache of answers from a QA system

- A QA system answers questions using information in the KB

Thus this process can be bootstrapped: QA can help build the KB, and the KB can provide the evidence for QA. We kickstart the process by initially seeding the KB with extractions from individual sentences in the book, and then use QA over those extractions to rescore and refine the knowledge ("introspective QA").

2.1 Information Extraction

Our first step is to process the textbook text and extract semi-structured representations of its content. We extract two forms of the textbook's information:

Logical Forms (LFs): A parse-based logical form (LF) representation of the book sentences using the BLUE system (Clark and Harrison, 2008), e.g., from *"Metabolism sets limits on cell size"* we obtain:

(S (SUBJ ("metabolism"))
   (V ("set"))
   (SOBJ ("limit" ("on" ("size" (MOD ("cell"))))))

Triples: A set of arg1-predicate-arg2 triples extracted via a chunker applied to the book sentences, using Univ. Washington's ReVerb system (Fader et al, 2011), e.g., from *"Free ribosomes are suspended in the cytosol and synthesize proteins there."* we obtain:

["ribosomes"] ["are suspended in"] ["the cytosol"]

These extractions are the raw material for the initial textual KB.

2.2 Knowledge-Base Construction and Introspective Question-Answering

As the ontology for the TKB, we are using the pre-existing biology taxonomy (isa hierarchy) from the hand-build biology KB (part of the formal knowledge project). Initially, for each concept in that ontology, all the extractions "about" that concept are gathered together. An extraction is considered "about" a concept if the concept's lexical name (also provided in the hand-built KB) is the subject or object of the verb (for the LFs), or is the arg1 or arg2 of the triple (for triples). For example ["ribosomes"] ["are suspended in"] ["the cytosol"] is an extraction about ribosomes, and also about cytosol, and so would be placed at the Ribosome and Cytosol nodes in the hierarchy.

As the extraction process is noisy, a major challenge is distinguishing good and bad extractions. If we were using a Web-scale corpus, we could some function over frequency counts as a measure of reliability e.g., (Banko et al, 2007). However, given the limited redundancy in a single textbook, verbatim duplication of extractions is rare, and so instead we use textual entailment technology to infer when one extraction supports (entails) another. If an extraction has strong support from other extractions, then that increases the confidence that it is indeed correct. In other words, the system performs a kind of "introspective question-answering" to compute a confidence about each fact X in the KB in turn, by asking whether (i.e., how likely is it that) X is true, given the KB.

To look for support for fact X in the LF database, the system searches for LFs that are subsumed by X's LF. For example, "animals are made of cells" subsumes (i.e., is supported by) "animals are made of eukaryotic cells". In the simplest case this is just structure matching, but more commonly the system explores rewrites of the sentences using four synonym and paraphrase resources, namely: WordNet (Fellbaum, 1998); the DIRT paraphrase database (Lin and Pantel, 2001); the ParaPara paraphrase database (from Johns Hopkins) (Chan et al, 2011); and lexical synonyms and hypernyms from the hand-coded formal KB itself (Gunning et al, 2010). For example, the (LF of the) extraction:

> *Channel proteins help move molecules through the membrane.*

is supported (i.e., entailed) by the (LF of the) extraction:

> *Channel proteins facilitate the passage of molecules across the membrane.*

using knowledge that

IF X facilitates Y **THEN** X helps Y (DIRT)
"passage" is a nominalization of "move" (WN)
"through" and "across" are synonyms (ParaPara)

To look for support for fact X in the triple database, the system searches for triples whose arguments and predicate have word overlap with the (triple representation of) the assertion X, with a (currently ad hoc) scoring function determining confidence. (Linguistic resources could help with this process also in the future).

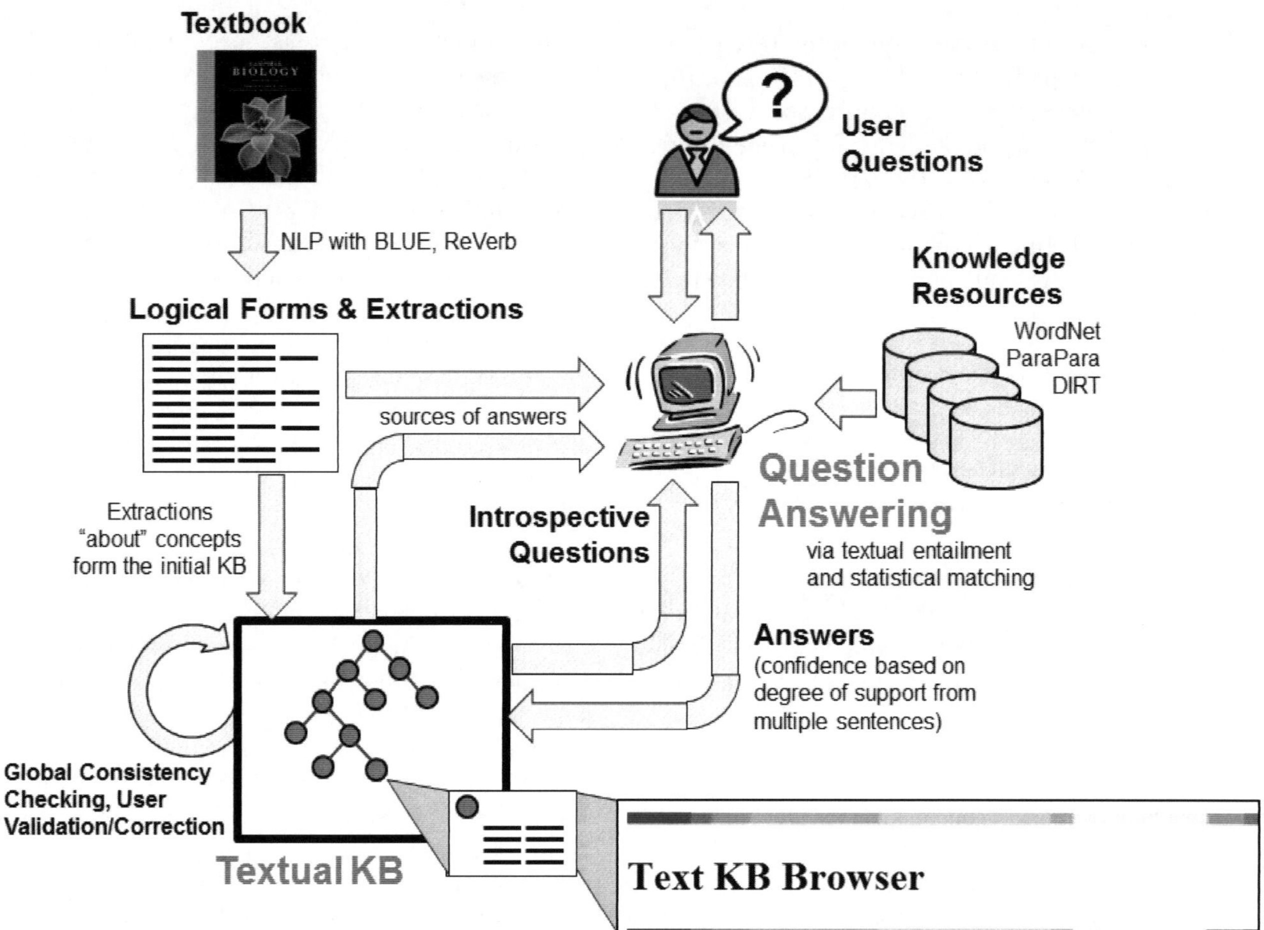

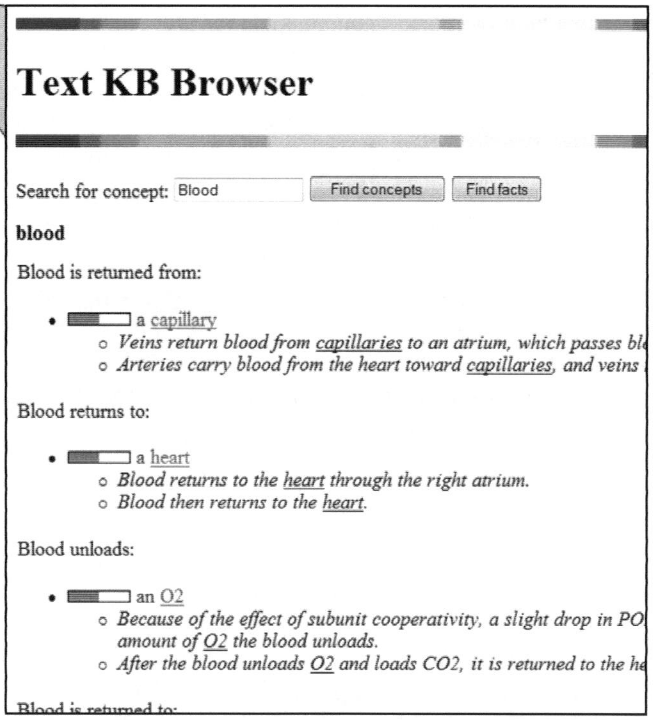

Figure 1: Extractions from the textbook are used for question-answering, and a selected subset form the initial text KB. Its contents are then verified (or refuted) via introspective QA, global consistency checks, and user validation. The resulting KB then assists in future QA.

Both of these methods are noisy: There are errors in the original extractions, the synonym databases, and the paraphrase databases, not to mention over-simplifications and context-dependence in the original book sentences themselves. To assign an overall confidence to an LF-based extraction entailed (supported) by multiple sentences in the TKB, we use machine learning to build a confidence model. Each (numeric) feature in this model is a combination (max, sum, min, etc.) of the individual entailment strengths that each sentence entails the extraction. Each individual entailment strength is a weighted sum of the individual paraphrase and synonym strengths it uses. By using alternative functions and weights, we generate a large number of features. Each final class is a numeric value on a 0 (wrong) to 4 (completely correct) scale. Training data was created by six biology students who scored approximately 1000 individual extractions (expressed as question-answer pairs) on the same 0-4 scale. A page from the TKB browser is shown in Figure 1 (the bars representing confidence in each assertion).

2.3 Knowledge Refinement

We have a preliminary implementation of the first two steps. This third step (not implemented) is to refine the textual KB using two methods:

- Global coherence constraints
- User ("crowd") verification/refinement

Our goal with global coherence constraints is to detect and remove additional extractions that are globally incoherent, even if they have apparent sentence-level support, e.g., as performed by (Carlson et al., 2010, Berant et al., 2011). Our plan here is to identify a "best" subset of the supported extractions that jointly satisfies general coherence constraints such as:

transitivity: $r(x,y) \wedge r(y,z) \rightarrow r(x,z)$
reflexivity: $r(x,y) \leftrightarrow r(y,x)$
irreflexivity: $r(x,y) \leftrightarrow \sim r(y,x)$

For example, one of the (biologically incorrect) assertions in the TKB is "Cells are made up of organisms". Although this assertion looks justified from the supporting sentences (including a bad paraphrase), it contradicts the strongly believed assertion "Organisms are made up of cells" stored elsewhere in the TKB. By checking for this global consistency, we hope to reduce such errors.

In addition, we plan to allow our biologists to review and correct the extractions in the KB in a "crowd"-sourcing-style interaction, in order to both improve the TKB and provide more training data for further use.

2.4 Performance Task

We have a clear end-goal, namely to answer students' questions as they read the eBook and do homework, and we have collected a large set of such questions from a group of biologists. Questions are answered using the QA methods described in step 2, only this time the questions are from the students rather than introspectively from the KB itself. The textual KB acts as a second source of evidence for generating answers to questions; we plan to use standard machine learning techniques to learn the appropriate weights for combining evidence from the original book extractions vs. evidence from the aggregated and refined textual assertions in the textual KB.

3. Discussion

Although preliminary, there are several interesting points of note:

1. We have been using a (pre-built) ontology of concepts, but not of relations. Thus there is a certain amount of semi-redundancy in the assertions about a given concept, for example the fact "Ribosomes make proteins" and "Ribosomes produce proteins" are both the TKB as top-level assertions, and each shows the other supports it. It is unclear whether we should embrace this semi-duplication, or move to a set of predefined semantic relationships (essentially canonicalizing the different lexical relationships that can occur).
2. Our QA approach and TKB contents are largely geared towards "factoid" questions (i.e., with a single word/phrase answer). However, our target task requires answering other kinds of questions also, including "How..." and "Why..." questions that require a short description (e.g., of a biological mechanism). This suggests that additional information is needed in the TKB, e.g., structures such as

   because(*sentence1,sentence2*)

   We plan to add some semantic information extractors to the system to acquire some types of relationships demanded by our question corpus, augmenting the more factoid core of the TKB.
3. We are combining two approaches to QA, namely textual inference (with logical forms), and structure matching (with ReVerb triples), but could benefit from additional approaches. Textual inference is a "high bar" to cross - it is reasonably accurate when it works, but has low recall. Conversely, structure matching has higher coverage but lower precision. Additional methods that lend extra evidence for particular answers would be beneficial.
4. We are in a somewhat unique position of having a formal KB at hand. We are using it's ontology both as a skeleton for the TKB, and to help with "isa" reasoning during word matching and textual inference. However, there are many more ways that it can be exploited, e.g., using it to help generate textual training data for the parts of the book which it does cover.
5. While there are numerous sources of error still in the TKB, two in particular stand out, namely

the lack of coreference resolution (which we currently do not handle), and treating each sentence as a stand-alone fact (ignoring its context). As an example of the latter, a reference to "the cell" or "cells" may only be referring to cells in that particular context (e.g., in a paragraph about eukaryotic cells), rather than cells in general.

6. We are also in the process of adding in addition supporting texts to the system (namely the biology part of Wikipedia) to improve the scoring/validation of textbook-derived facts.

References

Banko, M., Cafarella, M., Soderland, S., Broadhead, M., Etzioni, O. Open Information Extraction from the Web. IJCAI 2007.

Berant, J., Dagan, I., Goldberger, J. Global Learning of Focused Entailment Graphs. ACL 2011.

Carlson, A. Betteridge, J., Wang, R.C., Hruschka, E.R., Mitchel, T.M. Coupled Semi-Supervised Learning for Information Extraction. In Proceedings of the ACM International Conference on Web Search and Data Mining (WSDM), 2010.

Chan, C., Callison-Burch, C., Van Durme, B. Reranking Bilingually Extracted Paraphrases Using Monolingual Distributional Similarity. In Proceedings of GEometrical Models of Natural Language Semantics (GEMS-2011).

Clark, P., Harrison, P. Boeing's NLP System and the Challenges of Semantic Representation. In Proc SIGSEM Symposium on Text Processing (STEP'08), 2008.

Clark, P. Harrison, P. 2009. An inference-based approach to textual entailment. In Proc TAC 2009 (Text Analysis conference).

Fader, A., Soderland, S., Etzioni, O. Identifying Relations for Open Information Extraction. EMNLP 2011.

Fellbaum, C. "WordNet: An Electronic Lexical Database." Cambridge, MA: MIT Press, 1998.

Gunning, D., et al., Project Halo Update - Progress Toward Digital Aristotle In AI Magazine (vol 31 no 3), 2010.

Lin, D. and Pantel, P. 2001. Discovery of Inference Rules for Question Answering. *Natural Language Engineering* 7 (4) pp 343-360.

Knowledge Extraction and Joint Inference Using Tractable Markov Logic

Chloé Kiddon and **Pedro Domingos**
Department of Computer Science & Engineering
University of Washington
Seattle, WA 98105
{chloe,pedrod}@cs.washington.edu

Abstract

The development of knowledge base creation systems has mainly focused on information extraction without considering how to effectively reason over their databases of facts. One reason for this is that the inference required to learn a probabilistic knowledge base from text at any realistic scale is intractable. In this paper, we propose formulating the joint problem of fact extraction and probabilistic model learning in terms of Tractable Markov Logic (TML), a subset of Markov logic in which inference is low-order polynomial in the size of the knowledge base. Using TML, we can tractably extract new information from text while simultaneously learning a probabilistic knowledge base. We will also describe a testbed for our proposal: creating a biomedical knowledge base and making it available for querying on the Web.

1 Introduction

While structured sources of information exist, so much of human knowledge is found only in unstructured text that it is crucial we learn how to mine these unstructured sources efficiently and accurately. However, knowledge extraction is only half the battle. We develop knowledge bases not to be standalone structures but instead to be tools for applications such as decision making, question answering, and literature-based discovery. Therefore, a knowledge base should not be a static repository of facts; it should be a probabilistic model of knowledge extracted from text over which we can infer new facts not explicitly stated in the text.

Most current knowledge extraction systems extract a database of facts, not a true knowledge base. ReVerb (Etzioni et al., 2011) and TextRunner (Banko et al., 2007) are Web-scale knowledge extraction systems, but provide no clear method for reasoning over the extracted knowledge. Unsupervised Semantic Parsing (USP) and its successor Ontological USP (OntoUSP), learn more detailed ontological structure over information extracted from text, but they too do not build a coherent probabilistic knowledge base that can be reasoned with (Poon and Domingos 2009, Poon and Domingos 2010).

Some knowledge extraction systems have integrated rule learning. NELL learns rules to help extract more information, but the resulting knowledge base is still just a collection of facts (Carlson et al., 2010). The SHERLOCK system learns first-order Horn clauses from open-domain Web text, but the inferences allowed are not very deep and, like ReVerb and TextRunner, the database of facts is not structured into any useful ontology (Schoenmackers et al. 2008, Schoenmackers et al. 2010).

In this paper, we propose an unsupervised online approach to knowledge base construction that jointly extracts information from text and learns a probabilistic model of that information. For each input sentence, our approach will jointly learn the best syntactic and semantic parse for the sentence while using abductive reasoning to infer the changes to our knowledge base that best explain the information in the sentence. To keep this joint inference procedure tractable we will formulate our entire process in terms of Tractable Markov Logic. *Tractable Markov Logic (TML)* is a subset of Markov logic in

	Name	TML Syntax	Comments	Example
Rules	Subclass	`Is(C1,C2):w`		`Is(Lion,Mammal)`
	Subpart	`Has(C1,C2,P,n)`	`P`, `n` optional	`Has(EatingEvent,Animal,Eater)`
	Relation	`R(C,P1,...,Pn):w`	`¬R(...)` allowed	`Eats(EatingEvent,Eater,Eaten)`
Facts	Subclass	`Is(X,C)`	`¬Is(X,C)` allowed	`Is(Simba,Lion)`
	Subpart	`Has(X1,X2,P)`		`Has(TheLionKing,Simba,Protagonist)`
	Relation	`R(X,P1,...,Pn)`	`¬R(...)` allowed	`Defeats(TheLionKing,Simba,Scar)`

Table 1: The TML language

which exact inference is low-order polynomial in the size of the knowledge base (Domingos and Webb, 2012). TML is a surprisingly powerful language that can easily represent both semantic relations and facts and syntactic relations.

2 Tractable Markov Logic

Tractable Markov Logic (TML) (Domingos and Webb, 2012), is a tractable, yet quite powerful, subset of Markov logic, a first-order probabilistic language. A *Markov logic network (MLN)* is a set of weighted first-order logic clauses (Domingos and Lowd, 2009). Given a set of constants, an MLN defines a Markov network with one node per ground atom and one feature per ground clause. The weight of a feature is the weight of the first-order clause that originated it. The probability of a state $\mathbf{x}$ is given by $P(\mathbf{x}) = \frac{1}{Z}\exp\left(\sum_i w_i n_i(\mathbf{x})\right)$, where w_i is the weight of the ith clause, and n_i is the number of satisfied groundings of that clause. $Z = \sum_{\mathbf{x}} \exp(\sum_i w_i n_i(\mathbf{x}))$ is the partition function. A *TML knowledge base (KB)* is a set of rules with three different forms, summarized in Table 1. A TML rule `F` : w states that formula `F` has weight `w`. The conversion from rules in TML syntax to clauses in MLN syntax is straightforward. For details, see Webb and Domingos 2012.

Subclass rules define the hierarchy of classes in the TML KB. *Subpart rules* define decompositions of the part classes in the TML KB into their subpart classes. *Relation rules* define arbitrary relations between the subparts of a given class. There are three types of corresponding facts in TML that provide information about objects instead of classes: the classes of objects, the objects that are subparts of other objects, and relations between objects. Naturally, the facts in TML must be consistent with the structure set by the TML rules for the KB to be valid. For example, a fact can not define a subpart relation between two objects if that subpart relation does not exist as a rule between the classes of those objects.

There are a number of constraints on a set of TML rules for it to be a valid TML KB. The class hierarchy must be a forest, and subclasses of the same class are mutually exclusive. Also, the polarity of ground literals must be consistent among the descendants of an object's subparts under the same class. However, given these restrictions on the form of the TML KB, Theorem 1 of Domingos and Webb 2012 states that the partition function of a TML KB can be computed in time and space polynomial in the size of the knowledge base. The intuition behind this theorem is that traversing structure of the class hierarchy and part decomposition of the TML KB is isomorphic to the computation of the partition function of the corresponding MLN. Since the probability of a query can be computed as a ratio of partition functions, computing it is also tractable.

At first glance, it may seem that TML is a very restrictive language. However, TML is surprisingly flexible; it can compactly represent arbitrary junction trees and many high-treewidth models. The cost of using TML is that it cannot tractably represent all arbitrary networks, especially those with many dependencies between related objects (Domingos and Webb, 2012). However, when a network contains hierarchical structure, with bounds on the number of links between objects in different classes, the TML KB remains tractable. As shown in the success of OntoUSP, many statements in natural language can be semantically parsed into a hierarchical part/class structure. Syntax also has this kind of structure; smaller syntactic components form the subparts for larger components. We will now briefly describe how TML is a very natural fit for both the syntactic and semantic realms.

2.1 TML for syntactic parsing

Non-recursive probabilistic context-free grammars (PCFGs) (Chi, 1999) can be compactly encoded in TML. Non-terminals have class-subclass relationships to their set of productions. Each production is split into subparts based on the symbols appearing on its right-hand side. It is straightforward to show how to transform one of these grammars into a TML KB. (For a proof sketch see Domingos and Webb 2012.) Natural language is recursive, but fixing the number of recursive levels will allow for a grammar flexible enough for virtually all real sentences. Once we have the PCFG encoded in TML, we can find the most likely parse of a sentence using the standard TML inference algorithm.

2.2 TML for semantic parsing

TML closely mirrors the ontological structure of objects in the world. Objects are defined by class structure (e.g., monkeys are mammals), part decompositions (e.g., monkeys have a tail, legs, etc.), and relations (e.g., a monkey's tail is between its legs).

Text also frequently contains relations occurring between objects. These relations and constructs in natural language contain rich ontological structure; we hypothesize that this structure allows TML to compactly represent semantic information about relations and events. For example, to describe the food chain, we define a class for the eating relation with two subparts: the eater of the animal class and the eaten of the living thing class. This eating relation class would have subclasses to define carnivorous and vegetarian eating events and so on, refining the subpart classes as needed. Since animals tend to only eat things of one other class, the number of eating relation classes will be low, and the TML can tractably represent these relations. This approach can be easily extended to a hierarchy of narrative classes, which each contain up to a fixed number of events as subparts.

TML can also be used to deal with other types of phenomena in natural language. (Space precludes us from going into detail for many here.) For example, adding place markers to a TML KB is straightforward. A class can have a location subpart whose class is selected from a hierarchy of places.

3 TML for knowledge base construction

To create a knowledge base from unstructured text, we propose a joint inference procedure that takes as input a corpus of unstructured text and creates a TML knowledge base from information extracted from the text. For each sentence, this inference procedure will jointly find the maximum a posteriori (MAP) syntactic and semantic parse and abduce the best changes to the TML KB that explain the knowledge contained in the sentence. Unlike previous pipeline-based approaches to knowledge base construction where a sentence is parsed, facts are extracted, and a knowledge base is then induced, we propose to do the whole process jointly and online. As we infer the best parses of sentences, we are simultaneously learning a probabilistic model of the world, in terms of both structure and parameters.

We plan to develop our approach in stages. At first, we will take advantage of existing syntactic and semantic parsers (e.g., an existing PCFG parser + USP) to parse the text before converting to TML. We may also bootstrap our KB from existing ontologies. However, we will steadily integrate more of the parsing into the joint framework by replacing USP with a semantic parser that parses text straight into TML, and eventually replacing the syntactic parser with one formulated entirely in TML.

3.1 Inference

The probability of a joint syntactic parse T and semantic parse L for a sentence S using a TML KB K is $Pr(T, L|S) \propto \exp(\sum_i w_i n_i(T, L, S))$, where the sum is indexed over the clauses in the MLN created from converting K into Markov logic. Exact MAP inference is possible in MLNs formed from TML KBs. Therefore, finding the joint MAP syntactic and semantic parse for a sentence with a parser formulated as a TML KB is tractable. The tractability of inference is vital since the MAP parse of a sentence given a current state of the TML KB will need to be found frequently during learning.

Inference in a TML KB is low-order polynomial in the size of the KB. However, if the size becomes exponential, inference will no longer be tractable. In this case, we can utilize variational inference to approximate the intractable KB with the closest tractable one (Lowd and Domingos, 2010). However, in general, even if the full KB is intractable, the subset required to answer a particular query may be tractable, or at least easier to approximate.

3.2 Learning

As we parse sentences, we simultaneously learn the best TML KB that explains the information in the sentences. Given the MAP parse, the weights for the KB can be re-estimated in closed form by storing counts from previously-parsed knowledge and by using m-estimation for smoothing among the classes. However, we also need to search over possible changes to the part and class structure of the KB to find the state of the KB that best explains the parse of the sentence. Developing this structure search will be a key focus of our research.

We plan to take advantage of the fact that sentences tend to either state general rules (e.g., "Penguins are flightless birds") or facts about particular objects (e.g., "Tux can't fly"). When parsing a sentence that states a general rule, the structure learning focuses on how best to alter the class hierarchy or part decomposition to include the new rule and maintain a coherent structure. For example, parsing the sentence about penguins might involve adding penguins as a class of birds and updating the weight of the `CanFly(c)` relation for penguins, which in turn changes the weight of that relation for birds. For sentences that state properties or relations on objects, learning will involve identifying (or creating) the best classes for the objects and updating the weight of the property or relation involved. When learning, we will have to ensure that no constraints of the TML KB are violated (e.g., the class hierarchy must remain a forest).

3.3 Querying the database

Inferring the answer of a yes/no query is simply a matter of parsing a query, adding its semantic parse to the KB, and recomputing the partition function (which is tractable in TML). The probability of the query is the value of the new partition function divided by the old. For more substantive queries (e.g., "What does IL-13 enhance?"), the naïve approach would look at each possible answer in turn. However, we can greatly speed up this process using coarse-to-fine inference utilizing the class structure of the TML KB (Kiddon and Domingos, 2011).

4 Proposed testbed

As an initial testbed, we plan to use our approach to build a knowledge base from the text of PubMed[1] and PubMed Central[2], companion repositories of 21 million abstracts and 2.4 million full texts of biomedical articles respectively. PubMed is a good basis for an initial investigation of our methods for a number of reasons. A biomedical knowledge base is of real use and importance for biomedical researchers. PubMed is a good size: large and rich, but not Web-scale, which would require parallelization techniques beyond our proposal's scope. Also, since the repositories contain both abstracts and full-text articles, we can incrementally scale up our approach from abstracts to full text articles, until eventually extracting from both repositories. The biomedical domain is also a good since shallow understanding is attainable without requiring much domain knowledge. However, if needed, we can seed the knowledge base with information extracted from biology textbooks, biology ontologies, etc.

There will be many questions our KB cannot answer, but even if we are far from solving the knowledge extraction problem, we can do much better than the existing keyword-based retrieval offered by the repositories. We also plan to go further with our proposal and make our knowledge base available for querying on the Web to allow for peer evaluation.

5 Conclusion

We propose an approach to automatic knowledge base construction based on using tractable joint inference formulated in terms of Tractable Markov Logic. Using TML is a promising avenue for extracting and reasoning over knowledge from text, since it can easily represent many kinds of syntactic and semantic information. We do not expect TML to be good at everything, and a key part of our research agenda is discovering which language extraction and understanding tasks it is good at and which may need additional methods. We plan to use biomedical texts as a testbed so we may see how a knowledge base created using our approach performs in a large, real-world domain.

[1] http://www.ncbi.nlm.nih.gov/pubmed/

[2] http://www.ncbi.nlm.nih.gov/pmc/

Acknowledgments

This research was partly funded by ARO grant W911NF-08-1-0242, AFRL contract FA8750-09-C-0181, NSF grant IIS-0803481, ONR grant N00014-08-1-0670, and the National Science Foundation Graduate Research Fellowship under Grant No. DGE-0718124. The views and conclusions contained in this document are those of the authors and should not be interpreted as necessarily representing the official policies, either expressed or implied, of ARO, DARPA, AFRL, NSF, ONR, or the United States Government.

References

M. Banko, M. Cafarella, S. Soderland, M. Broadhead, and O. Etzioni. 2007. Open information extraction from the web. In *Proceedings of the Twentieth International Joint Conference on Artificial Intelligence*, pages 2670–2676.

A. Carlson, J. Betteridge, B. Kisiel, B. Settles, E.R. Hruschka Jr., and T.M. Mitchell. 2010. Toward an architecture for never-ending language learning. In *Proceedings of the Twenty-Fourth National Conference on Artificial Intelligence*, pages 1306–1313.

Z. Chi. 1999. Statistical properties of probabilistic context-free grammars. *Computational Linguistics*, 25:131–160.

P. Domingos and D. Lowd. 2009. *Markov Logic: An Interface Layer for Artificial Intelligence*. Morgan Kaufmann.

P. Domingos and W. A. Webb. 2012. A tractable first-order probabilistic logic. In *Proceedings of the Twenty-Sixth National Conference on Artificial Intelligence*.

O. Etzioni, A. Fader, J. Christensen, S. Soderland, and Mausam. 2011. Open information extraction: The second generation. In *Proceedings of the Twenty-Second International Joint Conference on Artificial Intelligence*, pages 3–10.

C. Kiddon and P. Domingos. 2011. Coarse-to-fine inference and learning for first-order probabilistic models. In *Proceedings of the Twenty-Fifth National Conference on Artificial Intelligence*, pages 1049–1056.

D. Lowd and P. Domingos. 2010. Approximate inference by compilation to arithmetic circuits. In *Advances in Neural Information Processing Systems*, pages 1477–1485.

H. Poon and P. Domingos. 2009. Unsupervised semantic parsing. In *Proceedings of the Conference on Empirical Methods in Natural Language Processing*, pages 1–10.

H. Poon and P. Domingos. 2010. Unsupervised ontology induction from text. In *Proceedings of the Association for Computational Linguistics*, pages 296–305.

S. Schoenmackers, O. Etzioni, and D. Weld. 2008. Scaling textual inference to the web. In *Proceedings of the Conference on Empirical Methods in Natural Language Processing*, pages 79–88.

S. Schoenmackers, O. Etzioni, D. Weld, and J. Davis. 2010. Learning first-order horn clauses from web text. In *Proceedings of the Conference on Empirical Methods in Natural Language Processing*, pages 1088–1098.

Entity Linking at Web Scale

Thomas Lin, Mausam, Oren Etzioni
Computer Science & Engineering
University of Washington
Seattle, WA 98195, USA
{tlin, mausam, etzioni}@cs.washington.edu

Abstract

This paper investigates entity linking over millions of high-precision extractions from a corpus of 500 million Web documents, toward the goal of creating a useful knowledge base of general facts. This paper is the first to report on entity linking over this many extractions, and describes new opportunities (such as corpus-level features) and challenges we found when entity linking at Web scale. We present several techniques that we developed and also lessons that we learned. We envision a future where information extraction and entity linking are paired to automatically generate knowledge bases with billions of assertions over millions of linked entities.

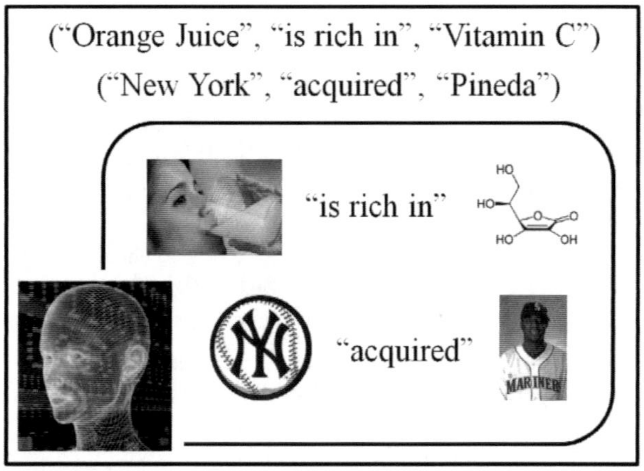

Figure 1: Entity Linking elevates textual argument strings to meaningful *entities* that hold properties, semantic types, and relationships with each other.

1 Introduction

Information Extraction techniques such as Open IE (Banko et al., 2007; Weld et al., 2008) operate at unprecedented scale. The REVERB extractor (Fader et al., 2011) was run on 500 million Web pages, and extracted 6 billion $(Subject, Relation, Object)$ extractions such as ("Orange Juice", "is rich in", "Vitamin C"), over millions of textual relations. Linking each textual argument string to its corresponding Wikipedia entity, known as *entity linking* (Bunescu and Paşca, 2006; Cucerzan, 2007), would offer benefits such as semantic type information, integration with linked data resources (Bizer et al., 2009), and disambiguation (see Figure 1).

Existing entity linking research has focused primarily on linking all the entities within individual documents into Wikipedia (Milne and Witten, 2008; Kulkarni et al., 2009; Dredze et al., 2010). To link a million documents they would repeat a million times. However, there are opportunities to do better when we know ahead of time that the task is large scale linking. For example, information on one document might help link an entity on another document. This relates to cross-document coreference (Singh et al., 2011), but is not the same because cross-document coreference does not offer all the benefits of linking to Wikipedia. Another opportunity is that after linking a million documents, we can discover systematic linking errors when particular entities are linked to many more times than expected.

In this paper we entity link millions of high-precision extractions from the Web, and present our initial methods for addressing some of the opportunities and practical challenges that arise when link-

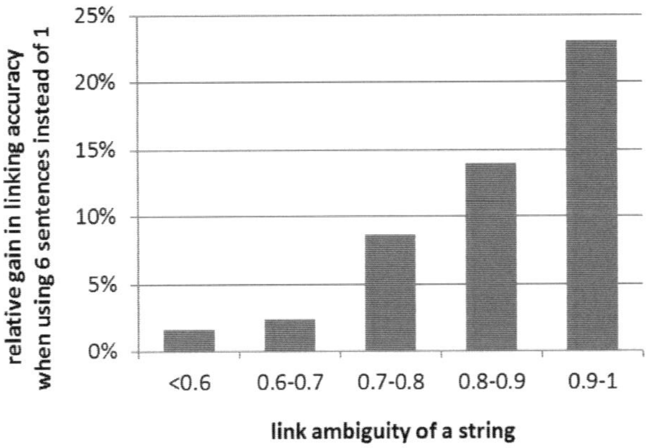

Figure 2: Context matching using more source sentences can increase entity linking accuracy, especially in cases where link ambiguity is high.

ing at this scale.

2 Entity Linking

Given a textual assertion, we aim to find the Wikipedia entity that corresponds to the argument. For example, the assertion ("New York", "acquired", "Pineda") should link to the Wikipedia article for *New York Yankees*, rather than *New York City*.

Speed is a practical concern when linking this many assertions, so instead of designing a system with sophisticated features that rely on the full Wikipedia graph structure, we instead start with a faster system leveraging linking features such as string matching, prominence, and context matching. (Ratinov et al., 2011) found that these "local" features already provide a baseline that is very difficult to beat with the more sophisticated "global" features that take more time to compute. For efficient high-quality entity linking of Web scale corpora, we focus on the faster techniques, and then later incorporate *corpus-level features* to increase precision.

2.1 Our Basic Linker

Given an entity string, we first obtain the most prominent Wikipedia entities that meet string matching criteria. As in (Fader et al., 2009), we measure prominence using inlink count, which is the number of Wikipedia pages that link to a Wikipedia entity's page. In our example, candidate matches for "New York" include entities such as:

- New York (State) at 92,253 inlinks
- New York City at 87,974 inlinks

entity	assertions	wiki inlinks	ratio
"Barack Obama"	16,094	16,415	0.98
"Larry Page"	13,871	588	23.6
"Bill Clinton"	5,710	11,176	0.51
"Microsoft"	5,681	12,880	0.44
"Same"	6,975	36	193

Table 1: The ratio between an entity's *linked assertion count* and its *inlink prominence* can help to detect systematic errors to correct or filter out.

- New York Yankees at 8,647 inlinks
- New York University at 7,983 inlinks

After obtaining a list of candidate entities, we employ a context matching (Bunescu and Paşca, 2006) step that uses cosine similarity to measure the semantic distance between the assertion and each candidate's Wikipedia article. For example, if our assertion came from the sentence "New York acquired Pineda on January 23," then we would calculate the similarity between this sentence and the Wikipedia articles for New York (State), New York City, etc.

As a final step we calculate a *link score* for each candidate as a product of string match level, prominence score and context match score. We also calculate a *link ambiguity* as the 2nd highest link score divided by the highest link score. The best matches have high link score and low link ambiguity.

2.2 Corpus-Level Features

This section describes two novel features we used that are enabled when linking at the corpus level.

2.2.1 Collective Contexts

One corpus-level feature we leverage here is *collective contexts*. We observe that in an extraction corpus, the same assertion is often extracted from multiple source sentences across different documents. If we collect together the various source sentences, this can provide stronger context signal for entity linking. While "New York acquired Pineda on January 23" may not provide strong signal by itself, adding another source sentence such as "New York acquired Pineda to strengthen their pitching staff," could be enough for the linker to choose the *New York Yankees* over the others. Figure 2 shows the gain in linking accuracy we observed when using 6 randomly sampled source sentences per assertion instead of 1. At each *link ambiguity* level, we took 200 random samples.

2.2.2 Link Count Expectation

Another corpus-level feature we found to be useful is *link count expectation.* When linking millions of general assertions, we do not expect strong relative deviation between the *number of assertions linking to each entity* and the *known prominence of the entities.* For example, we would expect many more assertions to link to "Lady Gaga" than "Michael Pineda." We formalize this notion by calculating an *inlink ratio* for each entity as the *number of assertions linking to it* divided by its *inlink prominence*.

When linking 15 million assertions, we found that ratios significantly greater than 1 were often signs of systematic errors. Table 1 shows ratios for several entities that had many assertions linked to them. It turns out that many assertions of the form "(Page, loaded in, 0.23 seconds)" were being incorrectly linked to "Larry Page," and assertions like "(Same, goes for, women)" were being linked to a city in East Timor named "Same." We filtered systematic errors detected in this way, but these errors could also serve as valuable negative labels in training a better linker.

2.3 Speed and Accuracy

Some of the existing linking systems we looked at (Hoffart et al., 2011; Ratinov et al., 2011) can take up to several seconds to link documents, which makes them difficult to run at Web scale without massive distributed computing. By focusing on the fastest local features and then improving precision using corpus-level features, our initial implementation was able to link at an average speed of 60 assertions per second on a standard machine without using multithreading. This translated to 3 days to link the set of 15 million textual assertions that REVERB identified as having the highest precision over its run of 500 million Web pages. On our Figure 2 data, overall linking accuracy was above 70%.

2.4 Unlinkable Entities

Aside from the speed benefit, another advantage of using the "extract then entity-link" pipeline (rather than entity linking all the source documents and then running extraction only for linked entities) is that it also allows us to capture assertions concerning the long tail of entities (e.g., "prune juice") that are not prominent enough to have their own Wikipedia article. Wikipedia has dedicated articles for "apple juice" and "orange juice" but not for "prune juice" or "wheatgrass juice." Searching Wikipedia for "prune juice" instead redirects to the article for "prune," which works for an encyclopedia, but not for many entity linking end tasks because "prunes" and "prune juice" are not the same and do not have the same semantic types. Out of 15 million assertions, we observed that around 5 million could not be linked. Even if an argument is not in Wikipedia, we would still like to assign semantic types to it and disambiguate it. We have been exploring handling these *unlinkable entities* over 3 steps, which can be performed in sequence or jointly:

2.4.1 Detect Entities

Noun phrase extraction arguments that cannot be linked tend to be a mix of entities that are too new or not prominent enough (e.g., "prune juice," "fiscal year 2012") and non-entities (e.g., "such techniques," "serious change"). We have had success training a classifier to separate these categories by using features derived from the Google Books Ngrams corpus, as unlinkable entities tend to have different usage-over-time characteristics than non-entities. For example, many non-entities are seen in books usage going back hundreds of years, with little year-to-year frequency variation.

2.4.2 Predict Types

We found that we can predict the Freebase types of unlinkable entities using instance-to-instance class propagation from the linked entities. For example, if "prune juice" cannot be linked, we can predict its semantic types by observing that the collection of relations it appears with (e.g., "is a good source of") also occur with linkable entities such as "orange juice" and "apple juice," and propagate the semantic types from these similar entities. Linking at Web scale means that unlinkable entities often have many relations to use for this process. When available, shared term heads (e.g., "juice") could also serve as a signal for finding entities that are likely to share semantic types.

	top assertions
rank by freq	"(teachers, teach at, school)" "(friend, teaches at, school)" "(Mike, teaches at, school)" "(biologist, teaches at, Harvard)" "(Jorie Graham, teaches at, Harvard)"
rank by link score	"(Pauline Oliveros, teaches at, RPI)" "(Azar Nafisi, teaches at, Johns Hopkins)" "(Steven Plaut, teaches at, Univ of Haifa)" "(Niall Ferguson, teaches at, NYU)" "(Ha Jin, teaches at, Boston University)"

Table 2: Ranking based on *link score* gives higher quality results than ranking based on *frequency*.

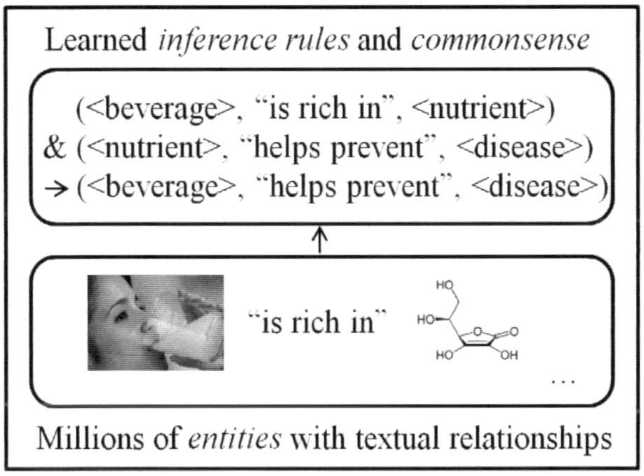

Figure 3: On top of an Entity Linked Open IE corpus we could learn *inference rules* and *commonsense knowledge*.

2.4.3 Disambiguation

In cases where we predict mutually exclusive types (e.g., *film* and *person* can be observed to be mutually exclusive in Freebase instances), this signifies that the argument is a name shared by multiple entities. We plan to use clustering to recover the most likely types of the multiple entities and then divide assertions among them.

3 Resources Enabled

We observed that entity linking of 15 million textual extractions enables several resources.

3.1 Freebase Selectional Preferences

Each Wikipedia entity that gets linked is easily annoted with its Freebase (Bollacker et al., 2008) semantic types using data from the Freebase Wikipedia Extraction (WEX) project. On the 15 million extractions, the entities that we linked to encompassed over 1,300 Freebase types. Knowing these entity types then allows us to compute the Freebase selectional preferences of all our textual relations. For example, we can observe from our linked entities that the "originated in" relation most often has types such as *food*, *sport*, and *animal breed* in the domain. Selectional preferences have been calculated for WordNet (Agirre and Martinez, 2002), but have not been calculated at scale for Freebase, which is something that we get for free in our scenario. Freebase has a much greater focus on named entities than WordNet, so these selectional preferences could be valuable in future applications.

3.2 Improved Instance Ranking Function

We observed *link score* to be a better ranking function than *assertion frequency* for presenting query results. For example, Table 2 shows the top results when searching the extractions for instances of the "teaches at" textual relation. When results are sorted by frequency in the corpus, assertions like "(friend, teaches at, school)" and "(Mike, teaches at, school)" are returned first. When results are sorted by *link score*, the top hundred results are all specific instances of professors and the schools they teach at, and are noticeably more specific and generally correct than the top frequency-sorted instances.

3.3 Inference

Disambiguated and typed entities are especially valuable for inference applications over extracted data. For example if we observe enough instances like "Orange Juice is rich in Vitamin C," "Vitamin C helps prevent scurvy," and "Orange Juice helps prevent scurvy," then we can learn the inference rule shown in Figure 3. (Schoenmackers et al., 2010) explored this, but without entity linking they had to rely on heavy filtering against hypernym data, losing most of their extraction instances in the process. We plan to explore how much gain we get in inference rule learning when using entity linking instead of hypernym filtering. Linked instances would also be higher precision input than what is currently available for learning implicit common sense properties of textual relations (Lin et al., 2010).

4 Conclusions

While numerous entity-linking systems have been developed in recent years, we believe that going forward, researchers will increasingly be considering the opportunities and challenges that arise when scaling up from the single document level toward the Web-scale corpus level. This paper is the first to run and report back on entity linking over millions of textual extractions, and we proposed novel ideas in areas such as corpus-level features and unlinkable entities. There are potentially many other corpus-level features and characteristics to explore, as well as additional challenges (e.g., how to best evaluate recall at this scale), and we look forward to seeing additional research in Entity Linking at Web scale over the coming years.

5 Acknowledgements

This research was supported in part by NSF grant IIS-0803481, ONR grant N00014-08-1-0431, and DARPA contract FA8750-09-C-0179, and carried out at the University of Washington's Turing Center.

References

Eneko Agirre and David Martinez. 2002. Integrating selectional preferences in wordnet. In *Proceedings of the first International WordNet Conference*.

Michele Banko, Michael J Cafarella, Stephen Soderland, Matt Broadhead, and Oren Etzioni. 2007. Open information extraction from the Web. In *Proceedings of IJCAI*.

Christian Bizer, Tom Heath, and Tim Berners-Lee. 2009. Linked data - the story so far. In *International Journal on Semantic Web and Information Systems (IJSWIS)*.

Kurt Bollacker, Colin Evans, Praveen Paritosh, Tim Sturge, and Jamie Taylor. 2008. Freebase: a collaboratively created graph database for structuring human knowledge. In *Proceedings of SIGMOD '08*, pages 1247–1250, New York, NY, USA.

Razvan Bunescu and Marius Paşca. 2006. Using encyclopedic knowledge for named entity disambiguation. In *Proceedings of the 11th Conference of the European Chapter of the Association of Computational Linguistics (EACL)*.

Silviu Cucerzan. 2007. Large-scale named entity disambiguation based on wikipedia data. In *Proceedings of EMNLP*.

Mark Dredze, Paul McNamee, Delip Rao, Adam Gerber, and Tim Finin. 2010. Entity disambiguation for knowledge base population. In *Proceedings of COLING*.

Anthony Fader, Stephen Soderland, and Oren Etzioni. 2009. Scaling Wikipedia-based named entity disambiguation to arbitrary Web text. In *IJCAI-09 Workshop on User-contributed Knowledge and Artificial Intelligence (WikiAI09)*.

Anthony Fader, Stephen Soderland, and Oren Etzioni. 2011. Identifying relations for open information extraction. In *Proceedings of EMNLP*.

Johannes Hoffart, Mohamed Amir Yosef, Ilaria Bordino, Hagen Fürstenau, Manfred Pinkal, Marc Spaniol, Bilyana Taneva, Stefan Thater, and Gerhard Weikum. 2011. Robust disambiguation of named entities in text. In *Proceedings of EMNLP*.

Sayali Kulkarni, Amit Singh, Ganesh Ramakrishnan, and Soumen Chakrabarti. 2009. Collective annotation of wikipedia entities in text. In *Proceedings of KDD*.

Thomas Lin, Mausam, and Oren Etzioni. 2010. Commonsense from the web: Relation properties. In *AAAI Fall Symposium on Commonsense*.

David Milne and Ian H. Witten. 2008. Learning to link with wikipedia. In *Proceedings of the 17h ACM International Conference on Information and Knowledge Management (CIKM)*.

Lev Ratinov, Dan Roth, Doug Downey, and Mike Anderson. 2011. Local and global algorithms for disambiguation to wikipedia. In *Proceedings of the Annual Meeting of the Association of Computational Linguistics (ACL)*.

Stefan Schoenmackers, Oren Etzioni, Daniel S. Weld, and Jesse Davis. 2010. Learning first-order horn clauses from web text. In *Proceedings of EMNLP*.

Sameer Singh, Amarnag Subramanya, Fernando Pereira, and Andrew McCallum. 2011. Large-scale cross-document coreference using distributed inference and hierarchical models. In *Proceedings of ACL*.

Daniel S. Weld, Raphael Hoffmann, and Fei Wu. 2008. Using wikipedia to bootstrap open information extraction. In *SIGMOD Record*.

Human-Machine Cooperation with Epistemological DBs: Supporting User Corrections to Knowledge Bases

Michael Wick
University of Massachusetts
140 Governor's Drive
Amherst, MA 01002
mwick@cs.umass.edu

Karl Schultz
University of Massachusetts
140 Governor's Drive
Amherst, MA 01002
kschultz@cs.umass.edu

Andrew McCallum
University of Massachusetts
140 Governor's Drive
Amherst, MA 01002
mccallum@cs.umass.edu

Abstract

Knowledge bases (KB) provide support for real-world decision making by exposing data in a structured format. However, constructing knowledge bases requires gathering data from many heterogeneous sources. Manual efforts for this task are accurate, but lack scalability, and automated approaches provide good coverage, but are not reliable enough for real-world decision makers to trust. These two approaches to KB construction have complementary strengths: in this paper we propose a novel framework for supporting human-proposed edits to knowledge bases.

1 Introduction

Knowledge bases (KB) facilitate real-world decision making by providing access to structured relational information that enables pattern discovery and semantic queries. However, populating KBs requires the daunting task of gathering and assembling information from a variety of structured and unstructured sources at scale: a complex multi-task process riddled with uncertainty. Uncertainty about the reliability of different sources, uncertainty about the accuracy of extraction, uncertainty about integration ambiguity, and uncertainty about changes over time.

While this data can be gathered manually with high accuracy, it can be achieved at greater scale using automated approaches such as information extraction (IE). Indeed manual and automated approaches to knowledge base construction have complementary strengths: humans have high accuracy while machines have high coverage. However, integrating the two approaches is difficult because it is not clear how to best resolve conflicting assertions on knowledge base content. For example, it is risky to just allow users to directly modify the KB's notion of "the truth" because sometimes humans will be wrong, sometimes humans disagree, and sometimes the human edits become out-of-date in response to new events (and should be later over-written by IE).

We propose a new framework for supporting human edits to knowledge bases. Rather than treating each human edit as a deterministic truth, each edit is simply a new piece of evidence that can participate in inference with other pieces of raw evidence. In particular, a graphical model of "the truth" contains factors that weigh these various sources of evidence (documents culled by a web spider, outputs from IE systems, triples pulled from semantic web ontologies, rows streamed from external databases, etc.) against edits provided by enthusiastic groups of users. Inference runs in the background—forever—constantly improving the current best known truth. We call this an epistemological approach to KB construction because the truth is never observed (i.e., provided deterministically from humans or IE), rather, it is inferred from raw evidence with inference. Further, because the truth is simply a random variable in a graphical model, we can jointly reason about the value of the truth as well as the reliability of human edits (which we save for future work).

In the next section we describe the task of constructing a bibliographic KB, motivate the importance of coreference, and describe how to enable human edits in this context. Then we empirically

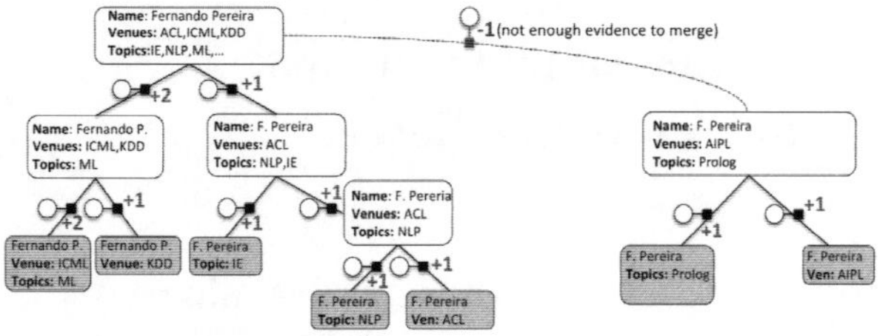

(a) **A recursive coreference model** with two predicted *Fernando Pereira* entities. Black squares represent factors, and the numbers represent their their log scores, which indicate the compatibilities of the various coreference decisions. There is not enough evidence to merge these two entities together.

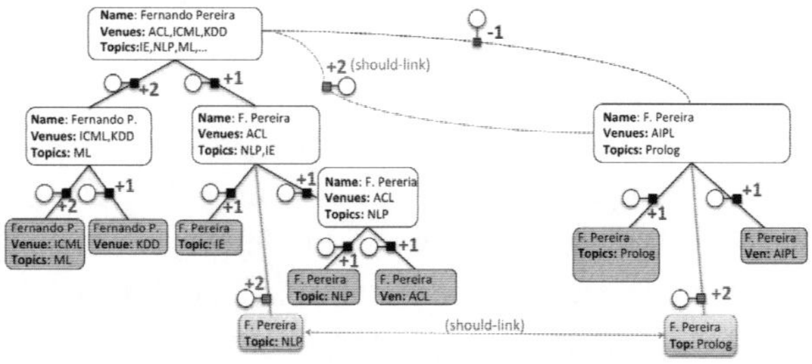

(b) **How a human edit can correct the coreference error** in the previous figure. A human asserts that the "Prolog F. Pereira is also the NLP F. Pereira." This statement creates two mentions with a should-link constraint. During inference, the mentions are first moved into different entities. Then, when inference proposes to merge those two entities, the model gives a small bonus to this possible world because the two should-link mentions are placed in the same entity.

Figure 1: A recall coreference error **(top)**, is corrected when a user edit arrives **(bottom)**.

demonstrate that treating user edits as evidence allows corrections to propagate throughout the database resulting in an additional 43% improvement over an approach that deterministically treats edits as the truth. We also demonstrate robustness to incorrect human edits.

2 Supporting Human Edits in a Bibliographic KB

Reasoning about academic research, the people who create it, and the venues/institutions/grants that foster it is a current area of high interest because it has the potential to revolutionize the way scientific research is conducted. For example, if we could predict the next hot research area, or identify researchers in different fields who should collaborate, or facilitate the hiring process by pairing potential faculty candidates with academic departments, then we could rapidly accelerate and strengthen scientific research. A first step towards making this possible is gathering a large amount of bibliographic data, extract mentions of papers, authors, venues, and institutions, and perform massive-scale cross document entity resolution (coreference) and relation extraction to identify the real-world entities.

To this end, we implement a prototype "epistemological" knowledge base for bibliographic data. Currently, we have supplemented DBLP[1] with extra mentions from BibTeX files to create a database with over ten million mentions (6 million authors, 2.3 million papers, 2.2 million venues, and 500k institutions). We perform joint coreference between authors, venues, papers, and institutions at this scale. We describe our coreference model next.

2.1 Hierarchical Coreference inside the DB

Entity resolution is difficult at any scale, but is particularly challenging on large bibliographic data sets or other domains where there are large numbers of mentions. Traditional pairwise models (Soon et al., 2001; McCallum and Wellner, 2003) of coreference—that measure compatibility between pairs of mentions—lack both scalability and modeling power to process these datasets. Instead, inspired by a recently proposed three-tiered hierarchical coreference model (Singh et al., 2011), we employ an alternative model that recursively structures entities into trees. Rather than measuring compatibilities between *all* mention pairs, instead, internal tree nodes might summarize thousands of leaf-level mentions, and compatibilities are instead measured between child and parent nodes. For example, a single intermediate node might compactly summarize one-hundred "F. Pereira" mentions. Compatibility functions (factors) measure how likely a mention is to be summarized by this intermediate node. Further, this intermediate node may be recursively summarized by a higher level node in the tree. We show an example of this recursive coreference factor graph instantiated on two entities in Figure 1a.

For inference, we use a modified version of the Metropolis-Hastings algorithm that proposes multiple worlds for each sample (Liu et al., 2000). In particular, each proposal selects two tree nodes uni-

[1] http://dblp.uni-trier.de/xml/

formly at random. If the nodes happen to be in the same entity tree, then one of the nodes is made the root of a new entity. Otherwise, the two nodes are in different entity trees, then we propose to merge the two sub-tree's together by either merging the second subtree into the first subtree, or merging the second subtree into the root of the first subtree. If two leaf-level nodes (mentions) are chosen, then a new entity is created and the two mentions are merged into this newly created entity. We describe these proposals and the hierarchical coreference model in more detail in a forthcoming paper (Wick et al., 2012).

2.2 Human edits for entity resolution

Broadly speaking, there are two common types of errors for entity coreference resolution: recall errors, and precision errors. A recall error occurs when the coreference system predicts that two mentions do not refer to the same entity when they actually do. Conversely, a precision error occurs when the coreference error incorrectly predicts that two mentions refer to the same entity when in fact they do not. In order to correct these two common error types, we introduce two class of user edits: *should-link* and *should-not-link*. These edits are analogous to *must-link* and *must-not-link* constraints in constrained clustering problems; however, they are not deterministic, but extra suggestions via factors.

Each coreference edit in fact introduces two new mentions which are each annotated with the information pertinent to the edit. For example, consider the recall error depicted in Figure 1a. This is a real error that occurred in our system: there is simply not enough evidence for the model to know that these two *Fernando Pereira* entities are the same person because the co-authors do not overlap, the venues hardly overlap, and the topics they write about do not overlap. A user might notice this error and wish to correct it with an edit: "user X declared on this day that the Fernando Pereira who worked with Prolog is the same Fernando Pereira who works on natural language processing (NLP)". Presenting this edit to the bibliographic database involves creating two mentions, one with keywords about Prolog and the other with keywords about NLP, and both are annotated with a note indicating user X's belief: "user x: should-link". Then, special factors in the model are able to examine these edits in the context of other coreference decisions. As Markov chain Monte Carlo (MCMC) inference explores possible worlds by moving mentions between entities, the factor graph rewards possible worlds where the two mentions belong to the same entity. For example, see Figure 1b. In our experiments, a similar coreference error is corrected by an edit of this nature.

3 Experiments on Author Coreference

For the purpose of these experiments we focus on the problem of author coreference, which is a notoriously difficult problem due to common first and last names, spelling errors, extraction errors, and lack of "within document boundaries."

In order to evaluate our approach, we label a highly ambiguous "F. Pereira" dataset from BibTeX files.[2] We select this first-initial last name combination because it is fairly common in Portugal, Brazil and several other countries, and as a result there are multiple prominent researchers in the field of computer science. We construct this dataset with two strategies. First, from a publicly available collection of BibTeX files, we identify citation entries that have an author with last name "Pereira" and first name beginning with "F." Each of the *Pereira* mentions gathered in this manner are manually disambiguated by identifying the real-world author to which they refer. Second, we identified five prominent *Pereira* entities from the initial labeling and for three of them we were able to find their publication page and enter each publication into our dataset manually. The number of mentions in the five entities is as follows: (181 mentions, 92 mentions, 43 mentions, 7 mentions, 2 mentions).

3.1 Human edits

We argued earlier that users should not be allowed to directly edit the value of the truth because of the complications that may arise: domain-specific constraint/logical violations, disagreement about the truth, incorrect edits, etc. In this section, we test the hypothesis that the epistemological approach is better able to incorporate human edits than a more direct approach where users can directly edit the database content. To this end, we design two experiments to evaluate database quality as the number of

[2] http://www.iesl.cs.umass.edu/data/bibtex

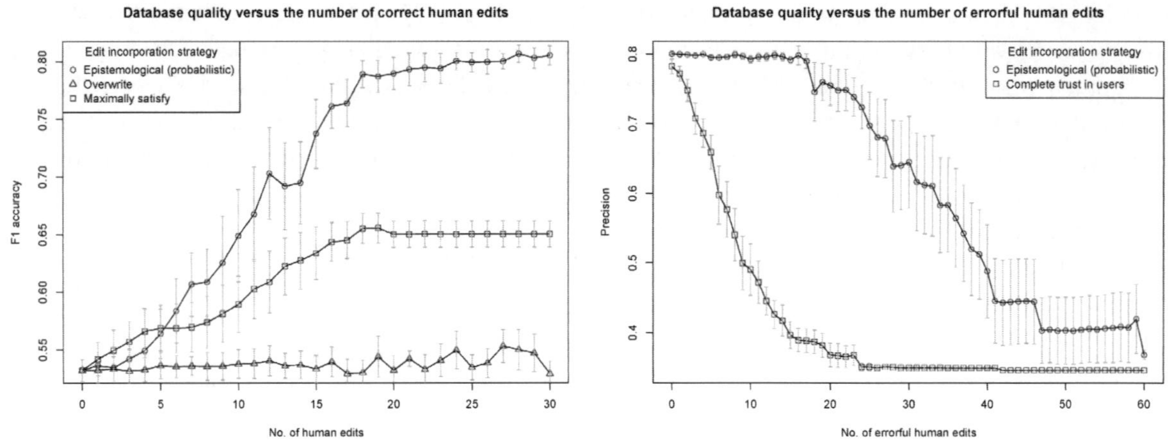

(a) Good quality human edits

(b) Poor quality human edits

Figure 2: Sampling Performance Plots for 145k mentions

human edits increase. In the first experiment, we stream "good quality" human edits to the database, and in the second experiment we stream "poor quality" human edits (we will define what we mean by this in more detail later). For these experiments, we first create an initial database using the mentions in the "F. Pereira" dataset, and run MCMC until convergence reaching a precision of 80, and F1 of 54.

Next, given this initial database of predicted author entities, we measure how both "good quality" (correct) and "poor quality" (incorrect) human edits influence the initial quality of coreference. Although assessing the quality of a user edit is a subjective endeavor, we are still able to implement a relatively objective measure. In particular, we take the set of *Pereira* author entities initially discovered in the "original" DB and consider all possible pairs of these entities. If merging a pair into the same entity would increase the overall F1 score we consider this a correct human edit; if the merge would decrease the score we consider this an incorrect edit. Note that this reflects the types of edits that might be considered in a real-world bibliographical database where a user would browse two author pages and decide (correctly or incorrectly) that they should be the same entity. For example, one of the good quality pairs we discover in this way encodes the simulated "user's" belief that the "the Fernando Pereira who works on NLP is the same Fernando Pereira who works on machine learning". An example of a poor quality edit is "the Fernando Pereira that researches NLP is the same Fernando Pereira that works on MPEG compression".

Once we have determined which author pairs result in higher or lower F1 accuracy, we can then construct simulated edits of various quality. We consider three ways of incorporating these edits into the database. The first approach, *epistemological*, which we advocate in this paper, is to treat the edits as evidence and incorporate them statistically with MCMC. We convert each entity pair into edit-evidence as follows: two mentions are created (one for each entity), the attributes of the entities are copied into the features of these corresponding mentions, and a *should-link* constraint is placed between the mentions. The second two approaches simulate users who directly modify the database content. The first baseline, *overwrite*, resolves conflicts by simply undo-ing previous edits and overwriting them, and the second baseline, *maximally satisfy*, applies all edits by taking their transitive closure.

Good quality edits

In Figure 2a we compare our *epistemological* approach to the two baselines *overwrite* and *maximally satisfy* on the set of good user edits (averaged over 10 random runs). What is interesting about this result is that the *epistemological* approach, which is not obligated to merge the edited entities, is actually substantially better than the two baselines (which are deterministically required to merge the edited entities (provided by a ground truth signal)). After some error analysis, we determine that a major reason for this improvement is that the user edits propagate beyond the entity pair they were initially intended to merge. In particular, as the user edits become applied, the quality of the entities increase. As the quality of the entities increase, the model is able to make more accurate decisions about other mentions that were errorfully merged. For example, we observed that after MCMC inference merged the *natural language processing Fernando* with the *machine learning Fernando*, that an additional 18 mentions were correctly incorporated into the new cluster by inference. In a traditional approach, these corrections could not propagate thus placing the burden on the users to provide additional edits.

Poor quality user edits

In Figure 2b we evaluate the robustness of our *epistemological* database to poor quality (incorrect) human edits. In this figure, we evaluate quality in terms of precision instead of F1 so that we can more directly measure resistance to the over-zealous recall-oriented errorful must-link edits. The baseline approach that deterministically incorporates the errorful edits suffers rapid loss of precision as entities become merged that should not be. In contrast, the *epistemological* approach is able to veto many errorful edits when there is enough evidence to warrant such an action (the system is completely robust for twenty straight errorful edits). Surprisingly, the F1 (not shown) of the epistemological database actually increases with some errorful edits because some of the edits are partially correct, indicating that the this approach is well suited for incorporating partially correct information.

4 Related Work

An example of a structured database where there is active research in harnessing user feedback is the DBLife project (DeRose et al., 2007). Chai et al. (Chai et al., 2009) propose a solution that exposes the intermediate results of extraction for users to edit directly. However, their approach deterministically integrates the user edits into the database and may potentially suffer from many of the issues discussed earlier; for example, conflicting user edits are resolved arbitrarily, and incorrect edits can potentially overwrite correct extractions or correct user edits.

There has also been recent interest in using probabilistic models for correcting the content of a knowledge base. For example, Kasneci et al. (Kasneci et al., 2010) use Bayesian networks to incorporate user feedback into an RDF semantic web ontology. Here users are able to assert their belief about facts in the ontology being true or false. The use of probabilistic modeling enables them to simultaneously reason about user reliability and the correctness of the database. However, there is no observed knowledge base content taken into consideration when making these inferences. In contrast, we jointly reason over the entire database as well as user beliefs, allowing us to take all available evidence into consideration. Koch et al (Koch and Olteanu, 2008) develop a data-cleaning "conditioning" operator for probabilistic databases that reduces uncertainty by ruling-out possible worlds. However, the evidence is incorporated as constraints that eliminate possible worlds. In contrast, we incorporate the evidence probabilistically which allows us to reduce the probability of possible worlds without eliminating them entirely; this gives our system the freedom to revisit the same inference decisions not just once, but multiple times if new evidence arrives that is more reliable.

5 Conclusion

In this paper we described a new framework for combining human edits with automated information extraction for improved knowledge base construction. We demonstrated that our approach was better able to incorporate "correct" human edits, and was more robust to "incorrect" human edits.

6 Acknowledgments

This work was supported in part by the CIIR, in part by ARFL under prime contract #FA8650-10-C-7059, in part by DARPA under AFRL prime contract #FA8750-09-C-0181, and in part by IARPA via DoI/NBC contract #D11PC20152. The U.S. Government is authorized to reproduce and distribute reprints for Governmental purposes notwithstanding any copyright annotation thereon. Any opinions, findings and conclusions or recommendations expressed in this material are those of the authors and do not necessarily reflect those of the sponsor.

References

Xiaoyong Chai, Ba-Quy Vuong, AnHai Doan, and Jeffrey F. Naughton. 2009. Efficiently incorporating user feedback into information extraction and integration programs. In *SIGMOD Conference*, pages 87–100.

Pedro DeRose, Warren Shen, Fei Chen, Yoonkyong Lee, Douglas Burdick, AnHai Doan, and Raghu Ramakrishnan. 2007. Dblife: A community information management platform for the database research community. In *CIDR*, pages 169–172.

Gjergji Kasneci, Jurgen Van Gael, Ralf Herbrich, and Thore Graepel. 2010. Bayesian knowledge corroboration with logical rules and user feedback. In *Proceedings of the 2010 European conference on Machine learning and knowledge discovery in databases: Part II*, ECML PKDD'10, pages 1–18, Berlin, Heidelberg. Springer-Verlag.

Christoph Koch and Dan Olteanu. 2008. Conditioning probabilistic databases. *Proc. VLDB Endow.*, 1:313–325, August.

Jun S. Liu, Faming Liang, and Wing Hung Wong. 2000. The multiple-try method and local optimization in metropolis sampling. *Journal of the American Statistical Association*, 96(449):121–134.

A. McCallum and B. Wellner. 2003. Toward conditional models of identity uncertainty with application to proper noun coreference. In *IJCAI Workshop on Information Integration on the Web*.

Sameer Singh, Amarnag Subramanya, Fernando C. N. Pereira, and Andrew McCallum. 2011. Large-scale cross-document coreference using distributed inference and hierarchical models. In *ACL*, pages 793–803.

Wee Meng Soon, Hwee Tou Ng, and Daniel Chung Yong Lim. 2001. A machine learning approach to coreference resolution of noun phrases. *Comput. Linguist.*, 27(4):521–544.

Michael Wick, Sameer Singh, and Andrew McCallum. 2012. A discriminative hierarchical model for fast coreference at large scale. In *Association for Computational Linguistics (ACL)*.

Annotated Gigaword

Courtney Napoles, Matthew Gormley, and Benjamin Van Durme
Human Language Technology Center of Excellence
Johns Hopkins University

Abstract

We have created layers of annotation on the English Gigaword v.5 corpus to render it useful as a standardized corpus for knowledge extraction and distributional semantics. Most existing large-scale work is based on inconsistent corpora which often have needed to be re-annotated by research teams independently, each time introducing biases that manifest as results that are only comparable at a high level. We provide to the community a public reference set based on current state-of-the-art syntactic analysis and coreference resolution, along with an interface for programmatic access. Our goal is to enable broader involvement in large-scale knowledge-acquisition efforts by researchers that otherwise may not have had the ability to produce such a resource on their own.

1 Introduction

Gigaword is currently the largest static corpus of English news documents available. The most recent addition, Gigaword v.5 (Parker et al., 2011), contains nearly 10-million documents from seven news outlets, with a total of more than 4-billion words. We have annotated this collection with syntactic and discourse structure, for release to the community through the Linguistic Data Consortium (LDC) as a static, large-scale resource for knowledge acquisition and computational semantics. This resource will (1) provide a consistent dataset of state-of-the-art annotations, over which researchers can compare results, (2) prevent the reduplication of annotation efforts by different research groups, and (3) "even the playing field" by better enabling those lacking the computational capacity to generate such annotations at this scale.

The Brown Laboratory for Linguistic Information Processing (BLLIP) corpus (Charniak et al., 2000) contains approximately 30-million words of Wall Street Journal text, annotated with automatically derived Treebank-style parses and part-of-speech tags. This was followed by the BLLIP North American News Text corpus (McClosky et al., 2008), containing approximately 350-million words of syntactically parsed newswire.

Through the Web-as-Corpus kool ynitiative (WaCky) project, two large-scale English corpora have been created.[1] The ukWaC corpus was developed by crawling the `.uk` domain, resulting in nearly 2-billion words then annotated with part-of-speech tags and lemmas (Ferraresi et al., 2008). ukWaC was later extended to include dependency parses extracted using the MaltParser (Nivre et al., 2007) (PukWaC). PukWaC thus represents a large amount of British English text, less formally edited than newswire. The WaCkypedia_EN corpus contains roughly 800-million tokens from a 2009 capture of English Wikipedia, with the same annotations as PukWaC.

Here we relied on the Stanford typed dependencies, rather than the Malt parser, owing to their relative dominance in recent work in distributional semantics and information extraction. In comparison to previous annotated corpora, Annotated Gigaword is a larger resource, based on formally edited ma-

[1] `http://wacky.sslmit.unibo.it/doku.php?id=corpora`

terial, that has additional levels of annotation, and reflects the current state of the art in text processing.

In particular, our collection provides the following for English Gigaword v.5 (referred to as *Gigaword* below):

1. tokenized and segmented sentences,
2. Treebank-style constituent parse trees,
3. syntactic dependency trees,
4. named entities, and
5. in-document coreference chains.

The following provides motivation for such a resource, the tools employed, a description of the programmatic interface provided alongside the data, and examples of ongoing work already enabled by this resource.

2 Motivation

Our community has long had a strong dependence on syntactically annotated corpora, going back at least as far as the Brown corpus (Francis and Kučera, 1964 1971 1979). As manual annotation of syntactic structure is expensive at any large scale, researchers have regularly shifted their reliance to automatically parsed corpora when concerned with statistics of co-occurrence.

For example, Church and Hanks (1990) pioneered the use of Pointwise Mutual Information (PMI) in the field, with results provided over syntactic derivations on a 44-million-word corpus of newswire, showing correlations such as the verb *drink/V* associating with direct objects *martinis*, *cup_water*, *champagne*, *beverage*, *cup_coffee*, and so on. This was followed by a large number of related efforts, such as that by Lin and Pantel (2001): Discovery of Inference Rules from Text (DIRT), aimed at building a collection of paths sharing distributionally similar nominal anchors, over syntactic dependency structures automatically derived from newswire text.

While these efforts are popularly known and constitute established methodological baselines within knowledge acquisition and computational semantics, the underlying annotated corpora are not public resources. As such, direct comparison to their methods are difficult or impossible.

Further examples of popularly known results that are difficult to reproduce include the large-scale information extraction results surrounding TextRunner (Yates et al., 2007), or the script induction efforts first described by Chambers and Jurafsky (2008). In the latter, coreference chains were required in addition to syntactic parsing: a further computationally expensive requirement.

Often researchers will provide full resultant derived resources, such as the DIRT rules or narrative chains (Chambers and Jurafsky, 2010). While this is to be encouraged (as opposed to merely allowing limited web-based access), there are likely a number of researchers that would prefer to tune, adapt, and modify large-scale extraction algorithms, if only they had ready access to the preprocessed collections that led to such resources. This is especially the case now, as interest in Vector Space Models (VSMs) for semantics gain increased attention within Cognitive (Mitchell and Lapata, 2010) and Computer (Turney and Pantel, 2010) Science: such models are often reliant on co-occurrence counts derived over large numbers of syntactically analyzed sentences.

3 Annotations

Gigaword was annotated in three steps: (1) preprocess the data and identify which sentences were to be annotated, (2) derive syntactic parses, and (3) post-process the parsed output to derive syntactic dependencies, named entities, and coreference chains. The second step, parsing, took the majority of our efforts: 10.5 days, using 16 GB of memory and 8 cores per Gigaword file. Using six machines, each with 48 cores and 128 GB of memory, we parsed roughly 700-thousand lines per hour.

3.1 Preprocessing

Gigaword has an SGML-style markup which does not differentiate between different types of body text. For example, list items are not distinguished from complete sentences. Therefore, we coarsely identified all non-sentential lines (list items) by lines with more than one character preceding the first non-space character, after inspection of several randomly sampled documents.

The remaining lines from the `<HEADLINE>` and

<TEXT> fields were segmented into sentences using the open-source tool Splitta, which reported the lowest error rate for English sentence segmentation (Gillick, 2009). Sentences were tokenized using a Penn-Treebank tokenizer (from the Stanford CoreNLP toolkit[2]). We skipped all sentences with more than 100 tokens because we observed that these sentences were often the result of sentence segmentation failure or concatenated list items. In total, we parsed 183,119,464 sentences from the collection. Our release includes information about which sentences were omitted. In an initial estimate of one file containing 548,409 sentences, we dropped 1,197 sentences due to length constraints, which is less than one percent of the total sentences.

3.2 Parsing

We have Penn-Treebank-style parses for the 183-million sentences described above, using the state-of-the-art co-trained English parser described in Huang et al. (2010). After consulting the authors, we used the self-trained (using product model) sixth-round grammar (ST-Prod grammar), because it had high accuracy[3] without the exceptional computational burden of a full product of grammars (which was expected to provide only slight improvement, but at significant computational cost).

3.3 Post-Syntactic Processing

We modified the Stanford CoreNLP pipeline to make use of the parse trees from the previous step, in order to then extract dependency structures, named entities, and coreference chains.[4]

Three types of dependency structures were generated and stored: basic typed dependencies, collapsed dependencies, and collapsed dependencies with conjunction dependencies propagated. See de Marneffe and Manning (2008) for details.

We used the best performing coreference-resolution system (Lee et al., 2011) to extract coreference chains over the approximately 180-million sentences in the <TEXT> of each document.

[2]http://nlp.stanford.edu/software/corenlp.shtml

[3]Avg. F score = 91.4 on WSJ sec 22

[4]The Stanford CoreNLP pipeline assumes all aspects of processing are performed with its own tools; the modifications were required to replace the parsing component with an external tool.

3.4 Storage

The data is stored in a form similar to the original Gigaword formatting along with XML annotations containing our additional markup. There is one file corresponding to each file distributed with the Gigaword corpus. The total uncompressed size of the collection is 400 GB, while the original Gigaword is about 26 GB, uncompressed.

4 Programmatic Access

We provide tools for reading the annotated data, including a Java API which provides convenient object representations for the contents of the XML files. Where appropriate, we use the original Stanford toolkit objects, such as *TypedDependency* and *WordLemmaTag*.

We also provide a suite of command-line tools, built on the Java API, for writing out each individual type of annotation in a common text annotation format. For example, one can print out only the part-of-speech tags, or only the dependencies for all the documents in an annotated file.

To parse the XML, we use the VTD-XML[5] parsing model (Zhang, 2008) and its open-source implementation for a 64-bit Java Virtual Machine. The VTD-XML parser allows for random access, while maintaining a very small memory footprint by memory mapping the XML file and maintaining an in-memory index based on the Virtual Token Descriptor (VTD), a concise binary encoding of the XML tokens. Building on VTD-XML, we also provide a streaming mode that processes and keeps in memory only one news document at a time.

The efficiency and ease of extensibility of our tool are a byproduct of it being built on the VTD-XML library. As an example, to parse one XML file (470 MB) consisting of 33,108 sentences into an object-oriented representation of the dependency parses and accumulate sufficient statistics about dependency edge counts requires just over 30 seconds using a 64 MB of heap space and a single core of an Intel Xeon 2.66 Ghz CPU.

[5]http://vtd-xml.sourceforge.net

Path	Gloss	Cos
NNS:nsubj:VBD← *dived*→VBD:dobj:NN	X dived Y	1.0000
NNS:nsubj:VBD←*slumped* →VBD:dobj:NN	X slumped Y	0.9883
NNS:nsubj:VBD←*plunged*→VBD:dobj:NN	X plunged Y	0.9831
NNS:nsubj:VBD←*gained*→VBD:dobj:NN	X gained Y	0.9831
NNS:nsubj:VBD←*soared*→VBD:dobj:NN	X soared Y	0.9820
NNS:nsubj:VBD←*leapt*→VBD:dobj:NN	X leapt Y	0.9700
NNS:nsubj:VBD←*eased*→VBD:dobj:NN	X eased Y	0.9700
NNS:pobj:IN←of←IN:prep:NN←index←NN:nsubj:VBD←*rose*→VBD:dobj:NN	X's index rose Y	0.9685
NNS:nsubj:VBD←*sank*→VBD:dobj:NN	X sank Y	0.9685
NNS:pobj:IN←of←IN:prep:NN←index←NN:nsubj:VBD←*fell*→VBD:dobj:NN	X's index fell Y	0.9621

Table 1: Relations most similar to "X dived Y" as found in Annotated Gigaword using approximate search.

Path	Gloss	Cos
NN:nsubj:VBD←*gained*→VBD:dobj:NNS	X gained Y	1.0000
NN:nsubj:VBD←*climbed*→VBD:dobj:NNS	X climbed Y	0.9883
NN:nsubj:VBD←*won*→VBD:dobj:NNS	X won Y	0.9808
NN:nsubj:VBD←*rose*→VBD:dobj:NNS	X rose Y	0.9783
NN:nsubj:VBD←*dropped*→VBD:dobj:NNS	X dropped Y	0.9743
NN:nsubj:VBD←*edged*→VBD:dobj:NNS	X edged Y	0.9700

Table 2: Relations most similar to "X gained Y" as found in Annotated Gigaword using approximate search.

5 Example Applications

The following gives two examples of work this resource and interface have already enabled.[6]

5.1 Shallow Semantic Parsing

Ongoing work uses this resource to automatically extract relations, in the spirit of Lin and Pantel (2001) (DIRT) and Poon and Domingos (2009) (USP). First, DIRT-like dependency paths between nominal anchors are extracted and then, using these observed nominal arguments to construct feature vectors, similar paths are discovered based on an approximate nearest-neighbor scheme as employed by Ravichandran et al. (2005). For example, the most similar phrases to "X dived/gained Y" found using this method are shown in Tables 1 and 2 (e.g. *the Nasdaq dived 3.5 percent*). Deriving examples such as these required relatively minor amounts of effort, but only once a large annotated resource and supporting tools became available.

[6]Both applications additionally rely on the Jerboa toolkit (Van Durme, 2012), in order to handle the large scale of features and instances extractable from Annotated Gigaword.

5.2 Enabling Meaning-preserving Rewriting

In a related project, Annotated Gigaword enabled Ganitkevitch et al. (2012) to perform large-scale extraction of rich distributional signatures for English phrases. They compiled the data into a flat corpus containing the constituency parse, lemmatization, and basic dependencies for each sentence. For each phrase occurring in the sentence, contextual features were extracted, including:

- Lexical, lemma, and part-of-speech n-gram features, drawn from an m-word window to the right and left of the phrase.
- Features based on dependencies for both links into and out of the phrase, labeled with the corresponding lexical item, lemma, and part of speech. If the phrase was syntactically well-formed, lexical, lemma, and part-of-speech features for its head were also included.
- Syntactically informed features for constituents governing the phrase, as well as for CCG-style slashed constituent labels for the phrase, into individual features by governing constituent and left- or right-missing constituent.

These features extracted from Annotated Gigaword were successfully used to score paraphrase similarity in a text-to-text generation system. Due to its much more diverse feature set, the resulting collection of 12-million rich feature vectors yielded significantly better output (as judged by humans) than a vastly larger collection of 200-million phrases derived from a web-scale n-gram corpus.

6 Conclusion

As interest in methods requiring large-scale data continues to grow, it becomes ever more important that standard reference collections of preprocessed collections be made available. Annotated Gigaword represents an order of magnitude increase over syntactically parsed corpora currently available via the LDC. Further, it includes Stanford syntactic dependencies, a shallow semantic formalism gaining rapid community acceptance, as well as named-entity tagging and coreference chains. Throughout we have relied on state-of-the-art tools, providing researchers a level playing field to experiment with and compare methods for knowledge acquisition and distributional semantics.

Acknowledgments

The authors wish to thank Juri Ganitkevich, Xuchen Yao, Chris Callison-Burch, Benjamin Shayne and Scott Roberts for their feedback and assistance. This work was partly supported by the National Science Foundation under Grant Nos. DGE-0707427 and DGE-1232825, and by the Johns Hopkins University Human Language Technology Center of Excellence.

References

Nathanael Chambers and Dan Jurafsky. 2008. Unsupervised learning of narrative event chains. In *Proceedings of the Annual Meeting of the Association of Computational Linguistics: Human Language Technologies (ACL08: HLT)*, pages 789–797, Columbus, Ohio. Association for Computational Linguistics.

Nathanael Chambers and Dan Jurafsky. 2010. A database of narrative schemas. In *Proceedings of the Seventh International Conference on Language Resources and Evaluation (LREC'10)*, Valletta, Malta. European Language Resources Association (ELRA).

Eugene Charniak, Don Blaheta, Niyu Ge, Keith Hall, John Hale, and Mark Johnson. 2000. *BLLIP 1987-89 WSJ Corpus Release 1*. Linguistic Data Consortium.

Kenneth Ward Church and Patrick Hanks. 1990. Word association norms, mutual information, and lexicography. *Computational Linguistics*, 16(1):22–29.

Marie-Catherine de Marneffe and Christopher D. Manning. 2008. Stanford typed dependencies manual. *http://nlp.stanford.edu/software/dependencies_manual.pdf*.

Adriano Ferraresi, Eros Zanchetta, Marco Baroni, and Silvia Bernardini. 2008. Introducing and evaluating ukWaC, a very large web-derived corpus of English. In *Proceedings of the 4th Web as Corpus Workshop (WAC-4) Can we beat Google*, pages 47–54.

W. Nelson Francis and Henry Kučera. 1964, 1971, 1979. A Standard Corpus of Present-Day Edited American English, for use with Digital Computers (Brown).

Juri Ganitkevitch, Benjamin Van Durme, and Chris Callison-Burch. 2012. Monolingual distributional similarity for text-to-text generation. In *Proceedings of the First Joint Conference on Lexical and Computational Semantics (*SEM)*.

Dan Gillick. 2009. Sentence boundary detection and the problem with the US. In *Proceedings of Human Language Technologies: The 2009 Annual Conference of the North American Chapter of the Association for Computational Linguistics, Companion Volume: Short Papers*, pages 241–244, Boulder, Colorado. Association for Computational Linguistics.

Zhongqiang Huang, Mary Harper, and Slav Petrov. 2010. Self-training with products of latent variable grammars. In *Proceedings of the 2010 Conference on Empirical Methods in Natural Language Processing*, pages 12–22, Cambridge, MA. Association for Computational Linguistics.

Heeyoung Lee, Yves Peirsman, Angel Chang, Nathanael Chambers, Mihai Surdeanu, and Dan Jurafsky. 2011. Stanford's multi-pass sieve coreference resolution system at the CoNLL-2011 shared task. In *Proceedings of the Fifteenth Conference on Computational Natural Language Learning: Shared Task*, pages 28–34, Portland, Oregon, USA. Association for Computational Linguistics.

Dekang Lin and Patrick Pantel. 2001. DIRT: Discovery of inference rules from text. In *Proceedings of the seventh ACM SIGKDD international conference on Knowledge discovery and data mining*, KDD '01, pages 323–328, New York, NY, USA. ACM.

David McClosky, Eugene Charniak, and Mark Johnson. 2008. *BLLIP North American News Text, Complete*. Linguistic Data Consortium.

Jeff Mitchell and Mirella Lapata. 2010. Composition in distributional models of semantics. *Cognitive Science*, 34(8):1388–1429.

Joakim Nivre, Johan Hall, Jens Nilsson, Atanas Chanev, Gülşen Eryiğit, Sandra Kübler, Stetoslav Marinov, and Erwin Marsi. 2007. MaltParser: A language-independent system for data-driven dependency parsing. *Natural Language Engineering*, 13(02):95–135.

Robert Parker, David Graff, Junbo Kong, Ke Chen, and Kazuaki Maeda. 2011. *English Gigaword Fifth Edition*. Linguistic Data Consortium.

Hoifung Poon and Pedro Domingos. 2009. Unsupervised semantic parsing. In *Proceedings of the 2009 Conference on Empirical Methods in Natural Language Processing*, pages 1–10, Singapore. Association for Computational Linguistics.

Deepak Ravichandran, Patrick Pantel, and Eduard Hovy. 2005. Randomized algorithms and NLP: Using locality sensitive hash functions for high speed noun clustering. In *Proceedings of the 43rd Annual Meeting of the Association for Computational Linguistics (ACL'05)*, pages 622–629, Ann Arbor, Michigan. Association for Computational Linguistics.

Peter D. Turney and Patrick Pantel. 2010. From frequency to meaning: Vector space models of semantics. *Journal of Artificial Intelligence Research (JAIR)*, 37(1):141–188.

Benjamin Van Durme. 2012. Jerboa: A toolkit for randomized and streaming algorithms. Technical Report 7, Human Language Technology Center of Excellence, Johns Hopkins University.

Alexander Yates, Michele Banko, Matthew Broadhead, Michael Cafarella, Oren Etzioni, and Stephen Soderland. 2007. TextRunner: Open information extraction on the web. In *Proceedings of Human Language Technologies: The Annual Conference of the North American Chapter of the Association for Computational Linguistics (NAACL-HLT)*, pages 25–26, Rochester, New York, USA. Association for Computational Linguistics.

Jimmy Zhang. 2008. VTD-XML: XML processing for the future (Part I). http://www.codeproject.com/Articles/23516/VTD-XML-XML-Processing-for-the-Future-Part-I.

Rel-grams: A Probabilistic Model of Relations in Text

Niranjan Balasubramanian, Stephen Soderland, Mausam, and Oren Etzioni
Turing Center, Department of Computer Science and Engineering
Box 352350
University of Washington
Seattle, WA 98195, USA
{niranjan,soderlan,mausam,etzioni}@cs.washington.edu

Abstract

We introduce the Rel-grams language model, which is analogous to an n-grams model, but is computed over relations rather than over words. The model encodes the conditional probability of observing a relational tuple R, given that R' was observed in a window of prior relational tuples. We build a database of Rel-grams co-occurence statistics from ReVerb extractions over 1.8M news wire documents and show that a graphical model based on these statistics is useful for automatically discovering event templates. We make this database freely available and hope it will prove a useful resource for a wide variety of NLP tasks.

1 Introduction

The Google N-grams corpus (Brants and Franz, 2006) has enjoyed immense popularity in NLP and has proven effective for a wide range of applications (Koehn et al., 2007; Bergsma et al., 2009; Lin et al., 2010). However, it is a lexical resource and provides only local, sentence-level information. It does not capture the flow of *semantic* content within a larger document or even in neighboring sentences.

We introduce the novel Rel-grams database[1] containing corpus statistics on frequently occurring sequences of open-domain relational tuples. Rel-grams is analogous to n-grams except that instead of word sequences within a sentence, it tabulates relation sequences within a document. Thus, we expect Rel-grams to model semantic and discourse-level regularities in the English language.

[1]available at *relgrams.cs.washington.edu*.

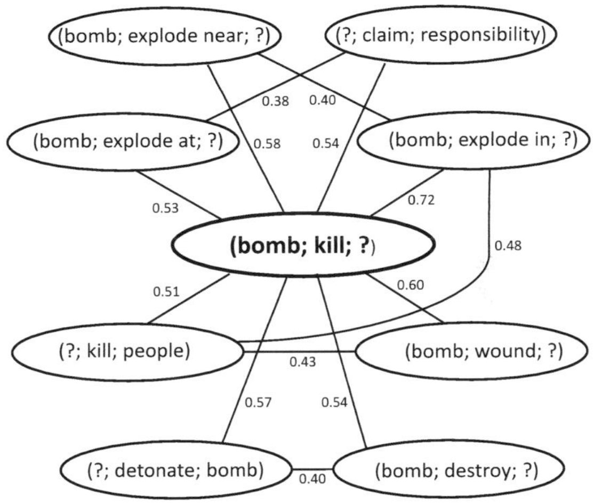

Figure 1: Part of a sub-graph that Rel-grams discovers showing relational tuples strongly associated with *(bomb; kill; ?)*

We have compiled a Rel-grams database from 1.8 million New York Times articles from the Gigaword corpus (Gigaword, 2011). The implementation is linear in the size of the corpus and easily scaled to far larger corpora. Rel-grams database facilitates several tasks including:

Relational Language Models: We define a relational language model, which encodes the probability of relational tuple R, having observed R' in the k previous tuples. This can be used for discourse coherence, sentence order in summarization, *etc.*

Event Template Construction: We cluster commonly co-occuring relational tuples as in Figure 1 and use them as the basis for open event templates (see Table 2). Our work builds on and generalizes earlier efforts by Chambers and Jurafsky (2011).

Expectation-driven Extraction: The probabilities output by the relational language model may be used to inform an information extractor.

As has been the case with n-gram models and resources such as DIRT (Lin and Pantel, 2001), we expect the community to suggest additional applications leveraging this large scale, public resource. An intriguing possibility is to use Rel-grams in document-level extraction or summarization to assess the discourse coherence of alternate hypotheses in a decoding step in much the same way that n-grams have been used in speech or statistical MT.

2 Rel-grams & Relational Language Model

We build a relational language model that specifies the probability of observing the next relational tuple in a sequence of tuples. As an approximation, we estimate bi-gram probabilities. Formally, we use $P_k(R|R')$ as the probability that R follows R' within a distance of k tuples, as a delta-smoothed estimate:

$$P_k(R|R') = \frac{\#(R, R', k) + \delta}{\#R' + \delta \cdot |V|} \quad (1)$$

where, $\#(R, R', k)$ is the number of times R follows R' in a document within a distance of k tuples. $k = 1$ indicates consecutive tuples in the document. $\#R'$ is the number of times R' was observed in the corpus. $|V|$ is the number of unique tuples in the corpus. Notice that, similar to typical language models, this is a sequential model, though we can define undirected models too.

We can use inference over the relational language model to answer a variety of questions. As an example, we can compute the semantic coherence of a document D by converting it into a sequence of relational tuples $< R_1, ..., R_n >$ and computing the joint probability of observing the document D:

$$P(D) = P_{seq}(< R_1, ..., R_n >) \quad (2)$$

$$= P(R_1) \prod_{i=2}^{n} P_1(R_i|R_{i-1}) \quad (3)$$

This can be used to score alternate sequences of tuples in a decoding step, ranking the coherence of alternate versions of a generated document or summary.

Another use of the relational language model is to assess the likelihood of a tuple R given a set of tuples within a window of k tuples. This can serve as a verification during NLP tasks such as extraction.

Table 1: Generalized tuples with the highest conditional probability given *(treasury bond; fall; ?)*. Our model matches well with human intuition about semantic relatedness.

Predicted tuples	Argument values
1.(bond; fall; ?)	point, percent
2.(yield; rise; ?)	point, percent
3.(report; show; ?)	economy, growth
4.(bond; yield; ?)	percent, point
5.(index; rise; ?)	percent, point
6.(federal reserve; raise; ?)	rate, interest rate

2.1 The Rel-grams Database

As a first step towards building the relational language model, we extract relational tuples from each sentence in our corpus using ReVerb, a state-of-the-art Open IE system (Fader et al., 2011). This extracts relational tuples in the format (arg1; rel; arg2) where each tuple element is a phrase from the sentence. We construct a relational database to hold co-occurrence statistics for pairs of tuples found in each document as shown in Figure 2. The database consists of three tables: a *Tuples* table maps each tuple to a unique identifier; *BigramCounts* stores the co-occurrence frequency, a count for a pair of tuples and a window k; *UniCounts* counts the number of times each tuple was observed in the corpus. We refer to this resource as the Rel-grams database.

Query Language: The relational nature of the Rel-grams database allows for powerful querying using SQL. For example, the database can be used to find the most frequent Rel-grams, whose first tuple has *bomb* as the head of its arg1 and has *explode near* as its predicate (with no constraints on arg2). We find that the views in which one or more of the elements in a tuple is a wild-card, are often useful (as in this example). We call these generalized tuples. We materialize tables for generalized tuples in advance to improve query performance.

The Rel-grams database aggregates important information regarding the occurence of semantic relations in documents and allows general querying capability. We envision the database to be also useful for several other tasks such as building event templates (Section 3).

We populated the Rel-grams database using ReVerb extractions from a subset of 1.8 million New York Times articles from the Gigaword corpus. To reduce sparsity, we represented the arguments and

Tuples

Id	Arg1Head	RelNorm	Arg2Head
...	...	...	...
...	...	...	...
13	bomb	explode near	market
...	...	...	...
20	bomb	kill	people
...	...	...	...
...	...	...	...

UniCounts

Id	Count
...	..
...	..
13	45
...	..
20	37
...	..
...	..

BigramCounts

T1	T2	Window	Count
...	...	...	...
13	20	3	12
13	20	9	16
...	...	...	...
20	13	5	2
20	13	7	5
...	...	...	...

Figure 2: Rel-grams Database

relation phrases by their stemmed head words, including prepositions for the relation phrases. The database consisted of over 97M entries.

2.2 Evaluation

First, we evaluated the relational language model to test if the conditional probabilities $P_k(R'|R)$ (Equation 1) reflect semantic relatedness between tuples. We took 20 arbitrary generalized tuples R' and obtained the top 50 tuples $\{R\}$ with highest conditional probability $P_5(R|R')$. Annotators considered each R to be correct if there was a close semantic relation with R', not necessarily synonymy. We found high precision, over 0.96, for the top 50 predicted tuples. Table 1 shows the top few tuples associated with the generalized tuple *(treasury bond; fall; ?)*. Notice that including an argument adds essential information to otherwise vague relation phrase such as "fall", "rise", "show", or "yield".

Next, we evaluated the relational language model on a pseudo-disambiguation task: distinguishing between randomly generated documents and original news articles. We created a test set as follows. From a random sample of the AFP portion of the Gigaword corpus, we selected the first ten documents that covered a non-redundant set of topics such as sports, politics, etc. Then, we pooled the sentences from these ten documents and built pseudo-documents by randomly sampling sentences from this pool.

Given a document, D, we extract the sequence of relational tuples $< R_1, ..., R_n >$. Then, we compute the likelihood of observing this sequence as shown in Equation 2 with window size k set to 5. To account for sparsity, we employ back-off models that switch to conditional probabilities of generalized tuples. We normalize the likelihoods to account for different length sequences.

The average likelihood of original news articles was 2.5 times higher than that of pseudo-documents created from a randomly sampled sentences. This suggests that relational language model captures important semantic information.

3 Event Template Discovery

The Rel-grams database can also be used to identify groups of tuples that frequently co-occur with each other in a specific event or scenario. In particular, we are motivated by the task of automatically building event templates. We cast this a clustering problem on a graph of relation tuples (Rel-graphs).

3.1 Rel-graphs

We define Rel-graphs as an undirected weighted graph $G = (V, E)$, whose vertices (V) are generalized relation tuples, and whose weighted edges (E) represent the strength of co-occurrences between each pair of tuples. We generalize each relation tuple by replacing either argument with a wild-card obtaining (arg1; rel; ?) and (?; rel; arg2). We then create edges for all pairs of these generalized tuples that co-occurred at least five times in the Relgram database. To assign edge weights, we choose normalized point-wise mutual information (PMI), which is computed as follows:

$$PMI(R, R') = \log\left\{\frac{\#(R, R', k) + \#(R', R, k)}{\#R \, \#R'}\right\}$$

where, $\#(R, R', k) + \#(R', R, k)$ is the number of times R and R' co-occur within a window of k, which we set to 10 for this experiment. We normalize the PMI score by the maximum marginal probability of the tuples. The resulting graph consisted of more than 320K vertices and more than 2M edges.

3.2 Event Templates from Clustering

Tightly connected clusters on the Rel-graphs represent frequently co-occurring tuples. These clusters may be viewed as representing event templates,

Table 2: A sample of the 50 highest connectivity Rel-clusters. We show only the first few nodes of each cluster and the highest frequency argument values for the open slot. About 89% of nodes in these 50 clusters are relevant.

Top Nodes	Arguments	Top Nodes	Arguments	Top Nodes	Arguments
(suit; seek; ?)	damages, status	(disease; cause ; ?)	death, virus	(sale; increase; ?)	percent, year
(lawsuit; file in; ?)	court, state	(study; show ; ?)	drug, people	(sale; account; ?)	revenue,sale
(case; involve; ?)	woman, company	(people; die; ?)	year, disease	(profit; rise; ?)	percent, pound
(suit; accuse; ?)	company, Microsoft	(disease; kill; ?)	people, woman	(share; fall; ?)	percent, cent
(?; file; suit)	group, lawyer	(?; treat; disease)	drug, cell	(share; rise; ?)	percent, penny
(suit; allege; ?)	company, fraud	(?; kill; people)	bomb, attack	(analyst; survey by; ?)	bloomberg,zacks
Top Nodes	**Argument Values**	**Top Nodes**	**Argument Values**	**Top Nodes**	**Argument Values**
(film; win; ?)	award, prize	(state; allow ; ?)	doctor, company	(patriot; play; ?)	game, sunday
(film; receive; ?)	review, rating	(law; require ; ?)	company, state	(patriot; in; ?)	game,league
(film; earn; ?)	year, million	(state; require; ?)	company, student	(patriot; win; ?)	game, super bowl
(?; make; film)	director, studio	(state; pass; ?)	law, legislation	(patriot; get; ?)	break, player
(film; get; ?)	nomination, review	(state; use; ?)	money, fund	(patriot; lose; ?)	game, sunday
(?; see; film)	people, anyone	(?; require; state)	bill, Congress	(?; rush; yard)	smith, williams

where the arguments are the entities (slots) in the event and the relation phrase represents their roles.

We employed Markov clustering (Van Dongen, 2008) to find tightly connected clusters on the Rel-graphs. Markov clustering finds clusters efficiently by simulating random walks on the graph.[2] The clustering produced 37,210 clusters for our Rel-graph, which we refer to as Rel-clusters.

We observed that our clusters often included tuples that were only weakly connected to other tuples in the cluster. To prune unrelated tuples, we devise a two step process. First, we select the top three most connected vertices within the cluster. Starting with these three vertices, we compute a subgraph including the direct neighbors and all their pairwise edges. We then sort the vertices in this sub-graph based on their total edge weights and select the top 50 vertices. Figure 1 shows a portion of such a cluster, with vertices strongly connected to (bomb; kill; ?) and all edges between those vertices.

Table 2 shows the top nodes for a sample of high connectivity Rel-clusterswith the two most frequent argument values for their wildcard slot.

3.3 Evaluation

First we evaluated the semantic cohesiveness of a random sample of the 50 clusters with highest connectivity. We found that about 89% of the nodes in each cluster were semantically related to the implicit topic of the cluster.

Next, we evaluate Rel-clusters with an independent gold standard. We compare against MUC-4 templates for terrorist events: bombing, attack, kidnapping, and arson. MUC-4 templates have six primary extraction slots – perpetrator, victim, physical target (omitted for kidnapping), instrument (omitted for kidnapping and arson), date, and location.

To obtain Rel-clusters for these four terrorist event types, we look for clusters that include the seed extractions: *(bomb; explode; ?)*, *(attack; kill; ?)*, *(?; kidnap; ?)*, *(?; set fire; ?)*. We examine the argument values for these nodes to see whether the argument type corresponds to a slot in the MUC-4 event template and use it to compute recall.

Table 3 shows the performance our Rel-clusters and compares it with the MUC-4 template slots discovered by an unsupervised template extraction approach (Chambers and Jurafsky, 2011). We find that Rel-clusters were able to find a node with arguments for all six slots for bombing and attack event types. It had more difficulty with kidnapping and arson, missing the date and location for kidnapping and missing the victim and location for arson. Chambers missed one victim and did not include date or location for any template.

We view these as promising preliminary results but do not draw any strong conclusions on the comparison with Chambers and Jurafsky, as unlike our system, theirs was designed to produce not only templates, but also extractors for the slots.

In the future, we will automatically determine semantic types for the slots. We will also split slots that have a mixture of semantic types, as in the example of the arguments {percent, year} for the extraction *(sale; increase; ?)* in Table 2.

[2]We use an efficient sparse matrix implementation from `http://micans.org/mcl/` that scales linearly in the number of graph vertices.

Table 3: Both Rel-clusters and Chambers system discovered clusters that covered most of the extraction slots for MUC-4 terrorism events.

	Fraction of slots	
	Chambers	Rel-clusters
Bombing	0.50	1.00
Attack	0.67	1.00
Kidnapping	0.50	0.50
Arson	0.60	0.60
Average	0.57	0.77

4 Related Work

There has been extensive use of n-grams to model language at the word level (Brown et al., 1992; Bergsma et al., 2009; Momtazi and Klakow, 2009; Yu et al., 2007; Lin et al., 2010). Rel-grams model language at the level of relations. Unlike DIRT (Lin and Pantel, 2001), Rel-grams counts relation co-occurrence rather than argument co-occurence. And unlike VerbOcean (Chklovski and Pantel, 2004), Rel-grams handles arbitrary relations rather than a small set of pre-determined relations between verbs.

We build on prior work that learns narrative chains and narrative schema that link actions by the same protagonists (Chambers and Jurafsky, 2008; Chambers and Jurafsky, 2009), and work that extracts event templates from a narrowly focused corpus (Chambers and Jurafsky, 2011). Rel-grams finds more general associations between relations, and has made a first step towards learning event templates at scale.

5 Conclusions

This paper introduces the Rel-grams model, which is analogous to n-gram language models, but is computed over relations rather than over words. We construct the Rel-grams probabilistic graphical model based on statistics stored in the Rel-grams database and demonstrate the model's use in identifying event templates from clusters of co-occurring relational tuples. The Rel-grams database is available to the research community and may prove useful for a wide range of NLP applications.

6 Acknowledgements

This research was supported in part by NSF grant IIS-0803481, ONR grant N00014-08-1-0431, and DARPA contract FA8750-09-C-0179, and carried out at the University of Washington's Turing Center.

References

S. Bergsma, D. Lin, and R. Goebel. 2009. Web-scale N-gram models for lexical disambiguation. In *Proceedings of IJCAI*.

Thorsten Brants and Alex Franz. 2006. The Google Web1T 5-gram Corpus Version 1.1. LDC2006T13.

P. Brown, P. deSouza, R. Mercer, V. Della Pietra, and J. Lai. 1992. Class-based n-gram models of natural language. *Computational Linguistics*.

N. Chambers and D. Jurafsky. 2008. Unsupervised learning of narrative event chains. In *Proceedings of ACL-08: HLT*.

N. Chambers and D. Jurafsky. 2009. Unsupervised learning of narrative schemas and their participants. In *Proceedings of ACL*.

N. Chambers and D. Jurafsky. 2011. Template-based information extraction without the templates. In *Proceedings of ACL*.

T. Chklovski and P. Pantel. 2004. VerbOcean: Mining the web for fine-grained semantic verb relations. In *Proceedings of the Conference on Empirical Methods in Natural Language Processing (EMNLP-04)*, pages 33–40.

Anthony Fader, Stephen Soderland, and Oren Etzioni. 2011. Identifying relations for open information extraction. In *Proceedings of EMNLP*.

English Gigaword. 2011. http://www.ldc.upenn.edu/Catalog/catalogEntry.jsp?catalogId=LDC2011T07.

P. Koehn, H. Hoang, A. Birch, C. Callison-Burch, M. Federico, N. Bertoldi, B. Cowan, W. Shen, C. Moran, R. Zens, C. Dyer, O. Bojar, A. Constantin, and E. Herbst. 2007. Moses: open source toolkit for statistical machine translation. In *Proceedings of ACL*.

D. Lin and P. Pantel. 2001. DIRT – Discovery of Inference Rules from Text. In *Proceedings of KDD*.

D. Lin, K. Church, H. Ji, S. Sekine, D. Yarowsky, S. Bergsma, K. Patil, E. Pitler, R. Lathbury, V. Rao, K. Dalwani, and S. Narsale. 2010. New tools for Web-scale N-grams. In *Proceedings of LREC*.

S. Momtazi and D. Klakow. 2009. A word clustering approach for language model-based sentence retrieval in question answering systems. In *Proceedings of CIKM*.

S. Van Dongen. 2008. Graph clustering via a discrete uncoupling process. *SIAM Journal on Matrix Analysis and Applications*, 30(1):121–141.

L-C. Yu, C-H. Wu, A. Philpot, and E. Hovy. 2007. OntoNotes: sense pool verification using Google N-gram and statistical tests. In *Proceedings of OntoLex Workshop*.

Automatic Knowledge Base Construction using Probabilistic Extraction, Deductive Reasoning, and Human Feedback

Daisy Zhe Wang **Yang Chen** **Sean Goldberg** **Christan Grant** **Kun Li**
Department of Computer and Information Science and Engineering,
University of Florida
{daisyw,yang,sean,cgrant,kli}@cise.ufl.edu

Abstract

We envision an automatic knowledge base construction system consisting of three interrelated components. MADDEN is a knowledge extraction system applying statistical text analysis methods over database systems (DBMS) and massive parallel processing (MPP) frameworks; PROBKB performs probabilistic reasoning over the extracted knowledge to derive additional facts not existing in the original text corpus; CAMEL leverages human intelligence to reduce the uncertainty resulting from both the information extraction and probabilistic reasoning processes.

1 Introduction

In order to build a better search engine that performs semantic search in addition to keyword matching, a knowledge base that contains information about all the entities and relationships on the web and beyond is needed. With recent advances in technology such as cloud computing and statistical machine learning (SML), automatic knowledge base construction is becoming possible and is receiving more and more interest from researchers. We envision an automatic knowledge base (KB) construction system that includes three components: probabilistic extraction, deductive reasoning, and human feedback.

Much research has been conducted on text analysis and extraction at web-scale using SML models and algorithms. We built our parallelized text analysis library MADDEN on top of relational database systems and MPP frameworks to achieve efficiency and scalability.

The automatically extracted information contains errors, uncertainties, and probabilities. We use a probabilistic database to preserve uncertainty in data representations and propagate probabilities through query processing.

Further, not all information can be extracted from the Web (Schoenmackers et al., 2008). A probabilistic deductive reasoning system is needed to infer additional facts from the existing facts and rules extracted by MADDEN.

Finally, we propose to use human feedback to improve the quality of the machine-generated knowledge base since SML methods are not perfect. Crowdsourcing is one of the ways to collect this feedback and though much slower, it is often more accurate than the state-of-the-art SML algorithms.

2 System Overview

Our vision of the automatic knowledge base construction process consists of three main components as shown in Figure 1.

The first component is a knowledge extraction system called MADDEN that sits on top of a probabilistic database system such as BAYESSTORE or PrDB and treats probabilistic data, statistical models, and algorithms as first-class citizens (Wang et al., 2008; Sen et al., 2009). MADDEN specifically implements SML models and algorithms on database systems (e.g., PostgreSQL) and massive parallel processing (MPP) frameworks (e.g., Greenplum) to extract various types of information from the text corpus, including *entities*, *relations*, and *rules*. Different types of information are extracted by different text analysis tasks. For example, the

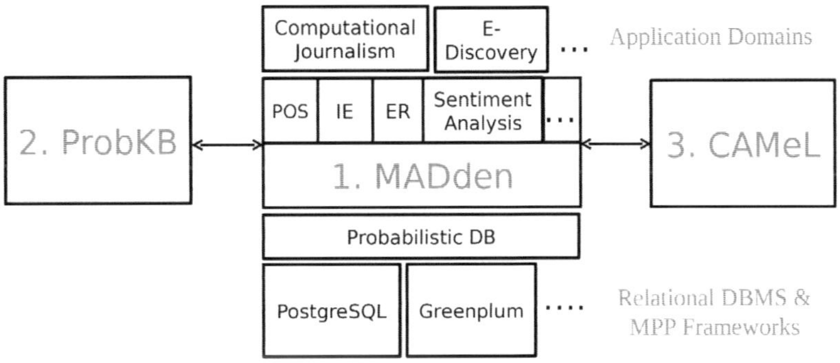

Figure 1: Architecture for Automatic Knowledge Base Construction

named entity recognition (NER) task extracts different types of *entities* including people, companies, and locations from text.

The second component is a probabilistic reasoning system called PROBKB. Given a set of entities, relations, and rules extracted from a text corpus (e.g., WWW), PROBKB enables large-scale inference and reasoning over uncertain entities and relations using probabilistic first-order logic rules. Such inference would generate a large number of new facts that did not exist in the original text corpus. The uncertain knowledge base is modeled by Markov logic networks (MLN) (Domingos et al., 2006). In this model, the probabilistic derivation of new facts from existing ones is equivalent to inference over the MLNs.

The third component is a crowd-based human feedback system called Crowd-Assisted Machine Learning or CAMEL. Given the set of extracted and derived facts, rules and their uncertainties, CAMEL leverages the human computing power from crowdsourcing services to improve the quality of the knowledge base. Based on the probabilities associated with the extracted and derived information in an uncertain knowledge base, CAMEL effectively selects and formulates questions to push to the crowd.

The resulting knowledge base constructed from the extraction, derivation, and feedback steps can be used in various application domains such as computational journalism and e-discovery.

3 MADDEN: Statistical Text Analysis on MPP Frameworks

The focus of the MADDEN project has been to integrate statistical text analytics into DBMS and MPP frameworks to achieve scalability and parallelization. Structured and unstructured text are core assets for data analysis. The increasing use of text analysis in enterprise applications has increased the expectation of customers and the opportunities for processing big data. The state-of-the-art text analysis and extraction tools are increasingly found to be based on statistical models and algorithms (Jurafsky et al., 2000; Feldman and Sanger, 2007).

Basic text analysis tasks include part-of-speech (POS) tagging, named entity extraction (NER), and entity resolution (ER) (Feldman and Sanger, 2007). Different statistical models and algorithms are implemented for each of these tasks with different runtime-accuracy trade-offs. An example entity resolution task could be to find all mentions in a text corpus that refer to a real-world entity X. Such a task can be done efficiently by approximate string matching (Navarro, 2001) techniques to find all mentions that approximately match the name of entity X. Approximate string matching is a high recall and low precision approach when compared to state-of-the-art collective entity resolution algorithms based on statistical models like Conditional Random Fields (CRFs) (Lafferty et al., 2001).

CRFs are a leading probabilistic model for solving many text analysis tasks, including POS tagging, NER, and ER (Lafferty et al., 2001). To support sophisticated text analysis, we implement four key methods: text feature extraction, inference over a

CRF (Viterbi), Markov chain Monte Carlo (MCMC) inference, and approximate string matching.

Text Feature Extraction: To analyze text, features need to be extracted from documents and it can be an expensive operation. To achieve results with high accuracy, CRF methods often compute hundreds of features over each token in the document, which can be high cost. Features are determined by functions over the sets of tokens. Examples of such features include: (1) dictionary features: *does this token exist in a provided dictionary?* (2) regex features: *does this token match a provided regular expression?* (3) edge features: *is the label of a token correlated with the label of a previous token?* (4) word features: *does this the token appear in the training data?* and (5) position features: *is this token the first or last in the token sequence?* The optimal combination of features depends on the application.

Approximate String Matching: A recurring primitive operation in text processing applications is the ability to match strings approximately. The technique we use is based on qgrams (Gravano et al., 2001). We create and index 3-grams over text. Given a string "Tim Tebow" we can create a 3-gram by using a sliding window of 3 characters over this text string. Given two strings we can compare the overlap of two sets of corresponding 3-grams and compute a similarity as the approximate matching score.

Once we have the features, the next step is to perform inference on the model. We also implemented two types of statistical inference within the database: Viterbi (when we only want the most likely answer from a linear-chain CRF model) and MCMC (when we want the probabilities or confidence of an answer from a general CRF model).

Viterbi Inference: The *Viterbi* dynamic programming algorithm (Manning et al., 1999) is a popular algorithm to find the top-k most likely labelings of a document for (linear-chain) CRF models.

To implement the Viterbi dynamic programming algorithm we experimented with two different implementations of macro-coordination over time. First, we chose to implement it using a combination of recursive SQL and window aggregate functions. We discussed this implementation at some length in earlier work (Wang et al., 2010). Second, we chose to implement a Python UDF that uses iterations to drive the recursion in Viterbi. In the Greenplum MPP Framework, Viterbi can be run in parallel over different subsets of the document on a multi-core machine.

MCMC Inference: MCMC methods are classical sampling algorithms that can be used to estimate probability distributions. We implemented two MCMC method: Gibbs sampling and Metropolis-Hastings (MCMC-MH).

The MCMC algorithms involve iterative procedures where the current values depend on previous iterations. We use SQL window aggregates for macro-coordination in this case, to carry "state" across iterations to perform the Markov-chain process. We discussed this implementation at some length in recent work (Wang et al., 2011). We are currently developing MCMC algorithms over Greenplum DBMS.

4 PROBKB: Probabilistic Knowledge Base

The second component of our system is PROBKB, a probabilistic knowledge base designed to derive implicit knowledge from entities, relations, and rules extracted from a text corpus by knowledge extraction systems like MADDEN. Discovering new knowledge is a crucial step towards knowledge base construction since many valuable facts are not explicitly stated in web text; they need to be inferred from extracted facts and rules.

PROBKB models uncertain facts as Markov logic networks (MLN) (Domingos et al., 2006). Markov logic networks are proposed to unify first-order logic and statistical inference by attaching a weight to each first-order formula (rule). These weights reflect our confidence of the rules being true. To obtain these weighted formulae, we have used natural language processing (NLP) methods to extract entities and relations as described in Section 3 and learned the formulae from the extractions.

One challenge in applying the MLN model is propagating the uncertainty of facts and rules in the inference process. A naive method may be discarding facts with low confidence using ad-hoc thresholds and heuristics, but we decided to maintain all the facts in our knowledge base regardless of their confidences. The rationale behind this is that some facts may have low confidence due to absence or inaccessibility of evidence rather than being incorrect; they may prove to be true when new extractions are available as supporting evidence.

We are experimenting on some state-of-the-art implementations of MLNs like TUFFY (Niu et al., 2011) as a base to develop our large-scale probabilistic inference engine. Taking the MLN and uncertain facts, rules, and their confidence as inputs, the system is able to answer queries like "how likely will Bob develop a cancer?". Though TUFFY is able to handle uncertainties resulted from extraction systems, it is no easy task for the system to scale up to tens of millions of facts and thousands of rules. To address this problem, we are currently researching several possible ways to parallelize the inference computation. One challenge for parallelization is data dependency: the result set (derived facts) of one rule may affect that of another. As a first attempt, we are looking at two different partitioning strategies: partition by rules and partition by facts.

In addition to partitioning techniques, we are also trying to evaluate the possibility of implementing MLNs on different MPP frameworks: Greenplum Database, HadoopDB, and Datapath (Arumugam et al., 2010). These database systems allow effective parallel processing of big data and running of inference algorithms, which is essential for scaling up probabilistic reasoning in the PROBKB project.

5 CAMEL: Crowd-Assisted Machine Learning

The final proposed component for automatic construction of a knowledge base is a crowd-based system, CAMEL, designed for improving uncertainty. CAMEL is built on top of an existing probabilistic knowledge or database like PROBKB and MADDEN.

In addition to using SML techniques for large scale analysis, an increasing trend has been to harness human computation in a distributed manner using crowdsourcing (Quinn et al., 2010; Sorokin and Forsyth, 2008). Benefits can be gained in problems that are too difficult or expensive for computers. Services like Amazon Mechanical Turk (AMT) (Ipeirotis, 2010) have led the way by setting up an infrastructure that allows payment for the combined resources of up to hundreds of thousands of people.

SML is not perfect: for some simple NLP tasks it achieves a relatively high accuracy while for other ones involving context and reasoning the results are much worse. Cases where the model is unable to adequately reason about a difficult piece of data introduces large uncertainties into the output. The need for a new type of data cleaning process has emerged. As discussed in Section 4, one approach is to threshold uncertainty and throw away those facts the machine is unable to reason about, leaving the knowledge base incomplete. Another approach is to convert these high uncertainty examples into questions for the crowd to answer.

The main tenets of CAMEL are its selection model and integration model as described below.

Selection Model: The first important feature of CAMEL is its ability to distinguish and select the most uncertain fields in the knowledge base. For tasks involving CRFs (MADDEN), each hidden node can be marginalized to find a probability distribution over the label space. From the marginal distribution, we can attach a *marginal entropy* to each node in the graph. Our algorithm selects the highest entropy node to be sent to the crowd. Additional research is being done to take advantage of specifics of the graph structure such as the connectivity and dependency relationships of each node.

Integration Model: Questions are posted on AMT and are answered by a number of different Turkers, generally three or five per question. The golden standard for aggregating the crowd response has been to take a majority vote. Since our system is built on top of a probabilistic knowledge base KB, we want to establish a distribution over the possible answers based on the received responses. We use the machinery of Dempster-Shafer's (DS) Theory of Evidence (Dempster, 1967; Shafer, 1976) for combining results in a probabilistic manner. Using an Expectation-Maximization algorithm proposed by Dawid and Skene (Dawid and Skene, 1979) for assessing Turker quality and confidence, answers are aggregated into a single distribution for reinsertion into the database. The more Turkers that are queried, the more fine-tuned the distribution becomes.

6 Conclusion

In this short paper, we described our vision of an automatic knowledge base construction system consisting of three major components—extraction, reasoning, and human feedback. The resulting system is expected to be scalable, efficient, and useful in vaiours application domains.

Acknowledgments

This material is based upon work supported by the national Science Foundation Graduate Research Fellowship under Grant No. DGE-0802270 and a generous gift from Greenplum.

References

Subi Arumugam, Alin Dobra, Christopher M. Jermaine, Niketan Pansare, and Luis Perez. 2010. The datapath system: a data-centric analytic processing engine for large data warehouses. In *Proceedings of the 2010 international conference on Management of data*, SIGMOD '10, pages 519–530, New York, NY, USA. ACM.

A. P. Dawid and A. M. Skene. 1979. Maximum likelihood estimation of observer error-rates using the em algorithm. *Applied Statistics*, 28(1):20–28.

A. P. Dempster. 1967. Upper and lower probabilities induced by a multivalued mapping. *Annals of Mathematical Statistics*, 38:325–339.

Pedro Domingos, Stanley Kok, Hoifung Poon, Matthew Richardson, and Parag Singla. 2006. Unifying logical and statistical ai. In *Proceedings of the 21st national conference on Artificial intelligence - Volume 1*, AAAI'06, pages 2–7. AAAI Press.

R. Feldman and J. Sanger. 2007. *The text mining handbook: advanced approaches in analyzing unstructured data*. Cambridge Univ Pr.

L. Gravano, P.G. Ipeirotis, H.V. Jagadish, N. Koudas, S. Muthukrishnan, L. Pietarinen, and D. Srivastava. 2001. Using q-grams in a dbms for approximate string processing. *IEEE Data Engineering Bulletin*, 24(4):28–34.

P.G. Ipeirotis. 2010. Analyzing the amazon mechanical turk marketplace. *XRDS: Crossroads, The ACM Magazine for Students*, 17(2):16–21.

D. Jurafsky, J.H. Martin, A. Kehler, K. Vander Linden, and N. Ward. 2000. *Speech and language processing: An introduction to natural language processing, computational linguistics, and speech recognition*, volume 2. Prentice Hall New Jersey.

John D. Lafferty, Andrew McCallum, and Fernando C. N. Pereira. 2001. Conditional random fields: Probabilistic models for segmenting and labeling sequence data. In *Proceedings of the Eighteenth International Conference on Machine Learning*, ICML '01, pages 282–289, San Francisco, CA, USA. Morgan Kaufmann Publishers Inc.

C.D. Manning, H. Schütze, and MITCogNet. 1999. *Foundations of statistical natural language processing*, volume 999. MIT Press.

Gonzalo Navarro. 2001. A guided tour to approximate string matching. *ACM Comput. Surv.*, 33(1):31–88, March.

Feng Niu, Christopher Ré, AnHai Doan, and Jude W. Shavlik. 2011. Tuffy: Scaling up statistical inference in markov logic networks using an rdbms. *CoRR*, abs/1104.3216.

A. Quinn, B. Bederson, T. Yeh, and J. Lin. 2010. CrowdFlow: Integrating Machine Learning with Mechanical Turk for Speed-Cost-Quality Flexibility. Technical report, University of Maryland, May.

Stefan Schoenmackers, Oren Etzioni, and Daniel S. Weld. 2008. Scaling textual inference to the web. In *Proceedings of the Conference on Empirical Methods in Natural Language Processing*, EMNLP '08, pages 79–88, Stroudsburg, PA, USA. Association for Computational Linguistics.

Prithviraj Sen, Amol Deshpande, and Lise Getoor. 2009. Prdb: managing and exploiting rich correlations in probabilistic databases. *The VLDB Journal*, 18(5):1065–1090, October.

G. Shafer. 1976. *A mathematical theory of evidence*. Princeton university press.

Alexander Sorokin and David Forsyth. 2008. Utility data annotation with Amazon Mechanical Turk. In *2008 IEEE Computer Society Conference on Computer Vision and Pattern Recognition Workshops*, pages 1–8. IEEE, June.

Daisy Zhe Wang, Eirinaios Michelakis, Minos Garofalakis, and Joseph M. Hellerstein. 2008. Bayesstore: managing large, uncertain data repositories with probabilistic graphical models. *Proc. VLDB Endow.*, 1:340–351, August.

Daisy Zhe Wang, Michael J. Franklin, Minos N. Garofalakis, and Joseph M. Hellerstein. 2010. Querying probabilistic information extraction. *PVLDB*, 3(1):1057–1067.

Daisy Zhe Wang, Michael J. Franklin, Minos Garofalakis, Joseph M. Hellerstein, and Michael L. Wick. 2011. Hybrid in-database inference for declarative information extraction. In *Proceedings of the 2011 international conference on Management of data*, SIGMOD '11, pages 517–528, New York, NY, USA. ACM.

Monte Carlo MCMC: Efficient Inference by Sampling Factors

Sameer Singh
University of Massachusetts
140 Governors Drive
Amherst MA 01003
sameer@cs.umass.edu

Michael Wick
University of Massachusetts
140 Governors Drive
Amherst MA 01003
mwick@cs.umass.edu

Andrew McCallum
University of Massachusetts
140 Governors Drive
Amherst MA 01003
mccallum@cs.umass.edu

Abstract

Conditional random fields and other graphical models have achieved state of the art results in a variety of NLP and IE tasks including coreference and relation extraction. Increasingly, practitioners are using models with more complex structure—higher tree-width, larger fan-out, more features, and more data—rendering even approximate inference methods such as MCMC inefficient. In this paper we propose an alternative MCMC sampling scheme in which transition probabilities are approximated by sampling from the set of relevant factors. We demonstrate that our method converges more quickly than a traditional MCMC sampler for both marginal and MAP inference. In an author coreference task with over 5 million mentions, we achieve a 13 times speedup over regular MCMC inference.

1 Introduction

Conditional random fields and other graphical models are at the forefront of many natural language processing (NLP) and information extraction (IE) tasks because they provide a framework for discriminative modeling while succinctly representing dependencies among many related output variables. Previously, most applications of graphical models were limited to structures where exact inference is possible, for example linear-chain CRFs (Lafferty et al., 2001). More recently there has been a desire to include more factors, longer range dependencies and larger numbers of more sophisticated features; these include skip-chain CRFs for named entity recognition (Sutton and McCallum, 2004), higher-order models for dependency parsing (Carreras, 2007), entity-wise models for coreference (Culotta et al., 2007) and global models of relations (Yao et al., 2010). The increasing sophistication of these individual NLP components compounded with the community's desire to model these tasks jointly across cross-document considerations has resulted in graphical models for which inference is computationally prohibitive. Even popular approximate inference techniques such as loopy belief propagation and Markov chain Monte Carlo (MCMC) may be prohibitive.

MCMC algorithms such as Metropolis-Hastings (MH) are usually efficient for graphical models because the only factors needed to score a proposal are those touching the changed variables. However, if the model variables have high degree (neighbor many factors), if computation of factor scores is slow, or if each proposal modifies a substantial number of variables (e.g. to satisfy deterministic constraints, such as transitivity in coreference), then even MH can be prohibitively slow. For example, the seemingly innocuous proposal changing the type of a single entity requires scoring a linear number of factors (in the number of mentions of that entity). Often, however, the factors are somewhat *redundant*, for example, not all the mentions of the "USA" entity need to be examined to confidently conclude that it is a COUNTRY.

In this paper we propose an approximate MCMC framework that facilitates efficient inference in high-degree graphical models. In particular, we approximate the acceptance ratio in the Metropolis-Hastings algorithm by replacing the exact model scores with a stochastic approximation. We propose two strategies for this approximation: static uniform sampling and adaptive confidence-based sampling, and demonstrate significant speedups on synthetic and real-world information extraction tasks.

MCMC is a popular method for dealing with large, dense graphical models for tasks in NLP and information extraction (Richardson and Domingos, 2006; Poon and Domingos, 2006; Poon et al., 2008; Singh et al., 2009; Wick et al., 2009). Popular probabilistic programming packages also rely on MCMC for inference and learning (Richardson and Domingos, 2006; McCallum et al., 2009), and parallel approaches to MCMC have also been recently proposed (Singh et al., 2011; Gonzalez et al., 2011). A generic method to speed up MCMC inference could have significant applicability.

2 MCMC for Graphical Models

Factor graphs represent the joint distribution over random variables by a product of factors that make the dependencies between the random variables explicit. Each (log) factor $f \in \mathcal{F}$ is a function that maps an assignment of its neighboring variables to a real number. The probability of an assignment y to the random variables, defined by the set of factors $\mathcal{F}$, is $P(y) = \frac{\exp \psi(y)}{Z}$ where $\psi(y) = \sum_{f \in \mathcal{F}} f(y)$ and $Z = \sum_y \exp \psi(y)$.

Often, computing marginal estimates of a model is computationally intractable due to the normalization constant Z, while maximum a posteriori (MAP) is prohibitive due to the search space. Markov chain Monte Carlo (MCMC) is an important tool for approximating both kinds of inference in these models. A particularly successful MCMC method for graphical model inference is Metropolis-Hastings (MH). Since sampling from the true model $P(y)$ is intractable, MH instead uses a simpler distribution $q(y'|y)$ that conditions on the current y and proposes a new state y' by modifying a few variables. This new assignment is then accepted with probability $\alpha = \min\left(1, \frac{P(y')}{P(y)} \frac{q(y|y')}{q(y'|y)}\right)$. Computing this acceptance probability is usually highly efficient because the partition function cancels, as do all the factors in the model that do not neighbor changed variables. MH can also be used for MAP inference; the acceptance probability is modified to include a temperature term: $\alpha = \min\left(1, \left(\frac{P(y')}{P(y)}\right)^{\tau}\right)$. If a cooling schedule is implemented for τ then the MH sampler for MAP inference can be seen as an instance of simulated annealing (Bertsimas and Tsitsiklis, 1993).

3 Monte Carlo MCMC

The benefit of MCMC lies in its ability to leverage the locality of the proposal. In particular, evaluation of each sample requires computing the score of all the factors that are *involved* in the change, i.e. all factors that neighbor any variable in the set that has changed. This evaluation becomes a bottleneck for tasks in which a large number of variables is involved in each proposal, or in which the model contains very high-degree variables, resulting in large number of factors, or in which computing the factor score involves an expensive computation, such as string similarity. Many of these arise naturally when performing joint inference, or representing uncertainty over the whole knowledge-base.

Instead of evaluating the log-score ψ of the model exactly, this paper proposes a Monte Carlo estimate of the log-score. In particular, if the set of factors for a given proposed change is $\mathcal{F}$, we use sampled subset of the factors $\mathcal{S} \subseteq \mathcal{F}$ as an approximation of the model score. Formally, $\psi(y) = \sum_{f \in \mathcal{F}} f(y) = |\mathcal{F}| \cdot \mathbb{E}_{\mathcal{F}}[f(y)]$ and $\psi_{\mathcal{S}}(y) = |\mathcal{F}| \cdot \mathbb{E}_{\mathcal{S}}[f(y)]$. We use $\psi_{\mathcal{S}}$ in the acceptance probability α to evaluate each sample. Since we are using a stochastic approximation to the model score, in general we expect to need more samples to converge. However, since evaluating each sample will be *much* faster ($O(|\mathcal{S}|)$ instead of $O(|\mathcal{F}|)$), we expect sampling overall to be faster. In the next sections we describe two strategies for sampling the set of factors $\mathcal{S}$.

3.1 Uniform Sampling

The most direct approach for subsampling the set of $\mathcal{F}$ is to perform uniform sampling. In particular, given a proportion parameter $0 < p \leq 1$, we select a random subset $\mathcal{S}_p \subseteq \mathcal{F}$ such that $|\mathcal{S}_p| = p \cdot |\mathcal{F}|$. Since this approach is agnostic as to the actual factors scores, $\mathbb{E}_{\mathcal{S}_p}[f] \equiv \mathbb{E}_{\mathcal{F}}[f]$. A low p leads to fast evaluation, however it may require a large number of samples due to the substantial approximation. On the other hand, although a high p will converge with fewer samples, evaluating each sample will be slow.

3.2 Confidence-Based Sampling

Selecting the best value for p is difficult, requiring analysis of the graph structure, and statistics on the distribution of the factors scores; often a difficult task for real-world applications. Further, the same value for p can result in different levels of approximation for different proposals, either unnecessarily accurate or restrictively noisy. We would prefer a strategy that adapts to the distribution of the scores.

Instead of sampling a fixed proportion, we can sample until we are confident that the current set of samples $\mathcal{S}_c$ is an accurate estimate of the true mean of $\mathcal{F}$. In particular, we maintain a running count of the sample mean $\mathbb{E}_{\mathcal{S}_c}[f]$ and variance $\sigma_{\mathcal{S}_c}$, using them to compute a confidence interval $I_{\mathcal{S}}$ around the estimate of the mean. Since the number of sampled factors $\mathcal{S}_c$ could be a substantial fraction of the set of factors $\mathcal{F}$,[1] we also incorporate *finite population control (fpc)* in our sample variance. We use the variance $\sigma^2_{\mathcal{S}_c} = \frac{1}{|\mathcal{S}_c|-1}\sum_{f\in\mathcal{S}_c}(f - \mathbb{E}_{\mathcal{S}_c}[f])^2$ to compute the interval $I_{\mathcal{S}_c} = 2z\frac{\sigma_{\mathcal{S}_c}}{\sqrt{|\mathcal{S}_c|}}\sqrt{\frac{|\mathcal{F}|-|\mathcal{S}_c|}{|\mathcal{F}|-1}}$, where $z = 1.96$, i.e. the 95% confidence interval. We iteratively sample factors without replacement from $\mathcal{F}$, until the confidence interval falls below a user specified threshold i. For proposals that contain high-variance factors, this strategy examines a large number of factors, while proposals that involve similar factors will result in fewer samples. Note that this user-specified threshold is agnostic to the graph structure and the number of factors, and instead directly reflects the distribution of the factor scores.

4 Experiments

4.1 Synthetic Entity Classification

Consider the task of classifying entities into a set of types, for example, POLITICIAN, VEHICLE, CITY, GOVERMENT-ORG, etc. For knowledge base construction, this prediction often takes place on the entity-level, as opposed to the mention-level common in traditional NLP. To evaluate the type at the entity-level, the scored factors examine features of all the entity mentions of the entity, along with the labels of all relation mentions for which it is an argument. See Yao et al. (2010) and Hoffmann et al. (2011) for examples of such models. Since a subset of the mentions can be sufficiently informative for the model, we expect our stochastic MCMC approach to work well.

We use synthetic data for such a model to evaluate the quality of marginals returned by the Gibbs sampling form of MCMC. Since the Gibbs algorithm samples each variable using a fixed assignment of its neighborhood, we represent generating a single sample as classification. We create models with a single unobserved variable (entity type) that neighbors many unary factors, each representing a single entity- or a relation-mention factor. Our synthetic models consist of random weights assigned to each of the 100 factors (generated from $\mathcal{N}(0.5, 1)$ for the true label, and $\mathcal{N}(-0.5, 1)$ for the false label).

We evaluate the previously described uniform sampling and confidence-based sampling, with several parameter values, and plot the L_1 error to the true marginals. We use the number of factors examined as a proxy for running time, as the effect of the steps in sampling are relatively negligible. The error in comparison to regular MCMC ($p = 1$) is shown in Figure 1, with standard error bars averaging over 100 models. Initially, as the sampling approach is made more stochastic (lowering p or increasing i), we see a steady improvement in the running time needed to obtain the same error tolerance. However, the amount of relative improvements slows as stochasticity is increased further, in fact for extreme values ($i = 0.05, p = 0.1$) the chains may perform worse than regular MCMC.

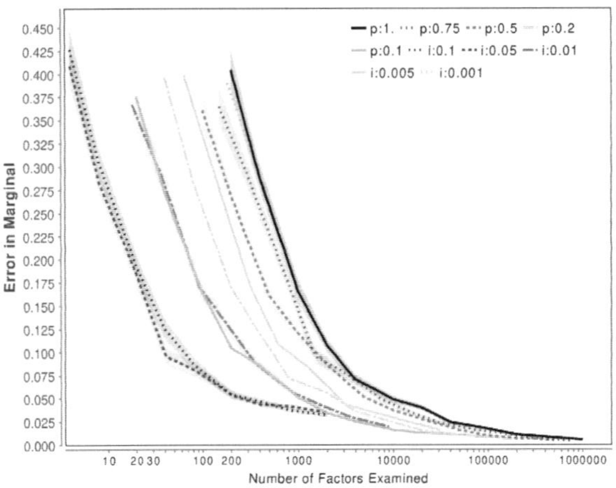

Figure 1: Synthetic Entity Classification

[1]Specifically, the fraction may be higher than 5%

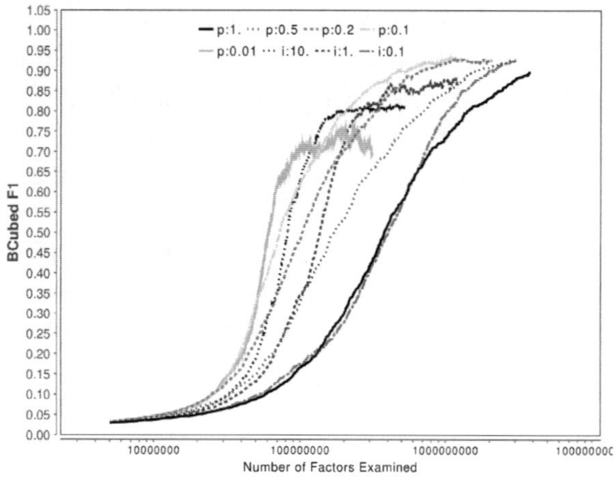

Figure 2: Entity Resolution over 5 million mentions.

Method	Factors Examined	Speedup
Baseline	1,395,330,603	1x
Uniform		
$p = 0.5$	689,254,134	2.02x
$p = 0.1$	206,157,705	6.77x
$p = 0.02$	142,689,770	9.78x
Variance		
$i = 0.1$	1,012,321,830	1.38x
$i = 1$	265,327,983	5.26x
$i = 10$	179,701,896	7.76x
$i = 100$	106,850,725	13.16x

Table 1: Speedups on DBLP to reach 80% B^3 F1

4.2 Large-Scale Author Coreference

Author coreference, the problem of clustering mentions of research paper authors into the real-world authors to which they refer, is an important step for performing meaningful bibliometric analysis. It is an instance of entity resolution, a clustering problem in which neither the identities or number of underlying entities is known. In this paper, the graphical model for entity resolution consists of observed mentions (m_i), and pairwise binary variables between pairs of mentions (y_{ij}) which represent whether the mentions are coreferent. A local factor for each y_{ij} has a high score if m_i and m_j are similar, and is instantiated only when $y_{ij} = 1$. Thus, $\psi(y) = \sum_e \sum_{m_i, m_j \in e} f(y_{ij})$. The set of possible worlds consists of all settings of the y variables such that they are consistent with transitivity, i.e. the binary variables directly represent a valid clustering over the mentions. Our proposal function selects a random mention, and moves it to a random entity, changing all the pairwise variables with mentions in its old and new entities. Thus, evaluation of such a proposal function requires scoring a number of factors linear in the size of the entities. However, the mentions are highly redundant, and observing only a subset of mentions can be sufficient.

Our dataset consists of 5 million BibTex entries from DBLP from which we extract author names, and features based on similarity between first, last names, and similarity among publication venues and co-authors. This DBLP dataset contains many large, "populous" clusters, making the evaluation of MCMC proposals computationally expensive. We also include some mentions that are labeled with their true entities, and evaluate accuracy on this subset as inference progresses. We plot *BCubed* F1, introduced by Bagga and Baldwin (1998), versus the number of factors examined (Figure 2). We also show accuracy in Table 1. We observe consistent speed improvements as stochasticity is increased. Our proposed method achieves substantial saving on this task, with a 13.16x speedup using the confidence-based sampler and 9.78x speedup using the uniform sampler. Our results also show that using extremely high confidence intervals and low sampling proportion can result in convergence to a low accuracy.

5 Conclusions

Motivated by the need for an efficient inference technique that can scale to large, densely-factored models, this paper considers a simple extension to the Markov chain Monto Carlo algorithm. By observing that many graphical models contain substantial redundancy among the factors, we propose a *stochastic* evaluation of proposals that subsamples the factors to be scored. Using two proposed sampling strategies, we demonstrate improved convergence for marginal inference on synthetic data. Further, we evaluate our approach on a large-scale, real-world entity resolution dataset, obtaining a 13x speedup on a dataset containing 5 million mentions.

Acknowledgements

We would like to thank the anonymous reviewers and Brian Martin for their valuable feedback. This work was supported in part by the Center for Intelligent Information Retrieval, in part by ARFL under prime contract number is FA8650-10-C-7059, and the University of Massachusetts gratefully acknowledges the support of Defense Advanced Research Projects Agency (DARPA) Machine Reading Program under Air Force Research Laboratory (AFRL) prime contract no. FA8750-09-C-0181. The U.S. Government is authorized to reproduce and distribute reprint for Governmental purposes notwithstanding any copyright annotation thereon. Any opinions, findings and conclusions or recommendations expressed in this material are those of the authors and do not necessarily reflect those of the sponsor.

References

[Bagga and Baldwin1998] Amit Bagga and Breck Baldwin. 1998. Algorithms for scoring coreference chains. In *International Conference on Language Resources and Evaluation (LREC) Workshop on Linguistics Coreference*, pages 563–566.

[Bertsimas and Tsitsiklis1993] D. Bertsimas and J. Tsitsiklis. 1993. Simulated annealing. *Statistical Science*, pages 10–15.

[Carreras2007] Xavier Carreras. 2007. Experiments with a higher-order projective dependency parser. In *Proceedings of the CoNLL Shared Task Session of EMNLP-CoNLL 2007*, pages 957–961.

[Culotta et al.2007] Aron Culotta, Michael Wick, and Andrew McCallum. 2007. First-order probabilistic models for coreference resolution. In *North American Chapter of the Association for Computational Linguistics - Human Language Technologies (NAACL HLT)*.

[Gonzalez et al.2011] Joseph Gonzalez, Yucheng Low, Arthur Gretton, and Carlos Guestrin. 2011. Parallel gibbs sampling: From colored fields to thin junction trees. In *Artificial Intelligence and Statistics (AISTATS)*, Ft. Lauderdale, FL, May.

[Hoffmann et al.2011] Raphael Hoffmann, Congle Zhang, Xiao Ling, Luke Zettlemoyer, and Daniel S. Weld. 2011. Knowledge-based weak supervision for information extraction of overlapping relations. In *Annual Meeting of the Association for Computational Linguistics (ACL)*, pages 541–550, Portland, Oregon, USA, June. Association for Computational Linguistics.

[Lafferty et al.2001] John Lafferty, Andrew McCallum, and Fernando Pereira. 2001. Conditional random fields: Probabilistic models for segmenting and labeling sequence data. In *Proc. 18th International Conf. on Machine Learning*, pages 282–289. Morgan Kaufmann, San Francisco, CA.

[McCallum et al.2009] Andrew McCallum, Karl Schultz, and Sameer Singh. 2009. FACTORIE: Probabilistic programming via imperatively defined factor graphs. In *Neural Information Processing Systems (NIPS)*.

[Poon and Domingos2006] Hoifung Poon and Pedro Domingos. 2006. Sound and efficient inference with probabilistic and deterministic dependencies. In *AAAI Conference on Artificial Intelligence*.

[Poon et al.2008] Hoifung Poon, Pedro Domingos, and Marc Sumner. 2008. A general method for reducing the complexity of relational inference and its application to MCMC. In *AAAI Conference on Artificial Intelligence*.

[Richardson and Domingos2006] Matthew Richardson and Pedro Domingos. 2006. Markov logic networks. *Machine Learning*, 62(1-2):107–136.

[Singh et al.2009] Sameer Singh, Karl Schultz, and Andrew McCallum. 2009. Bi-directional joint inference for entity resolution and segmentation using imperatively-defined factor graphs. In *Machine Learning and Knowledge Discovery in Databases (Lecture Notes in Computer Science) and European Conference on Machine Learning and Principles and Practice of Knowledge Discovery in Databases (ECML PKDD)*, pages 414–429.

[Singh et al.2011] Sameer Singh, Amarnag Subramanya, Fernando Pereira, and Andrew McCallum. 2011. Large-scale cross-document coreference using distributed inference and hierarchical models. In *Association for Computational Linguistics: Human Language Technologies (ACL HLT)*.

[Sutton and McCallum2004] Charles Sutton and Andrew McCallum. 2004. Collective segmentation and labeling of distant entities in information extraction. Technical Report TR # 04-49, University of Massachusetts, July.

[Wick et al.2009] Michael Wick, Aron Culotta, Khashayar Rohanimanesh, and Andrew McCallum. 2009. An entity-based model for coreference resolution. In *SIAM International Conference on Data Mining (SDM)*.

[Yao et al.2010] Limin Yao, Sebastian Riedel, and Andrew McCallum. 2010. Collective cross-document relation extraction without labelled data. In *Empirical Methods in Natural Language Processing (EMNLP)*.

Probabilistic Databases of Universal Schema

Limin Yao **Sebastian Riedel** **Andrew McCallum**
Department of Computer Science
University of Massachusetts, Amherst
`{lmyao,riedel,mccallum}@cs.umass.edu`

Abstract

In data integration we transform information from a source into a target schema. A general problem in this task is loss of fidelity and coverage: the source expresses more knowledge than can fit into the target schema, or knowledge that is hard to fit into any schema at all. This problem is taken to an extreme in information extraction (IE) where the source is natural language. To address this issue, one can either automatically learn a latent schema emergent in text (a brittle and ill-defined task), or manually extend schemas. We propose instead to store data in a probabilistic database of *universal schema*. This schema is simply the union of all source schemas, and the probabilistic database learns how to predict the cells of each source relation in this union. For example, the database could store Freebase relations and relations that correspond to natural language surface patterns. The database would learn to predict what freebase relations hold true based on what surface patterns appear, and vice versa. We describe an analogy between such databases and collaborative filtering models, and use it to implement our paradigm with probabilistic PCA, a scalable and effective collaborative filtering method.

1 Introduction

Natural language is a highly expressive representation of knowledge. Yet, for many tasks databases are more suitable, as they support more effective decision support, question answering and data mining. But given a fixed schema, any database can only capture so much of the information natural language can express, even if we restrict us to factual knowledge. For example, Freebase (Bollacker et al., 2008) captures the content of Wikipedia to some extent, but has no *criticized*(Person,Person) relation and hence cannot answer a question like "Who criticized George Bush?", even though partial answers are expressed in Wikipedia. This makes the database schema a major bottleneck in information extraction (IE). From a more general point of view, data integration always suffers from schema mismatch between knowledge source and knowledge target.

To overcome this problem, one could attempt to manually extend the schema whenever needed, but this is a time-consuming and expensive process. Alternatively, in the case of IE, we can automatically induce latent schemas from text, but this is a brittle, ill-defined and error-prone task. This paper proposes a third alternative: sidestep the issue of incomplete schemas altogether, by simply combining the relations of all knowledge sources into what we will refer to as a *universal schema*. In the case of IE this means maintaining a database with one table per natural language surface pattern. For data integration from structured sources it simply means storing the original tables as is. Crucially, the database will not only store what each source table *does* contain, it will also learn a probabilistic model about which other rows each source table *should correctly* contain.

Let us illustrate this approach in the context of IE. First we copy tables such as *profession* from a structured source (say, DBPedia). Next we create one table per surface pattern, such as *was-criticized-by* and *was-attacked-by* and fill these tables with the entity pairs that appear with this pattern in some natural language corpus (say, the NYT Corpus). At this point, our database is a simple combination of a structured and an OpenIE (Etzioni et al., 2008) knowledge representation. However, while we insert this knowledge, we can learn a probabilistic model which is able to predict *was-criticized-by* pairs based on information from the *was-attacked-by* relation. In addition, it learns that the *profession* relation in Freebase can help disambiguate between physical attacks in sports and verbal attacks in politics. At the same time, the model learns that the natural language relation *was-criticized-by* can help predict the *profession* information in Freebase. Moreover, often users of the database will not need to study a particular schema—they can use their own expressions (say, *works-at* instead of *profession*) and still find the right answers.

In the previous scenario we could answer more questions than our structured sources alone, because we learn how to predict new Freebase rows. We could answer more questions than the text corpus and OpenIE alone, because we learn how to predict new rows in surface pattern tables. We could also answer more questions than in Distant Supervision (Mintz et al., 2009), because our schema is not limited to the relations in the structured source. We could even go further and import additional structured sources, such as Yago (Hoffart et al., 2012). In this case the probabilistic database would have integrated, and implicitly aligned, several different data sources, in the sense that each helps predict the rows of the other.

In this paper we present results of our first technical approach to probabilistic databases with universal schema: collaborative filtering, which has been successful in modeling movie recommendations. Here each entity tuple explicitly "rates" source tables as "I appear in it" or "I don't", and the recommender system model predicts how the tuple would "rate" other tables—this amounts to the probability of membership in the corresponding table. Collaborative filtering provides us with a wide range of scalable and effective machine learning techniques. In particular, we are free to choose models that use no latent representations at all (such as a graphical model with one random variable per database cell), or models with latent representations that do not directly correspond to interpretable semantic concepts. In this paper we explore the latter and use a probabilistic generalization to PCA for recommendation.

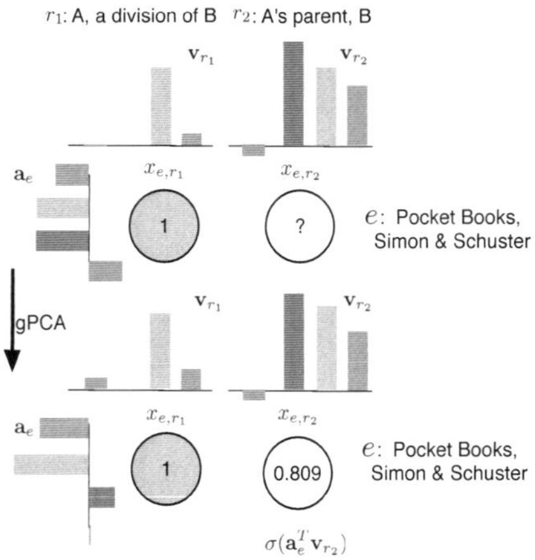

Figure 1: gPCA re-estimates the representations of two relations and a tuple with the arrival of an observation $r_1(e)$. This enables the estimation of the probability for unseen fact $r_2(e)$. Notice that both tuple and relation components are re-estimated and can change with the arrival of new observations.

In our experiments we integrate Freebase data and information from the New York Times Corpus (Sandhaus, 2008). We show that our probabilistic database can answer questions neither of the sources can answer, and that it uses information from one source to improve predictions for the other.

2 Generalized PCA

In this work we concentrate on a set of binary source relations $\mathcal{R}$, consisting of surface patterns as well as imported tables from other databases, and a set of entity pairs $\mathcal{E}$. We introduce a matrix $\mathbf{X}$ where each cell $x_{e,r}$ is a binary random variable indicating whether $r(e)$ is true or not. The upper half of figure 1 shows two cells of this matrix, based on the relations r_1 ("*a-division-of*") and r_2 ("'*s-parent,*") and the tuple e (Pocket Books, Simon&Schuster). Generally some of the cells will be observed (such as x_{e,r_1}) while others will be not (such as x_{e,r_2}).

We employ a probabilistic generalization of Principle Component Analysis (gPCA) to estimate the probabilities $P(r(e))$ for every non-observed fact $r(e)$ (Collins et al., 2001). In gPCA we learn a k-dimensional feature vector representation $\mathbf{v}_r$ for each relation (column) r, and a k-dimensional feature vector representation $\mathbf{a}_e$ for each entity pair e.

Figure 1 shows example vectors for both rows and columns. Notice that these vectors do not have to be positive nor sum up to one. Given these representations, the probability of $r(e)$ being true is given by the logistic function $\sigma(\theta) = \frac{1}{1+\exp(-\theta)}$ applied to the dot product $\theta_{r,e} \triangleq \mathbf{a}_e^{\mathsf{T}} \mathbf{v}_r$. In other words, we represent the matrix of parameters $\boldsymbol{\Theta} \triangleq (\theta_{r,e})$ using a low-rank approximation $\mathbf{AV}$ where $\mathbf{A} = (\mathbf{a}_e)_{e \in \mathcal{E}}$ and $\mathbf{V} = (\mathbf{v}_r)_{r \in \mathcal{R}}$.

Given a set of observed cells, gPCA estimates the tuple feature representations $\mathbf{A}$ and the relation feature representations $\mathbf{V}$ by maximizing the log-likelihood of the observed data. This can be done both in batch mode or in a more incremental fashion. In the latter we observe new facts (such as $r_1(e)$ in Figure 1) and then re-estimate $\mathbf{A}$ and $\mathbf{V}$. In Figure 1 we show what this means in practice. In the upper half we see the currently estimated representation $\mathbf{v}_{r_1}$ and $\mathbf{v}_{r_2}$ of r_1 and r_2, and a random initialization for the representation $\mathbf{a}_e$ of e. In the lower half we take the observation $r_1(e)$ into account and re-estimate $\mathbf{a}_e$ and $\mathbf{v}_{r_1}$. The new estimates can then be used to calculate the probability $\sigma(\mathbf{a}_e^{\mathsf{T}} \mathbf{v}_{r_2})$ of $r_2(e)$.

Notice that by incorporating new evidence for a given row, both entity and relation representations can improve, and hence beliefs across the whole matrix. In this sense, gPCA performs a form of joint or global inference. Likewise, when we observe several active relations for a new tuple, the model will increase the probabilistic association between theses relations and, transitively, also previously associated relations. This gives gPCA a never-ending-learning quality. Also note that it is easy to incorporate entity representations into the approach, and model selectional preferences. Likewise, we can easily add posterior constraints we know to hold across relations, and learn from unlabeled data.

3 Related Work

We briefly review related work in this section. Open IE (Etzioni et al., 2008) extracts how entities and their relations are actually mentioned in text, but does not predict how entities could be mentioned otherwise and hence suffer from reduced recall. There are approaches that learn synonym relations between surface patterns (Yates and Etzioni, 2009; Pantel et al., 2007; Lin and Pantel, 2001; Yao et al., 2011) to overcome this problem. Fundamentally, these methods rely on a *symmetric* notion of synonymy in which certain patterns are assumed to have the same meaning. Our approach rejects this assumption in favor of a model which learns that certain patterns, or combinations thereof, *entail* others in one direction, but not necessarily the other.

Methods that learn rules between textual patterns in OpenIE aim at a similar goal as our proposed gPCA algorithm (Schoenmackers et al., 2008; Schoenmackers et al., 2010). Such methods learn the structure of a Markov Network, and are ultimately bounded by limits on tree-width and density. In contrast, the gPCA learns a latent, although not necessarily interpretable, structure. This latent structure can express models of very high tree-width, and hence very complex rules, without loss in efficiency. Moreover, most rule learners work in batch mode while our method continues to learn new associations with the arrival of new data.

4 Experiments

Our work aims to predict new rows of source tables, where tables correspond to either surface patterns in natural language sources, or tables in structured sources. In this paper we concentrate on binary relations, but note that in future work we will use unary, and generally n-ary, tables as well.

4.1 Unstructured Data

The first set of relations to integrate into our universal schema comes from the surface patterns of 20 years of New York Times articles (Sandhaus, 2008). We preprocess the data similarly to Riedel et al. (2010). This yields a collection of entity mention pairs that appear in the same sentence, together with the syntactic path between the two mentions.

For each entity pair in a sentence we extract the following surface patterns: the dependency path which connects the two named entities, the words between the two named entities, and the context words of the two named entities. Then we add the entity pair to the set of relations to which the surface patterns correspond. This results in approximately 350,000 entity pairs in 23,000 relations.

Table 1: GPCA fills in new predicates for records

Relation	<-subj<-**own**->obj->**perc.**>prep->**of**->obj->	<-subj<-**criticize**->obj->
Obs.	Time Inc., American Tel. and Comms.	Bill Clinton, Bush Administration
New	United States, Manhattan	Mr. Forbes, Mr. Bush
	Campeau, Federated Department Stores	Mr. Dinkins, Mr. Giuliani
	Volvo, Scania A.B.	Mr. Badillo, Mr. Bloomberg

4.2 Structured Data

The second set of source relations stems from Freebase. We choose those relations that hold for entity pairs appearing in the NYT corpus. This adds 116 relations to our universal schema. For each of the relations we import only those rows which correspond to entity tuples also found in the NYT corpus. In order to link entity mentions in the text to entities in Freebase, we follow a simple string-match heuristic.

4.3 Experimental Setup and Training

In our experiments, we hold out some of the observed source rows and try to predict these based on other observed rows. In particular, for each entity pair, we traverse over all source relations. For each relation we throw an unbiased coin to determine whether it is observed for the given pair. Then we train a gPCA model of 50 components on the observed rows, and use it to predict the unobserved ones. Here a pair e is set to be in a given relation r if $P(r(e)) > 0.5$ according to our model. Since we generally do not have observed negative information,[1] we sub-sample a set of negative rows for each relation r to create a more balanced training set.

We evaluate recall of our method by measuring how many of the true held out rows we predict. We could use a similar approach to measure precision by considering each positive prediction to be a false positive if the observed held-out data does not contain the corresponding fact. However, this approach underestimates precision since our sources are generally incomplete. To overcome this issue, we use human annotations for the precision measure. In particular, we randomly sample a subset of entity pairs and ask human annotators to assess the predicted positive relations of each.

[1] Just because a particular e has not yet been seen in particular relation r we cannot infer that $r(e)$ is false.

4.4 Integrating the NYT Corpus

We investigate how gPCA can help us answer questions based on only single data source: the NYT Corpus. Table 1 presents, for two source relations (aka surface patterns), a set of observed entity pairs (Obs.) and the most likely inferred entity pairs (New). The table shows that we can answer a question like "Who owns percentages of Scania AB?" even though the corpus does not explicitly contain the answer. In our case, it only contains *"buy-stake-in*(VOLVO,SCANIA AB)."

gPCA achieves about 49% recall, at about 67% precision. Interestingly, the model learns more than just paraphrasing. Instead, it captures some notion of entailment. This can be observed in its asymmetric beliefs. For example, the model learned to predict *"professor-at*(K.BOYLE, OHIO STATE)" based on *"historian-at*(KEVIN BOYLE, OHIO STATE)" but would not make the inference *"historian-at*(R.FREEMAN,HARVARD)" based on *"professor-at*(R.FREEMAN,HARVARD)."

4.5 Integrating Freebase

What happens if we integrate additional structured sources into our probabilistic database? We observe that by incorporating Freebase tables in addition to the NYT data we can improve recall from 49% to 52% on surface patterns. The precision also increases by 2%.

Table 2 sums the results and also gives an example of how Freebase helps improve both precision and recall. Without Freebase, the gPCA predicts that Maher Arar was arrested in Syria—primarily because he lived in Syria and the NYT often talks about arrests of people in the city they live in[2]. After learning *placeOfBirth*(ARAR,SYRIA) from Freebase, the gPCA model infers *wasBornIn*(ARAR,SYRIA) as well as *grewUpIn*(ARAR,SYRIA).

[2] In fact, he was arrested in US

Table 2: Relation predictions w/o Freebase.

	without Freebase	with Freebase
Prec.	0.687	0.666
Rec.	0.491	0.520
E.g.	M. Arar, Syria (Freebase: placeOfBirth)	
Pred.	A was arrested in B	A was born in B
	A appeal to B	A grow up in B
	A, who represent B	A's home in B

5 Conclusion

In our approach we do not design or infer new relations to accommodate information from different sources. Instead we simply combine source relations into a universal schema, and learn a probabilistic model to predict what other rows the sources could contain. This simple paradigm allows us to perform data alignment, information extraction, and other forms of data integration, while minimizing both loss of information and the need for schema maintenance.

At the heart of our approach is the hypothesis that we should concentrate on building models to predict source data—a relatively well defined task—as opposed to models of semantic equivalence that match our intuition. Our future work will therefore investigate such predictive models in more detail, and ask how to (a) incorporate relations of different arities, (b) employ background knowledge, (c) optimize the choice of negative data and (d) scale up both in terms of rows and tables.

Acknowledgments

This work was supported in part by the Center for Intelligent Information Retrieval and the University of Massachusetts and in part by UPenn NSF medium IIS-0803847. We gratefully acknowledge the support of Defense Advanced Research Projects Agency (DARPA) Machine Reading Program under Air Force Research Laboratory (AFRL) prime contract no. FA8750-09-C-0181. Any opinions, findings, and conclusion or recommendations expressed in this material are those of the authors and do not necessarily reflect the view of DARPA, AFRL, or the US government.

References

Kurt Bollacker, Colin Evans, Praveen Paritosh, Tim Sturge, and Jamie Taylor. 2008. Freebase: a collaboratively created graph database for structuring human knowledge. In *SIGMOD '08: Proceedings of the 2008 ACM SIGMOD international conference on Management of data*, pages 1247–1250, New York, NY, USA. ACM.

Michael Collins, Sanjoy Dasgupta, and Robert E. Schapire. 2001. A generalization of principal component analysis to the exponential family. In *Proceedings of NIPS*.

Oren Etzioni, Michele Banko, Stephen Soderland, and Daniel S. Weld. 2008. Open information extraction from the web. *Commun. ACM*, 51(12):68–74.

Johannes Hoffart, Fabian M. Suchanek, Klaus Berberich, and Gerhard Weikum. 2012. Yago2: A spatially and temporally enhanced knowledge base from wikipedia. *Artificial Intelligence*.

Dekang Lin and Patrick Pantel. 2001. DIRT - discovery of inference rules from text. In *Knowledge Discovery and Data Mining*, pages 323–328.

Mike Mintz, Steven Bills, Rion Snow, and Daniel Jurafsky. 2009. Distant supervision for relation extraction without labeled data. In *Proceedings of the Joint Conference of the 47th Annual Meeting of the ACL and the 4th International Joint Conference on Natural Language Processing of the AFNLP (ACL '09)*, pages 1003–1011. Association for Computational Linguistics.

Patrick Pantel, Rahul Bhagat, Bonaventura Coppola, Timothy Chklovski, and Eduard Hovy. 2007. ISP: Learning Inferential Selectional Preferences. In *Proceedings of NAACL HLT*.

Sebastian Riedel, Limin Yao, and Andrew McCallum. 2010. Modeling relations and their mentions without labeled text. In *Proceedings of the European Conference on Machine Learning and Knowledge Discovery in Databases (ECML PKDD '10)*.

Evan Sandhaus, 2008. *The New York Times Annotated Corpus*. Linguistic Data Consortium, Philadelphia.

Stefan Schoenmackers, Oren Etzioni, and Daniel S. Weld. 2008. Scaling textual inference to the web. In *EMNLP '08: Proceedings of the Conference on Empirical Methods in Natural Language Processing*, pages 79–88, Morristown, NJ, USA. Association for Computational Linguistics.

Stefan Schoenmackers, Oren Etzioni, Daniel S. Weld, and Jesse Davis. 2010. Learning first-order horn clauses from web text. In *Proceedings of the 2010 Conference on Empirical Methods in Natural Language Processing*, EMNLP '10, pages 1088–1098,

Stroudsburg, PA, USA. Association for Computational Linguistics.

Limin Yao, Aria Haghighi, Sebastian Riedel, and Andrew McCallum. 2011. Structured relation discovery using generative models. In *Proceedings of the Conference on Empirical methods in natural language processing (EMNLP '11)*, July.

Alexander Yates and Oren Etzioni. 2009. Unsupervised methods for determining object and relation synonyms on the web. *Journal of Artificial Intelligence Research*, 34:255–296.

Using Textual Patterns to Learn Expected Event Frequencies

Jonathan Gordon
Department of Computer Science
University of Rochester
Rochester, NY, USA
jgordon@cs.rochester.edu

Lenhart K. Schubert
Department of Computer Science
University of Rochester
Rochester, NY, USA
schubert@cs.rochester.edu

Abstract

Commonsense reasoning requires knowledge about the frequency with which ordinary events and activities occur: How often do people eat a sandwich, go to sleep, write a book, or get married? This paper introduces work to acquire a knowledge base pairing factoids about such events with frequency categories learned from simple textual patterns. We are releasing a collection of the resulting event frequencies, which are evaluated for accuracy, and we demonstrate an initial application of the results to the problem of knowledge refinement.

1 Introduction

A general problem in artificial intelligence is knowledge acquisition: AI applications require both a background of general, commonsense knowledge about the world and the specific knowledge pertaining to the application's domain. This knowledge needs to be available in a form that facilitates reasoning, and it needs to be of high quality. While early work tended to hand-code knowledge – and this continues to be the preferred method for projects like Cyc (Lenat, 1995) – this is labor-intensive and neglects the systematic connection that can be made between natural language and representations suitable for inference. However, most efforts to acquire knowledge from text, such as KNEXT (Schubert, 2002), TEXTRUNNER (Banko et al., 2007), or DART (Clark and Harrison, 2009), are underspecified in a number of important respects, including word sense, quantificational structure, and the likelihood of their conclusions.

In this paper, we address the lack of information about the expected temporal frequency of ordinary events. While Gordon and Schubert (2010) addressed the problems of quantificational structure and strength for refining knowledge learned with KNEXT, they distinguish only three kinds of temporal predications:

- those that hold for the existence of the subject (*individual-level*), e.g., a house being big;
- those that hold at a specific moment in time (*non-repeatable stage-level*), e.g., a person dying; and
- those that hold at multiple moments in time (*repeatable stage-level*), which they quantify as "occasional" events, e.g., a person drinking a cup of coffee.

Repeatable stage-level predications vary from those done with great frequency, such as a person saying something, to those done quite infrequently, such as a woman giving birth. We will describe a simple method to learn rough frequencies of such events from text.

Our focus is on the commonsense knowledge needed for many AI applications, rather than more specific domain knowledge. This work looks for the frequency of everyday events – such as going to work – that might be mentioned in ordinary text like newspaper articles, rather than big events – like earthquakes devastating a city, which tend to be rare and unpredictable – or small events – like atoms decaying, which would typically escape our notice.

We are unaware of any previous work aimed at systematically learning the expected or normal frequency of events in the world. However, our basic approach to this problem aligns with a long-running line of work using textual references to learn specific kinds of world knowledge. This approach has been popular at least since Hearst (1992) used lexico-syntactic patterns like 'NP_0 such as $\{NP_1, NP_2, \ldots,$ (and|or)$\}$ NP_n' to learn hyponym relations, such as 'Bambara ndang is a bow lute' from large text corpora.

In addressing the problem of quantificational disambiguation, Srinivasan and Yates (2009) learn the expected sizes of sets of entities that participate in a relation; e.g., how many capitals a country has or how many cities a person tends to live in. They do this by using buckets of numeric phrases in hand-crafted extraction patterns like '(I|he|she) $\langle$word$\rangle$+ $\langle$numeric$\rangle$ $\langle$noun$\rangle$', which would match 'she visited four countries'. They apply these patterns to Google's Web1Tgram Corpus of n-grams.

Gusev et al. (2011) presented a similar approach to learning event durations using query patterns sent to a Web search engine, e.g., '$\langle$event$_{past}$ for * $\langle$bucket$\rangle$', where the bucket is a category in [seconds, minutes, hours, ..., decades] for classifying the event's expected duration. Both of these papers are notable for gaining wide coverage by indirectly using Web-scale text. However, they are limited by the brevity of patterns in n-grams and by the coarse matching abilities of Web queries, respectively. We will discuss these trade-offs and our approach, focusing on large offline corpora, in Section 2.

The contribution of this paper is the application of a traditional technique to a new problem. Temporal frequencies are of key importance to improving the quality of automatically learned knowledge for commonsense reasoning. Additionally, we hope that providing a knowledge base of expected frequencies for factoids about everyday events will serve as a new resource for other work in knowledge extraction and reasoning.

2 Textual Patterns of Frequency

The most direct linguistic expression of temporal frequency comes from frequency adverbs: words like *usually* and *always*, distinct in their meaning from other adverbs of quantification like *twice*. Sentences that contain a frequency adverb are referred to as *frequency statements*, e.g., 'John sometimes jogs in the park.' Frequency statements are interesting because their truth depends not just on the existence of some past events that support them but on a regular distribution of events in time. That is, saying that John 'sometimes jogs' means that it is a habitual rather than incidental activity.

As Cohen (1999) observes, much of our knowledge about the world is expressed through frequency statements, but it's not entirely clear what these sentences mean. From the perspective of knowledge extraction, they can seem quite opaque as their meaning seems to rely on our pre-existing ideas of what a normal temporal frequency for the event would be. For instance, to say that 'Mary snacks constantly' (or 'frequently' or 'occasionally') only makes sense if you already have in mind some range of frequencies that would be normal or unremarkable.

More absolute frequency adverbials, such as *daily*, *weekly*, or *every other week* avoid the problem of depending on a person's expectations for their meaning. However, these tend to occur with extraordinary rather than ordinary claims. For instance, in the British National Corpus we see

> 'Clashes between security forces and students had occurred almost daily.'
> 'New [viruses] are discovered every week'

Both of these are expressing surprising, unexpected information.

Following the example of Gordon and Schubert (2011) in considering "defied expectations", we look for textual expressions that indicate a person's frequency expectation has not been met and, looking at these in aggregate, we conclude what the original, implicit expectation is likely to have been. An example of such a defied expectation is

> 'Bob hasn't slept in two days.'

The production of sentences like this suggests that this is an unusually long gap between sleep periods for most people. We are unlikely to find many sentences saying, e.g., 'Bob hasn't slept in 2 hours' as this would not defy our expectation. (And while we will find exaggerations, such as 'I hadn't slept in weeks', the classification technique we describe will favor the smaller interval unless the counts for a longer interval are quite high.)

In this initial approach, we make use of two other patterns indicating temporal frequency. An additional indication of an upper-bound on how infrequent an event tends to be is a reference to the last time it was completed, or the next time it's anticipated, e.g., 'He walked the dog yesterday' or 'She'll go to the dentist next month'.

The other pattern is the use of *hourly*, *daily*, *every week*, etc. While frequency statements with such adverbs can be communicating a frequency that's much higher or lower than expected, they serve as an important source of information when we don't find matches for the defied expectations. They also occur as prenominal modifiers: For a factoid like 'A person may eat bread', we want to match references to 'his daily bread'. This use is presumptive and, as such, indicates a usual or expected frequency, as in 'our weekly meeting' or 'the annual conference'.

Method

Rather than relying on query-based retrieval from the Web, or on the use of n-gram databases, we have chosen to process a selection of large text corpora including the Brown Corpus (Kučera and Francis, 1967), the British National Corpus (BNC Consortium, 2001), the Penn TreeBank (Marcus et al., 1994), Gigaword (Graff et al., 2007), a snapshot of English Wikipedia (Wikipedia, 2009), a collection of weblog entries (Burton et al., 2009), and Project Gutenberg e-books (Hart and volunteers, 2006).

The motivation for doing so is the larger context offered and the flexibility of matching. Search engine queries for patterns are limited to quoted strings, possibly containing wildcards: There's no reasonable mechanism to prevent matching patterns nested in a sentence in an unintended way. For instance, searching for 'I hadn't eaten for months' can easily match not just the expected hyperbole but also sentences like 'I felt like I hadn't eaten for months'. Sets of n-grams pose the problem of limiting pattern length. While it's possible to chain n-grams for longer matches, this forfeits the guarantee of any actual sentence containing the match.

As a set of appropriate, everyday events abstracted away from specific instances, we used a corpus of factoids learned most frequently by the KNEXT knowledge-extraction system.[1] We heavily filtered the knowledge base both for quality (e.g., by limiting predicate names to known words) and to focus on those factoids describing the sort of action to which we want to assign a frequency. This included removing passives ('A person may be attacked') and subjects that aren't causal agents (according to WordNet). We abstracted multiple subjects to low common hypernyms for compactness and to focus on classes of related individuals, such as 'a parent', 'an executive', or 'a scholar'.

A good indication that a factoid can be annotated with a frequency is telicity: Telic verb phrases describe events rather than continuous actions or states. To check if the predication in a factoid is possibly telic, we look in the Google n-gram data set for short patterns. For each factoid of form (X Y Z*) and each set of indicators S,

(quickly|immediately|promptly)
(suddenly|abruptly|unexpectedly)
(inadvertently|unintentionally|deliberately|
unwittingly|purposely|accidentally)
(repeatedly|frequently)

we look for: 'S X Yed Z*', 'X Yed Z* S', and 'X S Yed Z*' where X is the subject, Yed is the past tense of the verb, and Z consists of any arguments. Any factoid with non-zero counts for more than one set of indicators was considered "possibly telic" and included for frequency extraction.

For each possibly telic factoid, we first determine whether it describes a regular event or not. A regular event doesn't need to be a rigid, scheduled appointment, just something done fairly consistently. 'Brush your teeth' is regular, while 'Overcome adversity' is not, depending instead on some scenario arising. Regularity can be indicated explicitly:

Ys/Yed regularly/habitually
Ys/Yed invariably/inveterately/unvaryingly
Ys/Yed like clockwork
Ys/Yed at regular intervals

It can also be suggested by a stated interval:

[1]Collections of KNEXT factoids can be browsed and are available for download at http://cs.rochester.edu/research/knext. Larger collections are available from the authors on request.

Ys/Yed hourly/daily/weekly/monthly/yearly/annually
Ys/Yed every hour/day/week/month/year
every hour/day/week/month/year X Ys/Yed

If we do not match enough of these patterns, we don't consider the factoid to be regular: It may be an occasional or existence-level predication, or we may just lack sufficient data to determine that it's regular.

For each regular-frequency factoid, we then check the corpora for matches in our three categories of patterns:

Explicit Frequency Matches These indicate the exact frequency but may be hyperbolic. The 'hourly' and 'every hour' style patterns used for checking regularity are explicit frequency indicators. In addition, if the factoid contains 'may have a Z', we search for the prenominal modifiers:

's/his/her/my/your/our
hourly/daily/weekly/monthly/yearly/annual Z

Defied Expectation Matches These indicate that people expect the activity to be done "at least *bucket* often". These include many small variations along these lines:

Hourly/multiple times a day:
Has X Yed this morning/afternoon/evening?
Didn't X Y this/last/yesterday morning/afternoon/evening?
Hasn't Yed for/in over an hour
Has not Yed for the whole/entire day

Daily/multiple times a week:
Have X not Yed today?
Did X not Y today/yesterday?
Had not Yed for/in more than N days
Haven't Yed for the whole/entire week

Weekly/multiple times a month:
Haven't X Yed this week?
Didn't X Y this/last week?
Hadn't Yed for more than a week
Had not Yed for the whole/entire month

Monthly/multiple times a year:
Hasn't X Yed this month?
Did X Y this/last month?
Hadn't Yed for over N months
Hadn't Yed for the whole/entire year

Yearly/multiple times a decade:
Have X Yed this year?
Didn't X Y this/last year?
Haven't Yed for/in over a year
Hadn't Yed for an entire decade

Last Reported Matches These are statements of the last time the predication is reported as being done or when it's expected to happen next. These are useful, as you wouldn't say 'I took a shower last year' if you take one daily. They indicate that the event happens "at most *bucket* often".

Hourly/multiple times a day:
Yed an hour ago
Yed earlier today
'll/will Y later today

Daily/multiple times a week:
Yed today/yesterday
Yed on Sunday/. . . /Saturday
'll/will Y tomorrow/Sunday/. . . /Saturday
'll/will Y on Sunday/. . . /Saturday

Weekly/multiple times a month:
Yed this/last week(end)
'll/will Y next week(end)

Monthly/multiple times a year:
Yed this/last month
'll/will X next month

Yearly/multiple times a decade:
Yed this/last year/season/spring/. . . /winter/January/. . . /December
'll/will Y next year/season/spring/. . . /winter/January/. . . /December

Decision For each of the three categories of patterns, we select the frequency bucket that it most strongly supports: We iterate through them from *hourly* to *yearly*, moving to the next bucket if its count is at least 2/3 that of the current one. For the 'last reported' matches, we go in the opposite direction: *yearly* to *hourly*.

From the three choices, the two buckets with the highest supporting counts are selected. If the range of these buckets is wide (that is, there is more than one intervening bucket), the bucket for a more frequent reading is chosen; otherwise, the less frequent one is chosen. This choice compensates for some hyperbole: If people claim they haven't slept for *days* and for *years*, we choose *days*. However, if we find that people haven't showered for *hours* or *days*, we choose days as a reasonable lower bound.

3 Evaluation

To evaluate how accurately this method assigns an expected frequency to a factoid, we sample 200 factoids that were classified as describing a regular occurrence. Each of these is verbalized as a conditional, e.g.,

> If a person drives taxis regularly, he or she is apt to do so daily or multiple times a week.
>
> If a male plays (video games) regularly, he is apt to do so daily or multiple times a week.

Note that we do not take the factoid to apply to all possible subjects, but for those it applies to, we're indicating our expected frequency. Arguments are taken to be narrow-scope, e.g., for 'a person may greet a friend', it can be a different friend for each greeting event rather than the same friend every time.

For each of the sampled factoids, two judges evaluated the statement "This is a reasonable and appropriately strong frequency claim (at least on some plausible understanding of it, if ambiguous)."

1. Agree
2. Lean towards agreement.
3. Unsure.
4. Lean towards disagreement.
5. Disagree.

The average rating for Judge 1 was 2.45, the average rating for Judge 2 was 2.46, and the Pearson correlation was 0.59.

A simple baseline for comparison is to assign the most common frequency ('daily') to every factoid. However, for this to be a fair baseline, this needs to be done at least for the entire possibly-telic KB, not just the factoids identified as being regular, as that classification part of the method being evaluated.This baseline was evaluated for 100 factoids, with an average ratings of 3.06 and 3.51 (correl. 0.66) – worse than 'unsure'. This result would be even lower if we applied this frequency to all factoids rather than just the telic ones: We would claim, for instance, that a person has a head daily.

The authors also judged a random sample of 100 of the factoids that were marked as not being regular actions. These were verbalized as denials of regularity:

> Even if a person files lawsuits at all, he or she doesn't do so regularly.

Of these, on average the judges indicated that 30 could reasonably be thought to be regular events that we would like to assign a frequency to.

Based on these encouraging preliminary results, we are releasing a corpus of the annotations for 10,000 factoids. This collection is available for download at http://cs.rochester.edu/research/knext.

One anticipated application of these annotations is as a guide in the sharpening (Gordon and Schubert, 2010) of KNEXT factoids into full Episodic Logic forms. For instance, from the factoid 'A person may eat lunch', we can select the correct episodic quantifier *daily*:

(all-or-most *x*: [*x* person.n]
  (daily *e*
    (some *y*: [*y* lunch.n]
      [[*x* eat.v *y*] ** *e*])))

That is, for all or most persons, there is a daily episode that is characterized by the person eating some lunch.

4 Future Work

There is room to improve the frequency labeling, for instance, using machine-learning techniques to combat sparsity issues by discovering new textual patterns for event frequencies. It would also be interesting to see how performance could be improved by automatically weighting the different patterns we've discussed as classification features.

5 Conclusions

The acquisition of temporal frequency information for everyday actions and events is a key problem for improving automatically extracted commonsense knowledge for use in reasoning. We argue that this information is readily available in text by looking at patterns expressing that a specific instance is at odds with the expected frequency, those that report frequencies explicitly, and those stating the last time such an event occurred. We find that a simple approach assigns event frequencies with good accuracy, motivating the release of an initial knowledge base of factoids with their frequencies.

Acknowledgements

This work was supported by NSF grants IIS-1016735 and IIS-0916599 and a subcontract to ONR STTR contract N00014-10-M-0297.

References

Michele Banko, Michael J. Cafarella, Stephen Soderland, Matt Broadhead, and Oren Etzioni. 2007. Open information extraction from the Web. In *Proceedings of the Twentieth International Joint Conference on Artificial Intelligence (IJCAI-07)*.

BNC Consortium. 2001. The British National Corpus, v.2. Dist. by Oxford University Computing Services.

Kevin Burton, Ashkay Java, and Ian Soboroff. 2009. The ICWSM 2009 Spinn3r dataset. In *Proceedings of the Third Annual Conference on Weblogs and Social Media (ICWSM 2009)*.

Peter Clark and Phil Harrison. 2009. Large-scale extraction and use of knowledge from text. In *Proceedings of the Fifth International Conference on Knowledge Capture (K-CAP 2009)*, pages 153–60.

Ariel Cohen. 1999. Generics, frequency adverbs, and probability. *Linguistics and Philosophy*, 22(3):221–253.

Jonathan Gordon and Lenhart Schubert. 2010. Quantificational sharpening of commonsense knowledge. In *Proceedings of the AAAI 2010 Fall Symposium on Commonsense Knowledge*.

Jonathan Gordon and Lenhart Schubert. 2011. Discovering commonsense entailment rules implicit in sentences. In *Proceedings of the EMNLP 2011 Workshop on Textual Entailment*.

David Graff, Junbo Kong, Ke Chen, and Kazuaki Maeda. 2007. *English Gigaword*. Linguistic Data Consortium.

Andrey Gusev, Nathanael Chambers, Pranav Khaitan, Divye Khilnani, Steven Bethard, and Dan Jurafsky. 2011. Using query patterns to learn the duration of events. In *Proceedings of the Ninth International Conference on Computational Semantics (IWCS '11)*, pages 145–154, Stroudsburg, PA, USA. Association for Computational Linguistics.

Michael S. Hart and volunteers. 2006. Project Gutenberg. www.gutenberg.org.

Marti A. Hearst. 1992. Automatic acquisition of hyponyms from large text corpora. In *Proceedings of the 14th International Conference on Computational Linguistics*, pages 539–545.

Henry Kučera and W. N. Francis. 1967. *Computational Analysis of Present-Day American English*. Brown University Press.

Douglas B. Lenat. 1995. Cyc: A Large-scale Investment in Knowledge Infrastructure. *Communications of the Association for Computing Machinery*, 38(11):33–48.

Mitchell P. Marcus, Beatrice Santorini, and Mary A. Marcinkiewicz. 1994. Building a large annotated corpus of english: The Penn Treebank. *Computational Linguistics*, 19(2):313–330.

Lenhart K. Schubert. 2002. Can we derive general world knowledge from texts? In *Proceedings of the 2nd International Conference on Human Language Technology Research (HLT02)*.

Prakash Srinivasan and Alexander Yates. 2009. Quantifier scope disambiguation using extracted pragmatic knowledge: Preliminary results. In *Proceedings of the Conference on Empirical Methods in Natural Language Processing (EMNLP)*.

Wikipedia. 2009. English Wikipedia snapshot, 2009-07-09. en.wikipedia.org.

Author Index